Make Yourself at HOME

Make Yourself at HOME

Family Life as a Key to Personal Growth

SARAH CHANA RADCLIFFE

Menucha Publishers

Menucha Publishers, Inc.
© 2012 by Menucha Publishers
Typeset and designed by Beena Sklare

ISBN: 978-1-61465-073-7

Published and distributed by
Menucha Publishers, Inc.
250 44th Street
Brooklyn, NY 11232
Tel/Fax: 718-232-0856
www.menuchapublishers.com
sales@menuchapublishers.com

Printed in Israel

CONTENTS

Acknowledgments...1

Introduction 3

PART ONE: MARRIAGE

You in Marriage 9

Is Marriage Always Hard?... 18

Stepping Up to the Plate 22

A Home of Our Own 26

Your Way and Mine...29

Just Do It...32

Say Thank You!..35

Whose Side Are You On, Anyway? 38

Keeping the Peace..42

Assertiveness Training...46

Just Trying to Be Helpful...50

A Difference of Opinion 53

Invitation to Fight..57

Blindsided.. 61

Stonewalling 64

What Does Hashem Want from Me? 68

The Camera Is Rolling 71

If You Make Him a King… 75

Date Night...79

PART TWO: PARENTING

You in Parenting..85

Marriage as a Parenting Tool 91

Laissez-Faire Parenting...95

Triangulation..99

You Owe Me.. 103

Over the Top 106

Mind Your Manners 109

Helping Kids Decide 113

Look, Ma, No Hands!.. 116

We'll Do It 120

The Strong-Willed Child.................................. 123

Please Stop Me!.. 127

He's Not Mine.. 130

Handling a Parenting Crisis............................. 133

Can't Relate 137

It's My Fault 141

A Rose by Any Other Name 144

Misbehavior or Something Else? 148

Let's Not Fight... 152

Addicted to Yelling 156

Think Ahead.. 160

Yell If You Want To 164

PART THREE: FAMILY LIFE

You in Family Life... 171

The Perfect Family 178

The Challenge of
Family Life 182

Self-Growth... 186

Seeing Yourself through Your Relationships 190

The Relationship Rule... 196

Getting What You Want..200

Siblings: Best Friends for Life? 203

Statute of Limitations 207

Misunderstood... 211

Who Is Responsible? 215

My Stress, Your Problem.. 219

Mixed Messages..223

Crazy-Making 227

When Is a Mother Not a Mother?.....................................233

PART FOUR: EXTENDING THE FAMILY

You in the Extended Family 239

Letting Go...245

Parenting Adult Children..248

Parents-in-Law 251

Child-in-Law Challenges 254

Mother-in-Law Trauma 258

Parenting in the Third Decade 262

PART FIVE: WORKING WITH EMOTIONS

Step Inside 269

Grown-Up Children 276

Self-Acceptance..280

The Turnaround 283

Everything Is Not Okay.......................................287

Sensitivity Training... 291

Don't Be Shy...295

Downtime 299

Rejected 303

Over and Over Again 306

My Right to Rant 310

Worrying 314

Moody, Grumpy, and Irritable Children 318

Nervous Habits..322

Phobias 326

Disorders of Impulse Control................................330

Teenage Moods and Mood Disorders....................334

Helping Children Deal with Loss 338

PART SIX: FESTIVALS AND FAMILY — SEASONS OF GROWTH

Good Shabbos 345

The King Will Answer on the Day We Call 349

Victory 352

It's Party Time! 355

Look Again 359

Planting Seeds 363

The Joy of Purim 366

When to Say No 370

The View from the Kitchen Window 374

Staying On Track 378

APPENDIXES:

Appendix 1: Marriage-Readiness Test 382

Appendix 2: The Parent's Top Ten 390

Appendix 3: Bach Flowers—Emotional First-Aid 394

ACKNOWLEDGMENTS

I am so grateful to Hashem for giving me the words and the opportunity to share them.

Thank you to Esther Heller for her persistence and encouragement to create this project. Everything takes time and effort, and so a little push in the right direction is always greatly appreciated! Thank you to Hirsch Traube for inviting me on board and for making this work available to readers who otherwise would have to continue to rip out pages of *Family First* to collect these articles on their own!

Thank you so much to *Mishpacha* magazine for giving me the opportunity to blend my love of Torah and psychology to make a positive difference in people's lives. It has been a wonderful experience working with the staff of *Family First*.

Thank you to my family for their ongoing love and support—and for helping me to "make myself at home."

Sarah Chana Radcliffe

INTRODUCTION

How do we become the people we are? Some of us credit or blame our parents for our personalities—both in terms of the genes they passed on to us and the way in which they raised us—but in truth, parents only provide a starting point for their children's personalities. It is true that people start out in life with certain inborn characteristics and tendencies, like being tenacious, anxious, sensitive, or hot-tempered, and then they learn from significant others—such as parents, siblings, and teachers— ways of behaving, thinking, and feeling. However, it's not parents, but Hashem Himself who determines the nature and impact of all physical, emotional, and environmental influences. Nonetheless, in the end, Hashem holds each of us accountable for whom we've become. In the end, it's up to *us* to make ourselves.

MOVING FORWARD

Many people live their lives responding to the challenge that each moment presents: "What's the weather like today—should I wear the light pink sweater or the warmer blue one? Are we out of milk? I'll run to the store. What should I make for tonight's dinner? Oops—I almost forgot—I have to take the kids for their dental checkup this afternoon. I wonder if I have time right now to return Aunt Faygie's call."

When do such people become the people they end up becoming? If we don't take matters into our own hands, there is a serious risk of growing into an older version of the person we were at age eight. However, in His kindness, Hashem often saves us from that fate by sending us circumstances in adulthood that *force* our growth and development. Unfortunately, many of these circumstances are painful or even traumatic ones. People who are sailing along worrying about the tasks of the day often get catapulted into higher spiritual levels through sudden tragedies and losses. Abuse, divorce, war, illness, death, disability, poverty—they're all superhighways to personal development (although risky ones, because we can all too easily fall right off the road). Indeed, even if we are spared from catastrophic events, we are routinely exposed to minor trials and tribulations that can nudge us along our growth curve. In fact, Hashem offers us a daily dose of such opportunities throughout our lives, most of them happening right at home.

STRIVING CONSCIOUSLY

The point of challenges and difficulties in family life is to help us *change*. We don't want to be the same as we were when we were in grade school. We want to be more mature, more resilient, more developed in every way. We want to be closer to the way Hashem wants us to be. The only way to get there is to be engaged in constant *teshuva*—self-correction. It might be our behavior that needs correction. Or perhaps it is our thinking process. Maybe it's a little of both. We might need to correct our relationship to ourselves, to others, or to Hashem.

Whatever we need to correct, we'll be able to find the inspiration and opportunity right at home. The situations that occur within our family relationships are perfect for prompting introspection. We can ask ourselves: "Is this child's behavior a reflection of my own? Is my spouse acting this way in reaction to something *I'm* doing? Is my sibling at war with me because she is evil or because I somehow bring out the worst in her?" We *can* ask these questions and use the answers to direct our next steps, but all too often we squander the opportunities for growth. Instead of examining ourselves and our roles in relationship challenges, we examine the behavior of everyone else! The child is difficult, the spouse is cold, the sister has a personality disorder. Even when these things are true, there is no reason to throw away the chance to improve *ourselves*. Yes, everyone has problems and weaknesses, including our family members and ourselves. We cannot become our greatest selves by focusing our attention on the behavior of others. We must focus our attention on ourselves.

Make Yourself at Home is a collection of articles—most of which first appeared in the *Family First* section of *Mishpacha* magazine—designed to help you engage in the process of making yourself into the person you want to be. They look at the way we fall into difficult places in family life, and they offer a helping hand out. As you read through them, see what part of the challenge, philosophy, or practical application might apply to you. Try *not* to spend much time thinking how they might apply to someone else in the family! Instead, aim to make *yourself*. Make yourself into the person that Hashem wants you to be. Make yourself—at home.

Part One

MARRIAGE

YOU
IN MARRIAGE

Marriage is a fascinating institution. Somehow, very young, inexperienced, immature people are supposed to select a partner with whom to spend the rest of their lives. Talk about big decisions! Selecting the "right" partner is virtually an impossible task. Even if the prospective mate seems "right" in the present moment, who's to say that the person won't become "wrong" some months or years later? After all, people change with the stresses of adulthood. Things happen—financial struggles, children, health issues, weight gain, family stress, challenging situations, even trauma—everything impacts on oneself and one's mate. Most likely, *both* people will change along the journey, eventually becoming virtually unrecognizable to each other. "Did I really marry *you*? Why would I have ever done such a thing?" people ask themselves.

According to secular images of marriage, the institution is all about romantic love. In popular culture, girl meets boy, they fall in love and get married and stay married (according to the modern fairy tale) only as long as they are still "in love." Hard as it is to believe, this superficial view of marriage is insinuating its way into our own mentality. Whereas Jews have a long tradition of stable family life that has been envied by the nations, many of us are opening our doors so wide that this alternative view of marriage is marching right in and making itself at home. We now expect to enjoy constant marital bliss with a person we adore and who loves us equally in return. When we hit a bump in the road—a fight, a rough spell, a bad year, or a disastrous decade—we become alarmed. This can't be right, we reason. Marriage is supposed to feel good. We look at our (disappointing, irritating, maddening, or hurtful) spouses and we realize that we must have "made a mistake." In fact, 99 percent of married people—Jewish and otherwise—think this at some point within their relationship.

Indeed, it *is* possible to make a mistake in choosing a spouse. Judaism acknowledges this by permitting divorce. If you happened to choose a violent partner; an intolerably addicted partner; one who becomes repulsive; one who abandons Torah; one who refuses intimacy; or one who is otherwise immoral, irresponsible, deviant, cruel, or dysfunctional, Hashem doesn't ask you to spend the rest of your life paying for this error. There is a way out. However, because of a poor understanding of human psychology and marriage, the vast majority of people outside the observant community now feel that the partner they chose is not fit for marriage. In fact, today, according to the research of world-renowned psychologist John Gottman, the chance of a first marriage ending in divorce over a forty-year period is 67 percent, with 50 percent of those failures occurring within the first seven years. Second marriages have an even higher divorce rate. In other words, secular marriage is not marriage at all as we understand the concept.

WHAT **IS** MARRIAGE?

First of all, marriage is meant to be a permanent, lifelong union. Divorce is to marriage what amputation is to medical treatment: a lifesaving intervention that occurs in exceptional circumstances. Divorce is *not* akin to a routine course of antibiotics meant to be utilized by the masses.

Second, marriage is meant to be a friendship, a loving companionship. Like all relationships, there will be times of greater and lesser closeness, more and less harmony, periods of greater ease and flow and periods with bumpier roads. It requires—like all friendships—nurturing, attention, and work. The special attribute of marriage is its unique, intimate bond, the joining of body and soul. This, too, is achieved and maintained through conscious effort and will vary in quality and intensity throughout the course of the relationship.

Third, marriage is meant to be a work in progress—a constant challenge. Indeed, it is the very challenge of marriage that produces its growth-enhancing properties. Only as a result of negotiating the challenge of marriage with humility, patience, courage, and determination can a person stretch into her greater, even greatest, self.

Finally, marriage is meant to be the cornerstone of a *bayis ne'eman b'Yisrael*—a partnership that forms an integral part of the extended Jewish soul. It is an enterprise that is both private and communal, and one that provides a stable, holy sanctuary in which to raise the next generation.

WHAT MARRIAGE ISN'T

Marriage isn't a romance novel. Marriage isn't a Hollywood movie. Marriage isn't something that can be observed by outsiders—it is only something that can be experienced by intimate participants. This last point is particularly important to know, because all too often people think they are looking at other people's happy marriages. In fact, if they are *seeing* it, then by definition they are not seeing *marriage*. Marriage is so private a relationship that only the two people who live it have any idea of what it is really like—and sometimes, only *one* of those people actually has any idea of what is really going on. As a marriage counselor with over thirty years' experience, I can tell you as an absolute fact that *none of us* knows what is going on behind other people's closed doors.

YOU IN YOUR MARRIAGE

As you negotiate your marriage relationship, you might find it helpful to keep the following tips in mind on a regular basis:

- **Hashem is always with you.**

- **Your mood and behavior affect your spouse.** Take care of yourself for everyone's sake! Do everything possible to achieve a happy, contented state of mind—find interesting work, engage in meaningful activities, build satisfying relationships, exercise regularly, seek personal therapy, and do whatever else contributes to your own well-being. Your well-being affects your marriage.

- **A successful marriage requires constant effort and attention throughout its entirety.** There is no time at which it is appropriate to sit back and relax. As therapist Bill O'Hanlon said, "Love is a verb"—an action word. *Your* action can build the love you want. Never take your spouse for granted. Always aim to have regular periods of private "friendship building" time throughout your day (even if only for a few dedicated minutes) and your week (even if only for an hour once a week). Do this for 120 years.

- **Keep attraction alive by keeping yourself attractive.** Yes it *does* matter, even after years of marriage. It matters a lot.

- **Your personal deficits will have a negative impact on your marriage, so try to improve in your weak areas.** Don't expect your spouse to adjust to you. Check how you are functioning in your anger management techniques, your spending habits, your habits of personal grooming, your organizational habits that impact on household management, your time management habits, the regulation of your moods, your addictions, your communication skills, and in every other area that can possibly affect your partner. Instead of asking your partner to work on his or her deficits, spend your energy working on your own!

- **Positive techniques like praise, encouragement, and rewards work much better than negative techniques like complaints, criticism, and anger.** Keeping your relationship upbeat, warm, and loving *prevents* conflict. It's okay to "fake it till you make it"—to act more cheerful than you feel.

When things are going poorly, you might find it helpful to keep the following tips in mind:

- **Try to address problems as soon as possible.** They're easier to fix when fresh.

- **You make as many mistakes as your spouse does.** Sometimes the very same ones and always different ones as well. Since we are always being judged by the *progress* we make from our starting point, it may well be that your spouse is more successful in spiritual growth than you are even when his behavior is far worse than yours. This can occur when you were at a higher starting point to begin with (for example, your spouse uses bad language, which is something you never do; your biggest communication error is that you are sometimes sarcastic), but your spouse improves more in his weak area than you do in yours (for instance, through tremendous will power, your spouse manages to completely stop using bad language while you only partially succeed in reducing your sarcasm).

- **When things are going badly in your marriage, your spouse is hurting as much as or even more than you are.** Remember that anger—both your own and your spouse's—is often a cover-up for deep hurt.

- **Your spouse wants you to love him but may not know how to earn your affection**.

- **In almost all cases, your spouse loves you; his hurtful behavior is almost always the result of skill deficits given to him by Hashem (largely through genetic tendencies and childhood experiences).** With your own wisdom and patience, you may be able to help your spouse acquire a better skill set. Each person raises his or her spouse in the same way that a person raises his or her children. Your job is to bring out the best in yourself and your spouse. Don't rely on your own resources to accomplish this enormous task: seek out teachers, spiritual guides, professional counseling, and other sources of support and wisdom. The road has been traveled before, and Hashem provides us with a map and a light; be careful not to follow directions offered by untrustworthy sources. There are those who will be happy to escort you to divorce court.

- **When things are going badly, you may be contributing to the problem through the way you react.** You can learn new ways to respond to provocation that may prevent fights and minimize difficult interactions. Read books, attend *shiurim*, get counseling, consult with your rabbi, and do whatever else you can to pick up new skills.

- **Some spouses are very difficult people.** They are grown-up versions of difficult children—youngsters who were bossy, aggressive, stubborn, inflexible, mean, impulsive, highly anxious, moody, and so on. If you have a spouse with personality challenges or a spouse who is dysfunctional in significant ways, Hashem knows that your marriage challenge is much greater than that of other people. Your task in such a marriage is not the same as the task of your friend who has a sweet, gentle, kind, helpful, responsible spouse. Your task might involve things like not succumbing to depression, rage, lack of faith, bitterness, jealousy, and other negative states. Your task might be managing to keep your home together in the best way possible so that your children will have stability. Your task might be to maintain as much peace as possible, even if deep love and affection may be unreasonable goals in your particular situation.

- **Nobody gets everything they want in life (healthy children, wealth, wonderful spouse, beauty, good friends, safe living conditions, and so on).** Try to be grateful for all your blessings, and remember that your challenges are for your spiritual benefit.

- **Divorce harms children, even though it is sometimes the only solution to a terrible situation.** It is *not* true that "if you're happy, your kids will be happy." On the contrary, a parent's happiness may very well be at his or her children's expense. In many cases of divorce, there is very often only one real choice—the parent's happiness or the children's. Research shows that divorce is preferable to a bad marriage for children only when the home is violent or completely dysfunctional.

Another option that may be open to someone suffering in marriage is to make the marriage more tolerable by getting all the help that is available, using all the tools that are available, grieving the loss of hope of having one's ideal marriage, accepting what is (at least for the time being), and pouring one's heart out to Hashem. Hashem does heed the prayers of the brokenhearted, and miracles do happen, despite what some people may say.

Add in this section your own marriage tips to keep in mind in good times and bad:

_____

_____

_____

_____

_____

_____

_____

_____

_____

_____

_____

_____

_____

_____

_____

_____

_____

_____

_____

_____

_____

_____

IS MARRIAGE ALWAYS HARD?

Somewhere, someone has won the marriage lottery. His or her spouse is patient, tolerant, wise, understanding and loving, generous, helpful, responsible, calm and caring. This spouse is a true tzaddik or *tzaddeikes*, a model for the rest of humanity to admire and emulate. He or she was a perfect child, an awesome adolescent, and now an amazing adult who has it all. While everyone wants to be married to such a spouse, the bulk of humanity has married normal people.

NORMAL PEOPLE

Normal people have their flaws. These are people who were regular kids—generally cheery but could be moody, sometimes mean, usually funny, sometimes lazy, often clever, making some friends and making some enemies. Talents and special qualities helped soften childish imperfections. They grew up to be good people who sometimes get it right and often get it wrong.

You married one. It is even possible that both you and your spouse are normal people. Normal spouses usually mean well but don't necessarily remember everything you say. They frequently don't listen in the first place. While they can be helpful, they are just as likely to make work for you and then fail to appreciate that you've done more than your share. They are loving—unless you irritate them, in which case they may become unkind or downright hurtful. Too stingy or too generous, insufficiently involved or too controlling, talking too much or not enough, normal people are out of balance on some of their character traits. It can be annoying. Under stress they sometimes fall apart completely, although some will shine in adversity. Most are well-intentioned but then fall off their diet, start smoking again, spend too much money, neglect important tasks, display inconsistencies and gaps in spiritual endeavors, and otherwise leave you feeling frustrated and disappointed a lot of the time. They're wonderful and yet difficult to live with.

PARTICULARLY CHALLENGING SPOUSES

Then, of course, there's another group of spouses. Your spouse may be in this group but you definitely are not. This is the "difficult spouse." Previously the difficult child and then the tough teen, this person still has a number of challenging characteristics. He or she fails to carry through on various responsibilities and so ends up being less than truthful in order to survive your wrath and his or her own shame. This person's flaws sometimes seem to exceed positive qualities just because they are so intense. Anger problems, parenting difficulties, addictions, serious mood issues or other mental health issues, money management issues, and other difficulties of adult functioning are common. The difficult spouse forces a normal spouse to develop extraordinary characteristics such as patience, self-control, empathy, perseverance, spiritual strength, and nerves of steel. Outside intervention is often required in order for a difficult spouse to be able to negotiate a successful marriage with a normal person. Life with a difficult spouse can be hard. But then, many things in life can be hard.

MAKING IT WORK

Jews have always been a light unto the nations when it comes to marriage. We have a good reputation for succeeding at family life—not because we find it easier than other people, but because we follow the excellent guidance of the Torah. Our marriages are challenging just like our lives are challenging. No matter how pleasant it all looks on the exterior, with rare exceptions, spousal relationships are complex and even difficult. Similarly, just as a few people are born to extreme wealth, almost everyone else must work hard to support their families. Hard work in money and in marriage is the norm, but we Jews are prepared for the task.

We have, to begin with, a spiritual frame of reference. Our difficulties are not meaningless struggles; they are challenges sent from Hashem to help us perfect ourselves. Instead of running from them to create easier, trouble-free lives, we tackle them head-on. We're not afraid of commitment or even of pain. We know there are treasures to be found in the recesses of broken hearts. Marital struggle leads us to deepen our prayers, seek counseling, improve our ways. It is a vehicle for growth, and growth is the purpose of our lives.

Our spouses' shortcomings are interesting but not nearly as interesting as our reactions to them. In order to successfully share a lifetime with a flawed human being, we must learn to be patient, tolerant, wise, understanding and loving, generous, helpful, responsible, calm, and caring. We must, in other words, become the tzaddik or *tzaddeikes* of our dreams. And then our spouse will have won the spousal lottery! Married couples share their prizes.

STEPPING UP TO THE PLATE

Our sages tell us it is good to marry young. And yet, youth brings with it some definite risks. Lack of experience alone is a hazard. Note that firstborns—whose parents are novices at the job when these offspring enter the picture—are more anxious than other people. In addition, certain traits associated with youth—reckless behavior, impulsivity, egocentricity, and others—can put a definite strain on marriage. Of course, age is no guarantee of having overcome the typical challenges of youth. There are some people who take a long time to grow up. While marriage itself forces some rapid maturity, it cannot single-handedly accomplish the whole task. We all know individuals in their thirties, forties, and beyond who, despite being married with children, are still quite immature. Unfortunately, immaturity in marriage and parenting can cause severe harm.

IRRESPONSIBILITY

A hallmark of immaturity is irresponsibility. The irresponsible adult hides his or her head in the sand, pretending that there are not serious consequences for irresponsible behavior. "Nothing will happen" is their motto. Like children, they do what suits them in the moment without regard for the future. There are many ways to be irresponsible in marriage. One is to engage in any life-threatening habit. Fast driving, smoking, dealing with the Mafia—anything that might shorten a person's life presents a risk of abandonment to that person's spouse. The Torah commands us to guard our souls and not take known safety risks. Our obligation is therefore both to Hashem and to our partner.

Irresponsibility can also come in the form of financial or legal risk taking. "I won't get caught" goes the childish belief. "I'm smarter than everyone else. I know how to prosper and get away with it." It is the same sentiment so common among those now sitting behind bars. The fast road often leads to slow recovery as extra costs are incurred. Whether through high-risk legal investing, chronic gambling, neglecting to pay bills, tax evasion, or any other scheme, taking the easy way out often creates incredible family hardship in the end.

Irresponsibility can take more mundane forms as well. The failure to carry through on tasks is a common form of irresponsible behavior. Failing to pay bills on time, not finishing projects that are needed for the family's welfare, even forgetting (regularly) to take out the garbage are all examples of irresponsibility that will inevitably cause marital (and thus familial) distress.

LYING

A behavior that is related to irresponsibility is lying. Those who have something to hide (like their irresponsible behavior) often become quite good at hiding it. Through various types of evasion and lying, they manage to delay the discovery of the truth. The keyword here is "delay," because eventually, it all comes out. Although having to learn that a spouse behaved poorly is disappointing and aggravating, it is nowhere near as destructive as learning that he or she has engaged in deception. Deception destroys the foundation of marriage, as trust is such an essential component of the marital bond. Those who lie to their spouses pay for temporary peace with permanent war. Once trust has been betrayed, the marriage begins to unravel. However, many people don't realize this until it is much too late.

SELFISHNESS

Selfishness, another trait of immaturity, refers to the tendency to consider one's needs while neglecting the needs of others. People who live in families cannot afford to be selfish. All members of a family affect each other. For instance, one person's mess creates an unpleasant environment for all and extra work for someone. When a married person does what's best for him or her without regard for how the spouse will be affected, the marriage will inevitably suffer. Imagine, for example, a person who claims that he needs to be out every night of the week with various activities and projects. If his wife agrees to his schedule, all is fine. But what if she doesn't? If he only does what works for him without regard for his wife's needs and wishes, he will harm his marriage. Similarly, a spouse who takes care of herself so much that her partner must do more than his share toward the functioning of the family, hurts the one she claims to love. In fact, selfish behavior always hurts one's spouse.

MOVING INTO MATURITY

Establishing harmony in marriage isn't a matter of good luck. It is the result of two people behaving well. While no one is perfect, all of us can work on reducing those behaviors that are known to harm our *shalom bayis*. Becoming one's best self enables one to enjoy the best marriage. It also provides the optimal model for one's children, giving them the greatest start in life.

A HOME OF OUR OWN

When a young couple first sets up their own home, there are many adjustments to be made. They are, after all, two very different people, with different ways of thinking, feeling, and functioning. While they probably share a view of the "big picture"—their general values, priorities, and *hashkafos*—they will soon learn how different they are on the details of life. The proverbial toothpaste issue (whether one squeezes the tube at the bottom or at the top) will soon color every aspect of life together: whether to spend money on restaurants or not; whether or not to leave dishes soaking in the sink; whether to call parents and in-laws daily, weekly, more often or less; and a million other dilemmas of daily living.

Not only do newly married people discover their different ways of behaving, but they also quickly learn that they have different ways of emoting. One may be expressive, loud, and dramatic, freely communicating joy, anger, shock, and any other passing emotion. Another may be reserved or even withdrawn, extremely reticent to express feelings. One may be talkative, wanting to share the minutiae of the day, while another may have very little to say on any topic. One may enjoy constant "together-time," while the other may value space and independence.

HANDLING THE DIFFERENCES

It is not the differences that make or break a marriage; it is the way the differences are handled. A good strategy is to "give up" right at the beginning of marriage. Don't fight to be right. Admit right away that there are different ways of doing things and different ways of being—all kosher. Give your spouse permission to be different from you and okay at the same time. Don't bother trying to impose *your* standards, *your* values, or *your* style on your spouse; instead, try to find a comfortable way of making a home that incorporates both realities.

Of course, most young people don't do any of this. Instead, they struggle to convince their partner that their own way is the right way and the partner's way is the wrong way. Throughout the early years of marriage, they try hard to stay the same as they were when they were single. They try hard to maintain the status quo, endeavoring to make their new home into a miniature replica of the one they just left. "My mother never had more than part-time cleaning help and she worked and raised a large family at the same time. Why should you need a full-time nanny with just one little baby in the house?"

The problem is that when two people try to make one home into the same as the one each just left, it can't work. Moreover, trying to make one's spouse into one's father or mother is as ridiculous as it is impossible. Marriage partners are unique individuals with the right to be different from Mom and Dad. In fact, marriage is a *new* world, a totally original creation of the two people who are building their home. It can be fun, exciting, and rewarding to embrace the challenge of bringing the best from both homes into the new one.

LEARNING AND GROWING

Marriage is meant to help us grow—not stay the same. A spouse can bring new perspectives and new information into one's life. There is no one way to wash a car, pay the bills, prepare dinners, and so on. Each spouse has something new to contribute. It's important to greet the innovations warmly, perhaps with curiosity but never with disdain. "That's an interesting way of doing it. I guess we could try it your way and see what happens." Each person can try to stretch a bit, sometimes using the wife's wisdom and experience and at other times using the husband's knowledge and know-how. Openness and flexibility along with the ability to compromise are traits that work best in marriage. Their opposites—closed-minded rigidity with a my-way-or-the-highway attitude—cause untold marital suffering. Nothing gets solved, and the couple's relationship is severely harmed. Controlling people may use intimidation, anger, withdrawal, and other forms of "punishment" and emotional warfare to get their way in marriage. While they may get their way over the details of how life should be lived, they will inevitably lose the love and respect of their spouse. It's a high price to pay for being "right" all the time. Such people are married to *themselves*, not to another person. Oneness in marriage comes from merging, not from standing one's own ground.

YOUR WAY
AND MINE

As we have seen, there is no simple black and white, but rather an inclusive awareness and appreciation of every aspect of creation. This *and* that. You *and* me. This child *and* that one.

This broad way of thinking can help us navigate family life. It may not be true, after all, that the toothpaste must be squeezed from the bottom of the tube. I mean, it works for *me* to do it that way, but I see that somehow you get toothpaste out of your tube even though you squeeze from the top (don't ask me how). Indeed, much of what I think is the one and only way really is the one and only way for *me*, the way that best suits my brain, my body, my psychological temperament. Hard as it is to believe, there may be another way for you—a way that works best for *your* physical and psychological makeup. Hashem made us both and made the world big enough to fulfill both our needs.

SHARING THE KITCHEN

Of course, when it comes down to sharing living space, we don't always see it that way. We experience the differences between us as a true challenge. The wife who soaks the *cholent* pot till she needs it next Friday may have trouble dealing with the husband whose sensitive nature cannot deal with the stress of a cluttered sink. The key to problem solving is respect. It is easy for intelligent grownups to figure out how to solve a sticky problem like this one, and if I offered you a hundred dollars to come up with a solution for this problem within the next five minutes, *all* of you would need to be paid. This is because the cholent pot is not the issue. Rather, the quarrel arises out of black-and-white thinking, an urge to believe that our own one way is the only way that life can be properly lived (note that even halacha is made of a stretchable fabric that bends to accommodate every situation and every person). The disrespect inherent in that thinking is what drives the battle.

"There is absolutely no reason to let a pot soak for a full week!" begins the husband. He judges his wife's behavior from his point of view and can see no merit in it. If you ask him why he's so upset about it, he'll explain that his wife is disorganized, scattered, self-centered, and even lazy. "If it bothers you that much, *you* can wash it right after Shabbos," retorts his partner. She's plenty upset herself, finding her husband to be critical, judgmental, and negative. "He's always finding fault with how I do things. He can't see the big picture: what a great mother I am, how many people look up to me, how much I accomplish in a day. For him, it's all about the cholent pot in the sink!"

INCLUSIVE THINKING

Marriage is an opportunity to discover that there are many ways of going about things. Men and women often find different ways according to typical gender differences. In fact, any two people from two different families will have lots of different ways. Even two people from the *same* family will have numerous different ways. Living in harmony requires recognizing that *all* ways make sense to the person who employs them. When there is an absolute right and wrong in a matter, the halacha steps in. However, when it comes to how many days a pot can sit in a sink, Hashem encourages *us* to answer the question with an eye on the bigger task of building marital harmony. Imagine the following dialogue:

"I know you let the cholent pot soak for the week because you've got so many other important and wonderful things to do; it's not the number 1 item on your priority list. That's what I love about you: that you're into everything and you do so much! I wouldn't want a wife who was boring. I'm just wondering, do you think you could let it soak in the basement out of my way? I just find it difficult to work around in the kitchen."

"No problem! I totally understand. You like a clean sink and I really appreciate that in you—believe me, I also love it that you keep things neat and organized around here. I'll get the pot out of your way until I'm ready to deal with it."

JUST DO IT

WIFE TO HUSBAND. When you ignore my birthday, it makes me feel unimportant. What I really want is for you to acknowledge my birthday.

HUSBAND. I don't do birthdays.

Really? You don't do birthdays? Surely you meant, "Before I was married, I never felt that celebrating birthdays was important. But now that I see how important the practice is to you, Dear Wife, I'll be *happy* to make that little change and begin celebrating birthdays right away!"

You meant this because you understand that the primary goal in marriage is to make your spouse happy. If you know that something will make him or her happy and it's within the realm of things you are capable of doing, you will do it. After all, your happy spouse is *your* happy marriage. (And of course, your unhappy spouse is *your* unhappy marriage!)

MARRIAGE *REQUIRES* CHANGING

Why would anyone do something or refrain from doing something, knowing that their actions will cause pain to their spouse? In other words, why would the husband in the birthday scenario respond the way he did? He's not an evil person or even a selfish person. He's just a man who hasn't yet realized that his task is to make his wife happy. He thinks that by making *himself* happy—doing what works for him—he'll experience the greatest happiness in the least amount of time. Unfortunately, he is *so* wrong! If he's married, he can't make himself happy at his wife's expense. He is no longer operating solo; everything he does and says is reflected right back to him. His wife is his mirror: smile at her and she smiles back. Frown at her, and she frowns back. Send a sour attitude and….guess what comes back? The same reality works for the wife. When they treat each other well, husband and wife both radiate in the glow of the love they express, and when they treat each other poorly, both suffocate in the cloud of gloom they generate.

Good treatment involves taking your spouse's wishes seriously. "I'd really like to spend more time with you," "I'd really appreciate it if you would hang up your clothes," "It would make me so happy if you would call my mom once in awhile," "I really need your help putting the kids to bed," "I prefer it when you wear your nice clothes around the house." Whatever it is that your spouse longs for—just *do it!* Making your spouse happy will make *you* happy and making your spouse miserable will cause you to suffer, too.

If you don't do it, consider how your spouse will feel. Even if he or she stops complaining to you about it, the dissatisfaction stays inside. People who come to marriage counseling after twenty-five years of marriage often complain that they have experienced disappointment about the same issues for the full two and a half decades. That's a lot of pain and negative energy. In fact, the reason people divorce after managing to stay married for so long is often that they can no longer tolerate the mound of hurt that has festered inside. Don't make the mistake of confusing your spouse's silence with compliance. You just might be too difficult to talk to; your spouse has chosen not to open up to you.

EXCEPTIONS TO THE RULE

Making your spouse happy need not involve making yourself crazy. Therefore, if what your spouse longs for is too difficult for you to do or outright unreasonable, adjustments must be made to the "just do it" rule. For things that are difficult, but not impossible nor strictly unreasonable, you can often modify the criteria for a better fit. If your spouse wants to celebrate birthdays with huge parties but you actually *hate* parties, you could offer to make him or her a party for every decade rather than every year. This would involve a stretch for you and a compromise for your spouse—both of which are marriage-minded activities. However, if your spouse asks you to wake up at three o'clock each morning, feel free to say "This is something I can't do." Additionally, if your spouse has excessive demands or endless requests, you needn't feel that you must comply with all of them in order to make him or her happy. Most likely, professional counseling can help sift out the reasonable from unreasonable wishes, helping both partners identify healthy limits.

Apart from these exceptions, get in the habit of asking yourself this question when your spouse wants something from you: "Can I do it (without undue pain and suffering)?" If the answer is yes, then just do it. If the answer is no, then ask yourself this question: "Can I find another way to do it that I *can* do?" If there are too many nos to both questions, then enlist the help of a professional if possible. Remember, both partners must work together to create the "just do it" marriage. So just do it.

SAY THANK YOU!

Wꞈe all love to feel appreciated. In fact, many serious marital problems occur because spouses do not feel sufficiently appreciated by each other. An unappreciated husband or wife feels invisible, unimportant, even uncared for. Most people know how to say thank you—they just don't do it. What goes wrong?

TEACHING METHODS

Parents can teach small children to *say* thank you but cannot necessarily teach them to *feel* thank you. Mommy serves a dish of ice cream to little Yossi. Yossi lifts his spoon, ready to dive right in, but Mommy remembers to teach him proper manners. "What did you forget to say, Yossi?" she asks. "Thank you," he utters quickly, with the spoon already halfway into his mouth. "You're welcome," she replies.

Similar scenes are repeated throughout the days and years until finally young Yossi becomes a *chasan*. His lessons served him well: he shows his *kallah* his excellent manners, right up until the last day of *sheva berachos*! But now he is a married man. His wife is "supposed to" wash his clothes for him, make him his meals, manage his house, and help him in a million other ways. When she fails to perform to his expectations, he makes his displeasure clear. When she does fulfill her tasks, he says nothing. After all, he reasons, it is her job. No one thanks him for doing what he is supposed to be doing. Why should he behave any differently?

For her part, Yossi's *kallah*, Etty, is pretty much the same. Her pleasant manners are now reserved for her friends, colleagues, and extended family members. She finds herself irritated with Yossi—mostly because he's so critical. She no longer tries so hard to please him and she doesn't feel that she needs to be positive with him because, after all, he's so negative with her. And around and around it goes.

HARDENED HEARTS

The couple's appreciation is smothered beneath deepening layers of irritation, anger, and resentment. Husband and wife focus their attention on what is lacking in the other, what has gone wrong, what has caused pain. Twenty years down the line, when the pile of negativity has reached the ceiling, these two may hardly like each other, let alone appreciate each other.

Disappointment and frustration about what we are *not* receiving often makes us blind to all the gifts we *are* receiving. In addition, festering wounds of the past ("He used to say horrible things to me") can erode our pleasure in current progress ("Yes, in the past ten years he stopped—but why should I show appreciation for *that*? He should never have behaved like that in the first place!"). We are unable to feel appreciation because we are mad.

CULTIVATING AND NURTURING APPRECIATION

The ability to feel appreciation is just as good for the person feeling it as it is for the recipient. When Etty can really feel appreciative for all the good that Yossi does, *she* will benefit in numerous ways. Her open and loving heart will pump positive energy into every cell of her body instead of pumping the poison of bitterness into her veins. These are not metaphors; appreciation generates healthy chemistry in the body, while anger generates a toxic chemical soup that, as both *Chazal* and medical science agree, not only causes constant unhappiness but also shortens one's life span. We all have a "right" to be mad—the people we live with tend to be imperfect somehow and end up hurting and disappointing us. However, we know that our irritations are sent by Hashem (even if they are hand-delivered by our spouse). We need to find ways to handle our frustrations and challenges without giving ourselves over to the *yetzer hara*—the force that strangles appreciation and love and drenches us in the muddy waters of angry entitlement.

For her own sake as well as for the sake of her husband and her marriage, Etty—along with all married individuals—needs to train her brain to search for and focus on any benefit bestowed by a spouse. Keeping a log really helps. This is a written reminder of benefits as they occur during each day. Review the log regularly. Put complaints and resentments in a *different folder*. While they must be attended to, they are separate and apart from all the good that one's spouse provides. Separating the lists in this way can give the brain the space it needs to recognize and enjoy all the good that Hashem sends via a spouse. Even when there are marital issues (as there inevitably are), a person with two separate lists will always be able to really feel and express the healing balm of appreciation.

WHOSE SIDE ARE YOU ON, ANYWAY?

The words "loyalty" and "love" both start with the letter *l*. Let's take this as a hint: the two are somehow related! Certainly, in the minds of many spouses, these two words are virtually synonymous. "If you loved me, you would take my side" is a common sentiment. "Since you aren't taking my side, it's obvious you don't love me" is its equally common corollary. Loyalty demonstrates love, and love demands loyalty.

THE LOYALTY CHALLENGE

The new *chasan* and *kallah* both feel loyalty. Not to each other, mind you. At this early stage of their relationship, they are much more likely to feel loyalty to the dear parents who raised them. Their long-standing bond with their family of origin (compared to the fledging bond with the new spouse) can create some challenging loyalty dilemmas.

Let's look at a typical example. Young Yanky is sitting with his wife and new baby at his parents' Shabbos table. Yanky's mother suggests that the young couple leave the baby with her for an evening during the week so they can go out together for a much-needed break. Her offer is generous and Yanky is appreciative. His wife Ruthie, however, bristles. She has no desire to leave her baby with her mother-in-law. In fact, she has no desire to leave her baby with anyone; she is happy to have the infant with her at all times. She thanks her mother-in-law for the kind offer, but declines; she doesn't want to be apart from the baby just yet. Mother-in-Law is astounded. This sounds a tad unhealthy to her, and she makes a tiny remark indicating her displeasure: "Well, to each their own." And the conversation ends.

Later that night, when the couple has returned home, a raging battle ensues. "Did you *hear* what your mother said to me?" Ruthie screams at her husband. "Did you hear how she *mocked* me? And you just sat there and said *nothing*! You never defended me at all. Your silence condoned her mistreatment of me and made me look like a fool! I can never forgive you for this."

Poor Yanky doesn't quite know what hit him. What did he do? Or not do? He's confused. He doesn't even remember his mother's remark. "You're imagining things," he says to his wife. "My mother would never insult you." His response, of course, only adds fuel to the fire. Ruthie becomes even more hysterical. "You're taking *her* side? You're *also* implying that I'm crazy? Well, let me tell you something, Yanky Goldman, you can just go home to your mother and stay with *her* if you like her so much! Ruthie slams the door as she marches off.

THE PAIN OF DISLOYALTY

Let's debrief the incident to find out what is bothering Ruthie so much. Here are the pertinent points to consider:

- **Ruthie is still newly married**. As such, she is not yet fully secure in her relationship with her husband. It will take many more years before their bond is cemented with certainty.

- **Ruthie understands nuances**. Although her mother-in-law didn't say all that much, Ruthie comprehended the full meaning behind the words (we humans can do that). She read her mother-in-law's disapproval accurately.

- **Yanky loves his mom**. He has a certain blind spot because of this. Also, he's a guy. Men are not always as sensitive to the nuances of emotional communications. He really didn't process the underlying meaning of his mother's words. To him, her innocent remark was just that—an offhand, innocent, true comment with no agenda.

- **Yanky is newly married**. He has no idea that his silence speaks volumes to his wife. He has no idea that he is *supposed* to verbally stand up for his wife whenever there is an expressed difference of opinion with others. He also does not yet fully comprehend his wife's emotional sensitivity and is still in the stage of discounting her feelings and perceptions. (He'll have to stop that soon, or he will suffer the consequences intensely!)

THE COST OF DISLOYALTY

Although incidents like this one may seem silly, it only takes a very few of them—sometimes only one—to create a traumatic crack in the foundation of a marriage. Due to lack of knowledge and inexperience, many couples make loyalty errors in their first year of marriage and then suffer the painful reverberations throughout their future decades. Slow learners may repeat disloyalty blunders for years before they fully appreciate the cost. To avoid needless suffering, keep the loyalty/love connection front and center in your relationship. Support your spouse's position when there is the slightest dissention from another person. "I trust Ruthie's judgment," would have been the simple, powerful statement that Yanky could have used. Insert your spouse's name into that statement and use the phrase as required in your own relationship; experience the remarkable positive consequences firsthand!

KEEPING THE PEACE

We've seen that harm can arise when a spouse fails to support his or her partner. For instance, when a woman feels insulted by her mother-in-law, she needs her husband to step in. When he fails to do so, she may turn on him in anger and hurt. We saw, too, that a husband in such a position may feel divided loyalties: he loves both his mother and his wife. Not wanting to hurt either of them, he may choose to be "blind" to his mother's insult, judge her favorably, and refrain from confrontation. While in his mind, he is keeping the peace, in his wife's mind, he is shirking his responsibility as a husband.

PARENTING PEACEKEEPERS

There are many types of familial peacekeepers. Take the case of Eli. He feels bad for his children because he thinks his wife Tamar is way too hard on them. Their fourteen-year-old son, Ari, is supposed to take the garbage out once a week. Ari tends to be forgetful, and there have been numerous occasions when the family has had to deal with the consequences of not having their garbage removed by the city workers. Tamar orders Eli to "take care of Ari's negligence and irresponsibility once and for all!" Naturally, Eli doesn't want to make a fuss. "It's almost Shabbos—you know how he is—he'll just get upset if I reprimand him. He's a good boy—he's just sometimes forgetful. If I see he hasn't done the job, I'll take the garbage out myself."

Eli's attitude infuriates his wife. What kind of *chinuch* is this? If he won't do it, then she'll have to do it herself. Now she's mad at *two* people: her son and her husband. She wonders why her husband can't support her parenting efforts. She feels utterly abandoned, and, after so many years of this sort of thing—absolutely enraged.

MARITAL PEACEKEEPERS

Marital peacekeepers also choose peace and quiet over open confrontation. They, too, will do anything to avoid a scene, ruffle someone's feelings or otherwise risk upsetting the status quo. Their discomfort with the discomfort of others prevents them from taking care of situations that require attention. For instance, Levi's brother Michael has a bad habit of making hurtful "jokes." Levi's wife, Atara, is often on the receiving end of these comments, and even though she's told Michael that she doesn't like his humor, Michael hasn't let up. Levi should really speak to his brother and try to get him to stop hurting Atara's feelings. However, Levi is a "peacemaker." He tells Atara that Michael is harmless, just immature, well-intentioned, and so on. He asks her to ignore it and not get all upset. Somehow, this doesn't work for Atara. She asks Levi to speak to Michael. Levi goes to Michael and says, "Hi, Bro!" and reports back to his wife that he spoke to Michael. Nothing changes.

PUBLIC PEACEKEEPERS

Orly is the peacekeeper in her family. Her husband, Mordy, on the other hand, is willing to stand up for what is right. For instance, Mordy will not accept incompetent service from someone who he is paying good money to. On many occasions, Mordy has insisted on his rights—not rudely, but definitely firmly—each time causing great embarrassment and discomfort to Orly. When Mordy asked the painter to return to their house to put on another coat of paint because the job was poorly done, Orly behaved in her typical way. She begged Mordy, "Just pay the poor man—he tried so hard!" Mordy then became upset with his wife, feeling that she wasn't backing him up on something that he was trying to do for the well-being of the family. It was *their* money that was being squandered, after all. Moreover, he felt she cared more about the feelings of the painter than she cared about his own.

TAKING CARE OF NUMBER 1

Although peacekeepers often seem to be protecting some innocent third party, in fact they are protecting *themselves.* Their spouses feel abandoned precisely because they *are* being abandoned. The peacekeeper cares first about him or herself (avoiding conflict because it is uncomfortable), second about the "innocent third party," and last (and least) about his or her spouse. Inevitably, there is a price to pay for this set of priorities.

One way that peacekeepers can avoid hurting their partners is by learning assertive communication strategies—techniques that allow for nonpainful confrontation and harmonious problem solving. Normally, peacekeepers fear *conflict*. However, as we will see in the next chapter, assertive communication is always respectful and caring. It helps prevent conflict because it is not *aggressive*, yet it helps set boundaries and effectively addresses issues (and shows marital support) because it is not *passive*.

ASSERTIVENESS TRAINING

Many times, the needs of one family member will be at odds with those of another family member. For instance, a woman's mother may need to be driven to numerous appointments, while the woman herself needs to take care of children, run a home, hold down a job, and make sure she maintains her own health. In such cases of competing needs, compromise is certainly possible. However, in certain relationships, one person tends to win (meaning, gets what he or she needs) while the other person tends to lose (doesn't get what he or she needs). Moreover, there are times in every relationship where a win-lose outcome is the only possible outcome: for instance, if one spouse wants to raise a family in California while the other wants to raise a family in Israel.

People who "lose" too often are at risk for sinking into depression or exploding into drastic action. It is important for every individual to learn the skills required for balancing their wins and losses.

PASSIVITY

The passive approach to negotiation involves giving up. It is often driven by fear of conflict or of not being loved. Although it may be the easier route in the moment, chronic passivity can destroy relationships. Passive partners may fail to act when action is called for, leading to deep resentment on the part of their spouses. Alternatively, passive partners may come to resent their spouses after years of squelching their own needs within the relationship. For instance, if the wife routinely gives in, thinking that a good wife has no right to have her needs met, she is at risk for coming to dislike her husband. Similarly, if a husband mistakenly feels that his job is to make his wife happy no matter what he personally feels and therefore takes the passive approach, doing *everything* her way, he may come to bitterly resent her.

Still, passivity is appropriate on occasion; it is important to allow others to "win" sometimes. In marriage, win-lose battles should work out about fifty-fifty, with the husband getting his way about half the time and the wife getting hers the other half. When issues can be settled with compromise, then husband and wife need to meet each other halfway. For instance, he wants to eat meals at home all the time while she wants to eat out once a week; they settle on eating out once a month.

AGGRESSIVENESS

At the other extreme is the person who aggressively pursues whatever he or she needs. This person steamrolls over others, disregarding their needs and feelings. "I don't care if you're busy—I need you at home in the morning to help get the kids ready for school and you have to be there!" The aggressive person is often willing to use unpleasant and frightening tactics like yelling, crying, threatening, insulting, stonewalling, and anything else that might convince the other party to capitulate. However, there are also quiet aggressive types who simply do what they want without regard for the effect it has on their partner.

Aggressive people don't trust that others care enough about them to want to make them happy. They use overly strong tactics because, deep down, they themselves are scared of being abandoned, mistreated, or otherwise unloved. Nonetheless, their communication strategy usually results in severely damaged relationships.

ASSERTIVENESS

Assertive communicators are polite and kind. They say what they have to say without provoking conflict. Their carefully chosen words, spoken gently and calmly, invite cooperation. They ask for what they want and need, feeling entitled to appropriate consideration. They are open to reasonable compromise when that is an option. "I realize you are busy in the mornings and you can't be here all the time. Tuesdays and Thursdays are the hardest for me because the baby needs attention just when I have to do car pool. If you could just do the car pool on those two days, I'll handle the other mornings myself. How do you feel about that solution?"

Assertive communicators recognize that they are *saving* their relationships by insisting that they get what they want approximately half the time. They know that if they get what they want more often than that, the family member they are taking advantage of will eventually hate them. They know, too, that if they get what they want less often than that, they will end up transgressing mitzvos such as not bearing hatred in their hearts or holding grudges against others. Therefore, when assertive communicators are dealing with aggressive non-negotiators, they seek professional help in order to preserve their spiritual integrity as well as the health of the relationship.

ASSESS YOURSELF

Does your spouse give you everything you want? Does your spouse get his or her way in almost every case? Either of these extremes can harm your marriage. Both husband and wife need to protect their relationship with the peaceful yet powerful strategy of assertiveness.

JUST TRYING TO BE HELPFUL

He's always telling me what I can do to improve myself. He thinks I need more friends; he tells me exactly how I should go about getting them. He thinks I need to take more classes, get more involved in community affairs, do more activities. If I don't take his advice, he gives me long lectures about what's wrong with my approach. And if I do take his advice, he rubs it in my face, saying things like, 'See? Didn't I tell you that it would work? I was right, wasn't I?' He makes me feel so inadequate."

"I'm only trying to help. She could accomplish so much more with her time. I've made her a schedule to follow—I do the same for myself and it works very well. I really push myself and as a result, I have accomplished a great deal in every area of my life. My wife's not achieving her full potential—she is basically lazy. She likes to be comfortable. She doesn't know what it means to set goals and work toward them. When I see her sitting and reading a novel, it really bothers me. This isn't the partner I want to share life with."

IRRECONCILABLE DIFFERENCES

When these two first came together, they were very much on the same page. They both said they wanted the same things in life. It was impossible to know at that time that they weren't speaking the same language. For instance, they both said how much they loved to have Shabbos guests. Who could know that by "Shabbos guests," *she* meant a small circle of friends and family members for daytime meals every other week or so, while *he* meant a large crowd of acquaintances from shul for each of the three Shabbos meals, every single Shabbos of the year? They had both agreed that it was important for a woman to stay at home with her children if it was financially possible. Who could know that in *her* mind, this conjured up a picture of taking the kids to parks and programs, while in *his* mind he saw a busy woman heading up a large volunteer organization, attending regular *shiurim* several times a week, and assisting her husband in his business? (Just like his mother did.) When they agreed that it was important to nurture personal physical health, she meant that having an annual checkup was essential. It turns out that he meant that one must exercise daily and hold to a strict dietary regimen *sans* junk food!

It became obvious fairly soon that Husband and Wife actually had very little in common and were in reality polar opposites. As might be expected, each had a different solution for dealing with their differences. Wife opted for a "live and let live" approach, content to allow her husband to do whatever he wanted to do as long as it didn't affect her directly. If he wanted to be busy 24/7, she accepted this, never asking him to come home and spend more time with her and the family. However, if he wanted to bring a dozen guests for meals, then she insisted that *he* prepare the food and clean up afterward, Husband resented her attitude. His approach was to help her "see the light." He began a relentless educational campaign with the goal of getting her to change her approach to life. He was certain that his was the superior and correct way of going about things. Moreover, he was disgusted by his wife's lack of accomplishment.

DEALING WITH THE CHALLENGE

One of the things that makes marriage so challenging is the necessity of accepting the intense differences perceived in one's spouse. People marry because they think they've found a perfect match (a carbon copy of themselves) and then they suffer intensely when they discover that their spouse is really so different. Yet, Hashem is the One who lures people into marriage with false appearances of similarity so that they will be forced to learn how to become accepting.

Try as one might, a person will not be able to *force* growth upon his or her partner. One spouse cannot make the other lose weight, become more spiritual, stop addictive behavior, stop being critical, become more social, become more ambitious, become calmer, become more affectionate, become less anxious, become more mature, or change in any other way. In fact, it's very hard for a person to change him or herself in any of these ways or in any way whatsoever. However, trying to change *oneself* is at least a proper goal and one that can certainly meet with some success. The first thing any married person might work on is his or her ability to love and accept a spouse just as he or she is—extreme differences and all. This task alone can keep a person busy for decades.

A DIFFERENCE
OF OPINION

HUSBAND. Shira's room is a disaster! We are absolutely negligent in allowing her to pile things up all over the place like that. There's no way she can find anything in there or even think straight. It's horrible for her!

WIFE. It's not that bad. There're just a few things she's got piled up on her dresser. She can find what she needs.

HUSBAND. The room is a nightmare! She can't function in there.

WIFE. It's just fine. She tends to put things down on her dresser, that's all. There's not that much there.

HUSBAND. No one should have to live in a room like that, and it's all our fault that we're not teaching her how to take care of her belongings!

WIFE. It's really not so terrible.

At the end of the conversation, both husband and wife are frustrated. Let's ask the husband how it felt for him:

HUSBAND. We obviously see things very differently. It's frustrating to have this kind of conversation (which, by the way, we have all the time). My wife just isn't willing to see my point, no matter how many times I say it.

Now let's ask the wife how she felt having the conversation:

WIFE. It's very annoying. He's not telling the truth. Shira's room isn't that bad—it's certainly not the disaster scene he seems to be describing. He exaggerates in order to make his point. I can't take him seriously.

WHO OWNS THE TRUTH?

The wife's opinion that her husband is not telling the truth is based on *her* truth. From *her* point of view, Shira's room is not in disarray. From *her* point of view, the few things that are sitting on the dresser are not problematic. From *her* point of view, the clutter will not ruin her daughter's life. From *her* point of view, her husband is lying.

The problem is that in marriage there are actually *two* points of view. The wife in our example has not yet acknowledged this reality and so measures her husband's comments only from *her* point of view. In her mind, she is the holder of the *truth*. She believes that she is objective in stating that Shira's room is not such a big problem. Some people will actually attempt to highlight the objectivity of their viewpoint by saying things like, "Nine out of ten people would agree with me on this," or "Ask anyone—your mother, brother, sister, and uncle—*anyone* would agree with what I'm saying." Again, the trouble with attempting to establish objective reality in marriage is that it is irrelevant. Who cares what *other* people have to say? The only opinion that really matters is the one of the person you are living with. Whether it is the wife or the husband who is the holder of the "truth," there will always be predictable negative consequences. It just doesn't work when you repeatedly disregard your spouse's opinion or feelings.

ALIENATION

Consistently ignoring or trying to invalidate your spouse's viewpoint does not get your spouse to see it your way. What it does accomplish is alienation. Your spouse feels misunderstood, alone, discounted, unimportant, and maybe even uncared for. Again, let's ask the husband in our example how he feels when this sort of conversation happens over and over again:

HUSBAND. I'm used to it now. She doesn't care what I think. I get the feeling she thinks I'm crazy or maybe stupid. She's always so right and I'm always so wrong. If I'm that wrong, why should I even offer my opinion? I should just let her do whatever she wants and quietly disappear. At the end of the day, it makes me feel really distant from her, because she isn't even interested in trying to understand what I'm saying.

ROOM ENOUGH FOR TWO

Marriages that can accommodate the two realities of husband and wife are happier. Instead of trying to convince your partner that he or she is wrong, spend your energy trying to understand and accept (not necessarily agree with) your partner's position. "What is it about Shira's room that you find so problematic?" Ask questions. Seek clarification. Acknowledge perception. "I see. That makes sense. Her dresser is full of stuff that doesn't belong there." Work toward addressing your spouse's concern. "What do you think we should do about it?" Your open and receptive attitude will help foster a similar receptivity in your spouse, making it easier for him or her to take *your* thoughts and feelings into serious consideration. Problems will become easier to solve. Conflict will be reduced. It's not about being right or wrong; it's about being respectful and caring. Put your relationship ahead of the "truth" by remembering that your spouse's truth is just as true as your own. Make your marriage big enough for two.

INVITATION TO FIGHT

S pouses bother each other in a number of small and large ways: someone "forgets" to wash a plate or shut a cupboard door, someone doesn't speak so nicely, someone is never available, someone isn't supportive when it comes to parenting, someone can't get along with the extended family, and so on and so forth. There are so many common issues that occur in marriage that it would be impossible to list them.

And yet, it is not these issues that destroy a marriage. Rather, it is *the way the issues are handled* that can cause so much trouble. When people don't know how to negotiate their issues kindly and respectfully, *then* the marriage will suffer.

RUFFLED FEATHERS

Let's say that a husband and wife agreed to spend a certain amount—and no more—on a new dining room table. With the husband's go-ahead, the wife picks out the table, has it sent to the house, and everything looks just lovely. Then, a few weeks later, a credit card bill arrives stating the way-too-much price of the table. The husband is, understandably, very upset. This isn't right! They made a deal! His wife apparently betrayed him, and he would not take this lightly. With credit card in hand, he storms into the room where his wife is reading quietly and lets out a roar that the children, neighbors, and bordering countries can hear.

In this scenario, the husband is issuing "an invitation to fight." Anger is catchy. If his wife isn't careful, she can find herself screaming just as loudly. "You weren't there—you don't understand—you think I have no brains. That was the last table in the store and the last store of the hundreds I already went to. I don't have time for this..." Of course, he'll scream back, but no matter how loudly each person speaks, no one can hear. No one is listening.

MAKING A POINT

We often issue invitations to fight when we have something very important to say. We'll say it louder, more harshly, sarcastically, insultingly, repeatedly. All of these unpleasant communication strategies usually lead in one direction: to a stressful and unproductive "fight."

THE CHOICE IS OURS

Fights don't happen *to* us and no one can fight "at" us. If one person is being verbally abusive, that is not called a fight. It is called "one person is being verbally abusive." A fight involves a minimum of two people. You must *join* a fight. But why would you want to? You can always choose to refuse the invitation to fight as if you are saying, "No thanks, not right now. I'm not in the mood." If your partner seriously wants to address an issue (big or small), you can let him or her know that you'd be happy to discuss it in a calm way at any time. In fact, it's a good idea to schedule a "calm meeting" for the purpose of resolving whatever issue is upsetting or concerning your spouse.

At some point, you might ask for a meeting to speak out the subject of "how issues are raised in this family." During this meeting you can address the fact that your spouse often speaks disrespectfully when he or she wants to raise an issue and that this makes it very difficult to have a serious, caring, respectful conversation about the matter. You can respectfully request that your partner make an effort to follow the rules of respectful speech and conduct when wanting to express a concern. You can point out how hurtful communications tend to backfire, causing relationship damage over time. In addition, you can point out that hurtful discussions never resolve the issues in a satisfactory way and are thus a sorry waste of time and energy.

RAISING AND RESPONDING TO ISSUES

Instead of picking fights, let your spouse know you have a concern and ask him or her to arrange a time to speak with you about the issue.

If your spouse raises an issue respectfully, respond respectfully. If you can't give the matter your full attention right at the time, state a time that you will be available for a fuller discussion.

If your spouse raises an issue disrespectfully, pause before responding—keep your mouth closed for a few moments. This will help prevent an adrenalin rush that leads to fights. With your mouth closed, you'll be able to actually *think*. You can then make your selection from the following "refuse the invitation to fight" menu:

- **Say nothing at all (if no response is called for)**

- **Make a brief acknowledgment to your spouse and a mental note to yourself to take up the issue again (in the near future) when you and your spouse are both calm.**

Remember, you can always refuse the invitation to fight. You'll be glad you did.

BLINDSIDED

Shaindy is delighted; her mother is busy babysitting while she and her husband Chaim are enjoying a long-awaited two-day vacation. They've decided to go to the city, where they can enjoy sightseeing, restaurants, and shopping. And now they find themselves in a charming boutique full of interesting knickknacks and accessories.

"Wow! Just look at this scarf!" Shaindy exclaims excitedly. "It matches *everything* in my wardrobe!"

"Don't buy it," growls Chaim. "You've spent too much already. This is why our credit card bill looks the way it does every month."

Shaindy drops the scarf, marches out of the store, and refuses to talk to Chaim for the remainder of their vacation.

SHAINDY'S PERSPECTIVE

"I was so excited about this holiday. We haven't been alone since

Dovey was born eight years ago. I was so looking forward to being together, being free of responsibility, and having some fun. For me, shopping is part of it. We never get to the city. It wasn't meant to be a shopping spree, but I definitely intended to pick up a couple of souvenirs. That scarf, for instance, would have been a constant reminder of a wonderful day in my marriage. That's why I dropped it like a hot potato once he bit my head off. I would have remembered his tone and the angry look on his face every time I put it on, and there was no way I wanted that memory! When he spoke to me like that—like he was my father or something—I felt shocked and disgusted. It came out of left field. I had been in such a good mood and then—pow! I was blindsided. After what he said and the way he said it, I didn't want to be with him anymore. I just wanted to be alone. That's why I stopped talking to him. He ruined my excitement, my fun, our closeness. He ruined everything!"

CHAIM'S PERSPECTIVE

"Yes, we were on holiday, and yes, shopping could have been a small part of it. But do you know how much that scarf cost? I saw the price tag! Shaindy is totally irresponsible. Sure, she wants a scarf, but she's not the one who will have to pay that bill when it rolls in at the end of the month. I try my hardest to take care of our family. I work day and night. It all falls on my shoulders. I'm the one who pays the bills and manages our finances. I've asked Shaindy repeatedly to take over the job or even sit down and do it with me, but she always tells me she's too busy. But then when I tell her she has to cut down on her spending, she treats me like I'm some sort of enemy! I'm doing it for us, for goodness' sake! I'm trying to be responsible. Is that some sort of crime? And when she picks up an item like that scarf, knowing full well that it is a luxury item we can't afford, I get mad. It feels like she doesn't care about me at all, like she doesn't even know me.

My stress means nothing to her—that's what it feels like. And then she thinks she's going to punish me by not talking for the rest of our vacation? She's punishing herself! She ruined our holiday."

PREVENTABLE PROBLEMS

As long as Shaindy and Chaim view life from their own unique perspectives, they will experience many hurt and lonely moments in their marriage. Inside their own heads and hearts, they cannot see their partner, the larger picture, or obvious solutions to their problems. For instance, in this particular case, an outsider could see that the "scarf problem" was preventable; having a clear discussion about the holiday budget *before* the holiday was one measure that could have been taken. Alternatively, if money issues have risen before in this marriage, noting them and taking steps to resolve them (possibly with professional help) could have helped prevent the sudden eruption of the issue "in the moment" (i.e., the blindsiding experience). If the couple had not yet acknowledged the presence of unresolved money issues, they could have at least used healthy communication skills to address the upset within minutes of its occurrence. For example, Shaindy and Chaim could have acknowledged that they were both pretty upset and needed a few minutes to calm down, after which they could calmly discuss the issue, striving to understand the other person's perspective and searching for ways to resolve it more or less happily for both of them. If they lacked the skill to do this, they could note that and plan to take steps to acquire the skills for the future. The holiday could have been saved.

Irreconcilable differences melt away when a husband and wife search for their common ground.

STONEWALLING

Some people act out. Others act in. Each of us does *something* with our stress. If we yell it out or hurl it out physically, we'll feel better at the cost of damaging our relationships. Everyone is familiar with the harm caused by loud, frightening conflict. What is less familiar is the equal harm accomplished through quiet, even silent, quarrel. The purposeful, noncommunication technique called "stonewalling" destroys trust, safety, and love. Avoidance of destructive conflict is meritorious when the issues are addressed. Avoidance of the issues is a whole other story.

THE SILENT TREATMENT

Some people have learned that the expression of anger is dangerous. As children, they may have been physically or emotionally punished for expressing their rage. They subsequently learned to keep their feelings to themselves, particularly when dealing with family members. When irritated, hurt, or bothered by others, they go silent. Instead of verbally communicating their displeasure, they sulk, showing displeasure through rigid body language and morose facial expressions. Verbal interaction is restricted to monosyllabic mumbles and family participation is limited to "work-to-rule." The stonewaller essentially withdraws until the painful energy has whistled slowly out of her system. This may take minutes, hours, days, or weeks.

Unfortunately, children who are exposed to this style of anger management often copy it. They grow up to silently withdraw in their own marriages, and they also continue the coping mechanism with their older parents, siblings, and sometimes their own children. In fact, some families are constantly alternating between "hot" and "cold" periods, with various factions speaking to each other and others withdrawing into silence. The "cold treatment" response to interpersonal stress becomes a painful and dysfunctional fact of family life.

REFUSAL TO PLAY BALL

Another form of withdrawal is called "blocking." In this form of stonewalling, a person refuses to answer questions or address issues. A spouse might say, "We need to talk about the credit card bill," and the blocker might respond, "Not now" (meaning "not ever"). If the spouse persists, the blocker might use emotional drama to emphasize refusal to engage: "I can't cope with this now! I told you I'm too stressed and I can't take anymore and you just don't get it!" Of course, if the stressed person comes back a little later to arrange for the credit card discussion to occur, the damage is minimized. However, if the person uses hysteria, anger, or any other form of upset in order to permanently block communication on a subject, the damage to the relationship will usually be severe. Partners learn to stop raising issues, keeping their thoughts to themselves. A "silent divorce" is always extremely dangerous, sometimes opening the door to legal divorce in the future.

Blockers rarely realize the consequences of their behavior. They use a short-term solution with long-term negative consequences. After all, blockers are not only successfully blocking stressful conversations, but they are also blocking interpersonal connection. By unilaterally withdrawing from discussion, spouses can severely harm their marriages. Parents who block communication with their kids model dysfunctional relational skills and also alienate their children. The only form of blocking that can safely be used in family relationships is "postponement." "This isn't a good time for me to talk with you about this. Can we do it tomorrow night after dinner?" Of course, it's essential to keep any postponed appointment!

I HEAR YOU

There is another type of stonewalling—more passive-aggressive in style. In this form of withdrawal a person purports to be cooperative. When asked by her spouse to organize the children's playroom, this person acknowledges the issue and actually agrees to attend to it. However, no action is ever taken. When confronted weeks or months later, the person agrees again and promises again to tend to it. And again, nothing happens. The passive-aggressive stonewaller often responds in this way to the majority of demands or wishes expressed by spouse or family members. Eventually the spouse or kids lose trust in the stonewaller. They may stop expressing their needs, resulting in a major disconnect in the relational bond. They start to feel unloved, expressing the sentiment that someone who loves them would care enough to address their concerns. Obviously, intense feelings of abandonment caused by stonewalling behavior can seriously threaten the integrity of family bonds.

No form of ignoring will work well in family life. On the contrary, the momentary relief it provides can cause untold long-term suffering. Having a difficult conversation or performing a difficult task isn't pleasant. However, it is one of the prices one pays for the privilege of enjoying positive family relationships. Conflict and responsibility are part and parcel of family living. Learning to face the tough stuff instead of avoiding it is essential to the development and maintenance of secure and loving relationships.

WHAT DOES HASHEM WANT FROM ME?

Dear Mrs. Radcliffe,

I have been living a life of desperation. I look like a perfectly normal frum mother working and taking care of her children. But if you could see inside of me you'd find a completely broken human being.

My husband has never been a true partner. He leaves all the discipline of the children to me (causing me to be "the bad one") and lets the kids get away with everything. He does not lead our family. In fact, he does only what he wants to do without regard for me or the children. For instance, he will stay out of the house every evening even if I beg him to help me do homework with the children or help me put them to bed. Whatever he has to do is always more important. I rarely make demands on him, so I would think that if I ask him one time for help, maybe he would do it, but he doesn't. I make his meals, clean the house, take care of the children, work outside of the home, and on top of all this, I have to do everything he wants because if I don't he makes me pay for it. For instance, if he decides we need to attend a particular simcha—even if I'm tired or if we've already been out too many times that week for the good of the children—then I'd better go or he will make my life even more miserable.

Through all of this I have been working so hard to better myself. I read mussar books and how-to books and I take classes. Like so many women, I really try hard to make changes. But I don't see the same effort in my husband. What is it that makes men think they don't have to lift a finger to try to become better partners?

I have thought about divorce, but in our frum world that is a terrible way for children to grow up, and even after they're married it's still a difficult situation (and my husband is a very vengeful person, so I know the payback would be enormous). But I feel so empty and lonely in our marriage. What does Hashem want from me? I am really at the end of my rope.

Drowning

Dear Drowning,

It is obvious that you are in tremendous pain. Year after year you have suffered from a lack of support and consideration and you can't continue this way. It is admirable that you have worked so hard to improve your own character—this really is the work of marriage and exactly what Hashem wants from you and all of us. However, it is not always sufficient to work on yourself through books and classes. We all have our blind spots and cannot really see how we may be contributing to a marital problem. A third party is needed in order to give accurate feedback to both husband and wife. To consider divorce without having tried several rounds of marriage counseling is unfair to yourself and your family. I say "several rounds," because it is not always the first counselor who can provide all the help that is needed. Sometimes it is the fifth! Still, divorce is so serious that it is worth going six weeks (give each a chance) to six counselors if necessary, until you find one that resonates with both you and your husband. Keep in mind that divorce may cast you into a state of poverty. Whatever marriage counseling costs, it is always less than the cost of divorce.

Let's assume for the sake of argument that after much marital counseling, it turns out that your husband is totally at fault and refuses to change his ways. (Hopefully this will not be the outcome of therapy, but the therapist cannot "force" anyone to change and it does sometimes happen this way.) Although the Torah permits divorce, let's further assume that you don't want to go this route for the reasons you gave above. Then, if you are to be truly happy despite a poorly behaved partner, you will have to accept your husband as he is and give up any further hope of change on his part. Once you completely stop hoping, you can get on with your life—being the happiest you can be through your own efforts. Keep in mind that losing a husband (to divorce or death) does not automatically confer happiness upon a person. Our happiness is ultimately a product of our own efforts (which we can certainly expend while still married). Having said all this, I truly hope that your counseling experience will have a positive outcome and you can live "happily ever after" with your husband.

THE CAMERA IS ROLLING

One of the main reasons that marital counseling is effective is that it shames people into behaving normally. Not that the therapist humiliates the client. Rather, the client humiliates *him-* or *herself* by revealing how he or she behaves at home. No one likes to admit that they shriek, make insulting remarks, slam doors, utter ugly threats, or otherwise behave not nicely. We don't want to expose actions that are blatantly selfish or outright cruel. Our partner's reflection of our behavior, now shared with a normal-looking outsider—the therapist—makes us look ridiculous. The marital counselor is an outside witness, a reality check for the client. *Gosh, this doesn't sound good, does it?* one wonders as he or she hears the description of things said and done that no one would be proud of. Even when one tries to explain oneself, the truth slaps him or her in the face: *there is no excuse or justification for behaving that way.* Explanations for crass behavior sound ludicrous to one's own ears.

In this way, marital counseling is a lot like Rosh Hashana. "The books are open"—or, in modern lingo, the camera is rolling. All our actions are being recorded. And we're going to have to watch the movie in front of a critical audience (Hashem). What we thought was private will now be exposed; our own embarrassment and remorse will help us repent. Everyone should have a few sessions of marital counseling at some point in their lives, just so that they can get a hint of the feeling that will come on Judgment Day.

KEEPING NOTES

Imagine that you and your spouse are in couples counseling. After every less-than-ideal interaction at home, your spouse pulls out a little black notebook and starts scribbling. You know that his or her impressions are being recorded for the sake of the upcoming therapy session. After a few weeks of this, you start to be more careful at home, tired of hearing your lesser self played back in front of the therapist. You want to make a good impression. "How was the week?" the therapist asks? "Amazing!" your spouse gushes. "Spouse was so kind, generous, thoughtful, helpful—I couldn't ask for more!" You blush, not only because you are bashful about the praise, but because you know that this is the way you should have been acting anyway.

Now imagine that you are not in marital counseling. Your home feels *private.* It seems that no one can see how you are behaving except your spouse (whose fault it is) and your kids (about whom you can't think right now in the middle of your intense aggravation, so their long-term development is not currently on your radar). You do what you want to do, allowing the *feelings* that drive your behavior to effectively wipe out your logical *thought* processes. There is no slowing down; no reflecting, analyzing, or strategizing; no attempt to align with Torah principles and directives. It's as if your soul has no access to your brain. Your evil inclination is the star of the movie you will watch on Judgment Day.

KEEP YOUR OWN NOTES

Fortunately, there is a way to preempt this disastrous scenario. *Take your own notes.* Keep a record of your behavior—not your spouse's—after each unpleasant incident. In your journal, you'll see entries like the following:

- **I raised my voice.**
- **I insulted my spouse.**
- **I was unreasonable.**
- **I was irritable.**
- **I glared.**
- **I used bad words.**
- **I was stubborn.**
- **I spoke *lashon hara*.**
- **I exaggerated to make my point.**

If you look carefully, you may notice an eerie resemblance of this list to another list: the Yom Kippur confessional. Odd coincidence.

MAKE IT PUBLIC

Now that you've got your written record of your own actions, *make it public.* Read it to Hashem each night (also known as *chesbon hane-fesh*). Read it to your spouse. Now, can you read it to a friend of yours? It starts to get tougher, doesn't it? The shame factor starts to kick in, the important stimulus for *teshuva.* Being so intimate and "friendly" with Hashem, we may actually feel less shame in confessing to Him than to a human being—at least until we get to Olam Habah (at which point the shame will *far* exceed anything we've ever felt down here). Alternatively, get your own therapist and read it to him or her (not like those clients who read *their spouse's list* to the therapist!). Or, ask your spouse to record your behavior, too, and take both lists to a couples therapist. Choose the most *painful* form of public exposure for the greatest gain at the greatest speed.

And remember, whether you take this initiative or not, *the camera is rolling.*

IF YOU MAKE HIM
A KING...

Guess what? Modern psychology is confirming what Torah has taught us long ago: men and women are psychologically different! Both men and women experience fear that affects their interactions and their feelings toward each other. However, the nature of their fears are different. Men's greatest emotional vulnerability is ego based—the fear of being shamed. This is thought to be related to men's inherent need to succeed at protecting and providing for their families. Women's greatest emotional vulnerability is connection based—the fear of being abandoned. This is thought to be related to women's greater physical vulnerability and resultant survival issues.

In marriage, these fears are constantly triggered. When a man is at home with his wife he may feel content and secure just knowing that she is in the kitchen preparing dinner while he is in his den studying or working. However, she may feel alone, lonely, and disconnected in the same scenario, because her husband is "far away" in his own world instead of coming close to her through physical proximity and verbal communication. When she complains to him that he is distant, she does so in order to pursue closeness. However, he experiences her complaint as proof of his failure. His resultant shame—the "hide and cover" emotion—hurts him, leading him to withdraw from her. The more she complains, the less he risks contact with her. The couple gets stuck in a painful cycle of mutual suffering.

It is possible for either partner to initiate behavior that will break the impasse. For instance, a man may make extra efforts to make his wife feel his love and presence; this will normally reduce her shaming behavior and he will then feel safer as well. Or, a woman may reduce her shaming behavior and use success-based strategies that will bring her husband closer to her while reducing his fear. For now, we will address only the woman's potential to initiate change, since an *eizer k'negdo* doesn't wait for her husband to figure out what to do!

UNDERSTANDING MALE SHAME

Let's look at the shaming process a little more closely. When men fail at anything, they can experience overwhelming shame, fueled by a flooding of cortisol and other chemical processes that cause defensive rage, anxiety, and other forms of emotional and physical upset. His response to her shaming is often either a temper tantrum or an emotional shutdown, followed by physical withdrawal. As we have already seen, this is the last thing that a woman wants to happen!

A woman can shame her husband in hundreds of ways. Here are some of the most popular:

- **Being unhappy (he feels he has "failed" to make his wife happy)**.
- **Criticizing or correcting him**.
- **Complaining or expressing dissatisfaction**.
- **Comparing him to others or praising other males**.
- **Asking someone else for help**.
- **Giving him unsolicited advice or instructions**.

Basically, any form of asking a man to be different or do something differently tends to be perceived *by him* as shaming. This, of course, poses a difficulty for a wife: how is she ever supposed to get him to *change*? She may want him to listen more, provide more help around the house, discipline the kids differently, talk more nicely to her mother, make more efforts to spend time with her, handle his business differently, and change in any number of endless ways. If she can't just tell him what she wants without initiating a downward spiral in the relationship, what *can* she do?

GETTING PEOPLE TO CHANGE

Women have already learned how to show respect for their children's feelings by limiting criticism and increasing positive attention for desirable behaviors. Using the CLeaR Method in marriage is every bit as powerful as it is in parenting. "CLeaR" stands for Comment, Label, and Reward—three *good feeling* communications designed to draw attention to and strengthen desirable behaviors. (Once the behavior is strengthened, the "reward" is discarded and the behavior is permanently maintained by consistent use of "comment and label.")

If a woman wants to increase a man's helpfulness, for instance, she can wait until he takes one plate off the table and then use her three steps: "Thank you for taking the plate, Yossi (Comment). That was so *thoughtful/helpful* of you (Label). Would you like to try one of those cookies I baked for the kids this afternoon? (Reward—as the saying goes, the way to a man's heart is through his stomach!)

In addition to targeting specific behaviors with the CLeaR Method, a woman can apply the 95–5 rule: 95 percent of all of her communication should *feel* good to her husband (for example, jokes, empathy, compliments, affection, listening, and so on). A tiny percentage of direct requests will then be benign. A man who receives so much positive attention is more secure and much more likely to *want* to please his wife in whatever way he can. Try these two techniques for yourself and see how they work in your marriage!

DATE NIGHT

When is a couple not a couple? When they have no personal relationship. It is possible for people to be married for twenty-five years and still have virtually no personal relationship. They may be excellent parenting partners. They may run an efficient home together (operating as "business" partners in creating and maintaining a viable, functional household). They may be a model of their individual, respective roles—he, an excellent husband and she, an excellent wife. They may be all of this and still not be a couple.

LONELY IN MARRIAGE

It is totally possible, and even fairly common, for a man or woman to actually be lonely in marriage. Although there is a person there at one's side, involved in every aspect of life, it is, oddly enough, not sufficient. Togetherness is not only a matter of undertaking projects together or sharing space. It is more a matter of sharing *souls*. The "oneness" we think of as the goal of marriage does not refer to one car, one house, or one income. It refers to one heart.

Yet many people have no idea of how to merge in such a way as to become one. They maintain their own inner worlds independently. A man, for example, keeps his thoughts and feelings to himself as he goes about his day. He lives his life, fulfilling his obligations and even pursuing his dreams—but he does so on his own. His wife similarly goes about her business in a world that is often very different from her husband's. She never had that much in common with him to begin with. Now, after many years of pursuing her own set of responsibilities and activities, she is no closer to common ground and perhaps even further than before. Unresolved resentments and disappointments built up over the decades have created additional walls between them. They are both quite lonely.

LOVING COMPANIONS

And yet, it could be so different. In fact, it's fairly easy to create a strong connection with one's spouse. It requires a little know-how and lots of commitment, but nothing else. Let's start with the know-how:

- **Invest in "date night."** This is a once-a-week date that must take place for the duration of a marriage. It can be a get-together of husband and wife that lasts anywhere from one hour to several hours, in or outside the home. It must be "couple time"—a time to be with each other as friends. No stressful conversation should take place (this isn't a meeting to discuss budget concerns, discipline issues, upset feelings, and so on). This is a time to relax together and either talk about things (see #2 below) or do activities together (see #3 below). *Do not be fooled* by the apparent simplicity of the Date Night concept: it is probably the *most important, most powerful, most frequently suggested* positive relationship activity suggested by marital counselors worldwide.

- **Get closer to each other through talking.** This means simple, straightforward, normal communication—not emotional talking, feeling talking, or relationship talking. This can occur on Date Night and also in shorter bursts throughout the week (i.e., during a ten-minute get-together in the evening). Suitable talking subjects include talking about an item heard on the news, something read in an article, a topic expressed in a book, a subject brought up by others at a gathering, and so on. If necessary, prepare in advance for talking time by reading and listening for potential subjects. When you talk about a subject, you reveal who you are—your thoughts, feelings, ideas, and values. Your spouse will get to know you better, which is the goal of the activity.

- **Get closer to each other through activities.** Again, this can occur on Date Night and also in shorter bursts during the week if it is possible. Doing a pleasurable, even "fun" activity together makes people feel closer to each other. Pick from the following suggestions or use your own ideas: cook a gourmet meal or dessert together; do a puzzle or play a game together; do a *chesed* project together; visit galleries or specialty stores together; learn a musical instrument (or complementary instruments) together; learn and do a craft together; create a family album or other family-related project together; take up a hobby together; learn together; exercise together; learn a language together; plan a vacation, renovation, celebration, or whatever together. The more you talk, laugh, and enjoy yourselves during your activity time, the closer you will feel.

- **Commit.** Even one hour a week of together time can create an ever-present, powerful, loving bond between a husband and wife. It can positively affect every other minute of the relationship, not only building a close relationship, but also reducing conflict and enhancing family life. Don't let life get in the way—*commit* to Date Night every single week. You and your children will be glad you did.

Part Two

PARENTING

YOU IN PARENTING

There are no adequate words to describe the experience of parenting. Sure, we can talk about joy, love, worry, panic, and rage. We can laugh till our sides split and cry till our hearts break. We can tell lots of stories. But we will never be able to adequately express the depth and breadth of the awesome journey of raising our children. So much of it rests inside our souls.

Are there words to describe what we feel as we first hold our baby in our arms? No. What words describe the feelings we have as that baby utters his first words, takes his first steps? What word accurately conveys the jumble of emotions we experience as that youngster moves away—first to a babysitter or preschool, then to camp, later still to out-of-town places of learning, and finally, please G-d, to the chuppah?

When a teacher or rebbe gives us disturbing news, we may grope for words—but find only a pit in our stomach. When, Heaven forbid, there is a serious health concern we may beg for words, but find only darkness, terror, and confusion. When the child him- or herself faces life's pains and struggles, we offer words, but we crumble wordless inside of ourselves.

The parenting journey is beyond words, with its ups and downs, its ecstasy and despair. It is an emotional roller coaster ride that can last an adult lifetime. Oh, it starts innocently enough. Many of us believe that our fierce love will make everything okay—our children will be happy, clever, successful in all aspects of their lives. They will love us just as we love them. We anticipate a smooth ride. And then, as this child grows and as more come or don't, as things unfold in more complicated ways than we anticipated, we go through various stages. There's fear and worry, of course. But denial helps in the beginning. Later there might be various types of loss, grief, disappointment, hurt, frustration, and anger. They will be plenty of confusion. Fortunately, happy times and comic relief inevitably boost our energy and we carry on. There's always hope.

Some people seem to face more challenges than others. Their genes, their childhoods, and their current circumstances may conspire to create enormous parenting challenges. And then there are always some parents who seem to glide through the parenting decades with a smile on their face. Rest assured, even "easy" parenting isn't easy! What parent hasn't nursed a feverish, vomiting child throughout the night and then had to rise early to carry on with business as usual? Even the most uneventful parenting journey is stressful, at times exhausting, and always deeply challenging. This is the way it is meant to be. The challenge that Hashem sends is individually tailored for our personal growth. We will have the parenting situation that is best for our spiritual journey.

As you are growing through your own parenting journey, you

may find it helpful to keep the following tips in mind:

- **It is not all up to you.** It is not all your fault, nor is it all to your credit. Hashem has given each of your children their unique pool of genes resulting in unique personalities, strengths, and weaknesses. Your child is influenced not only by you, but also by your spouse, your relatives, his or her peer group, teachers, rebbe'im, community, shul, neighborhood, and others. The culture you live in plays a role as well. The child's own free will is also at play. You can only do the best you can do with your part of the pie, which includes praying that all influences—including your own—will be beneficial and lead to blessing.

- **Take care of yourself so that you can take care of your family.** Your kids need you to be rested enough, happy enough, calm enough, and optimistic enough. If there is something in the way that prevents you from being in a good mood most of the time, get the help you need to fix it. Do it for your kids.

- **No one—not even you—knows everything. Get help along the way on the parenting journey.** Read books; take classes; talk to mentors, rabbi's, and professionals; attend parenting groups; talk to other parents; do whatever you can to expand your parenting options, gain broader perspective, and learn more. This approach not only reduces parenting stress, but it helps you to do the best you can for each child in the family. The more skilled you are in anything, the better you can do it. What is more important than parenting?

- **Despite your efforts, you will have to make mistakes sometimes, because Hashem made all of us limited and flawed.** There is no parent out there who is exempt from this rule.

- **It is more helpful to be compassionate toward yourself for**

your parenting errors than to be riddled with guilt and feelings of inadequacy. Feeling guilty keeps us stuck in the erroneous past, whereas self-forgiveness allows us to move forward into the more enlightened future. If you didn't make mistakes, you couldn't grow, and growing is the whole point of the parenting journey. Remember, Hashem could have made children come into the world already grown-up rather than in the infantile state (and this was, in fact, His original plan). Requiring parents to *raise* their children puts parents in a position to do constant self-analysis and self-correction. ("I'm sorry. I shouldn't have shouted at you. I lost control. I'm going to read the Iggeres HaRamban daily for the next forty days to help myself with this.")

- **Conveying love is the most important parenting tool because it allows you to have parenting power—the power to educate your child.** It is not enough that you feel love for your child; your child must *feel* your love. It is not enough that you *give* love to your child; it is essential that you don't undo its positive effects by giving an equal or greater or more intense amount of criticism, complaints, correction, or anger. If negativity gets in your way, get professional help. Do it for your kids.

- **Conveying love is the most important parenting tool, because it allows you to have a lifelong relationship with your children, as well as a relationship with your grandchildren.** Many parents lose their kids along the way, not because they don't love them, but because they fail to *convey* this love. Get the help you need in order to learn successfully how to convey love.

- **Don't fight with your spouse about parenting.** Your spouse is allowed to make parenting errors just like you are. Educate by praising and modeling.

- **If your spouse is abusive—actually abusive—to your children, do everything you can do to get professional and/or rabbinical help for the two of you.** Do whatever you must do to protect your home from verbal and physical violence.

- **Always generate positive pictures in your mind.** Picture each of your children thriving. Worry is a form of negative prayer: imagining awful scenario's not only scares *you*, but it also draws harmful spiritual energies that can increase the likelihood of bad things happening, Heaven forbid. Instead of worrying, attach yourself to Hashem through *emunah* and *bitachon*, trusting Him to bring your children to a safe harbor. Picture it.

Add your own tips to help you along your parenting journey:

_____

_____

_____

_____

_____

_____

_____

_____

_____

_____

_____

_____

_____

_____

_____

_____

_____

_____

_____

_____

_____

_____

MARRIAGE AS A
PARENTING TOOL

What kind of marriage do you want your kids to have?
There are no guarantees, of course. You may want the
sun, the moon, and the stars for your kids and then
things just don't turn out that way. Hashem has other plans for
them. However, this reality doesn't stop parents from trying their
best to give their kids the best opportunity for the best possible lives.
Nor should it. Parents are obligated to give their children the best
that they can in terms of education and guidance. What happens
after that is just not up to them.

So if it were in your power, what kind of marriage would you like
your children to have? Although individuals differ in the details,
most people seem to want their kids to have peaceful, loving relationships. They want their kids to enjoy happy marriages. If this is

your goal, the next question to ask is, what are you doing to equip your child to have this in his or her life?

CHILDREN LIVE OUR MARRIAGE

Your marriage is not a private affair between you and your spouse. Certainly there are private *aspects*, but by and large, your marital relationship is public property in your home. This means that anyone living in your home lives your marriage with you. The ones who are most impacted by this arrangement are your children.

Your children live and breathe your marriage. How many fights a month would you like your daughter to have with her husband? I'll bet you say "none." How many fights do *you* have monthly (daily, weekly, annually) with your spouse? Can you teach your daughter how fights are avoided if you haven't figured that out yourself? Can your daughter sit by your table for twenty years watching you insult and hurt each other and walk away knowing how to be kind and sensitive in provocative or stressful situations? Of course, it is possible that she'll do better than you for a myriad of reasons: better inborn "nature," other healthy models that she can observe, her own free will to improve herself, and your prayers for her, among other reasons. However, this does not exempt *you*, the parents, from providing the best education you can offer. Is *your* marriage the best educational opportunity you can offer?

MARRIAGE TEACHES LIFE SKILLS

Your marriage teaches your kids anger management skills, but it also teaches them much more: how to manage money, handle responsibilities, show love and affection, negotiate respectfully, and share space. Let's look at each of these marriage skills:

- **Money management.** Creating a budget and operating within it for the well-being of the family. Couples who do this together create an equal power base of two responsible adults. There are no fights in the house about financial irresponsibility or mismanagement. Children observe a secure model of adult responsibility and mutual respect.

- **Handling responsibilities.** Being accountable and responsible for various tasks, including being punctual, creating a respectful division of labor, waking up on time and by oneself, performing one's own duties without being nagged to do so, fulfilling one's commitments punctually and independently. Responsible parents will be two high-functioning adults rather than two children or one "parent" and one "child." The actual children in the house will experience security in the hands of true grown-ups and they will witness the model of grown-up functioning.

- **Showing love and affection.** The skill of making one's partner feel cherished and important. Adults can be giving or withholding. In warm marriages, the couple shows affection through acts of kindness, humor, affectionate words, generous compliments, expressions of appreciation, and gifts. Children learn that love is freely flowing and easy to give.

- **Negotiating respectfully.** Problem solving quietly and respectfully. Just because people don't fight doesn't mean they are negotiating in a healthy way. Some people just don't say anything. They let their spouse "bully" them, and they store away their resentment until they can no longer tolerate their partner. Silently swallowing one's upset can be as destructive as high drama. Negotiation involves both speaking and listening respectfully. Children need to witness this skill in order to learn how to do it.

- **Sharing space.** The ability to live with another person, taking into consideration their needs and preferences and finding a way to compromise. People who share space nicely make sure that all shared areas are comfortable for *both* people (i.e., neither intolerably neat nor intolerably messy). Children observe cooperation and mutual respect.

What kind of marriage are you showing your children? Are you teaching them both by your model and your instruction how to minimize conflict, increase love and harmony, and behave in an adult manner? Think about it. Act on it.

LAISSEZ-FAIRE PARENTING

L
aissez-faire" is French for "let people do as they please." Laissez-faire *parenting* is a style of raising children in which children are given more freedom and less rules. The laissez-faire parent (hereafter referred to as the "LFP") allows children to follow their own intuitions regarding bedtimes, study habits, eating habits, and other activities. The parent does not impose limits or guidelines except in rare circumstances (such as directing the child to get out of the road).

LFPs may adopt their way of raising kids for a number of reasons. Here are some of the more common ones:

- **Having a rational parenting philosophy.** Some people have studied various approaches to child rearing and have concluded that children do best when allowed to experience the consequences of their own actions. They reason that getting out of the child's way (so to speak), allows children to learn how to make their own decisions, solve their own problems, and draw their own conclusions. This sort of LFP has consciously and rationally selected this parenting approach.

- **Reacting to an overly strict or abusive childhood.** Some people adopt the LFP stance in order to spare their children the pain that they themselves suffered at the hands of overly rigid, punitive parents.

- **Compensating for an overly strict or abusive spouse.** Sometimes one spouse is too cold, too rule-oriented, or too harsh on the children. The other spouse tries to make up for the lack of warmth, love, and compassion of this parent by always being "nice" or "fun" or loving with the children. Instead of applying the 80:20 rule, this compensating parent applies the 100:0 rule, offering 100 percent good-feeling communications and completely avoiding not-so-good-feeling communications such as instructions, corrections, saying no, disciplining, and all other forms of parental guidance.

- **Being a "softy" by nature.** This LFP has a nonconfrontational nature and/or simply can't bring himself or herself to deny the kids anything they want. It breaks his or her heart to see a frustrated child who really wants candy at bedtime but can't have it—so he or she gives it to the youngster. This person might feel that childhood should be a protected time when children are free from the heavy demands that they will later experience in life—therefore, if the child isn't in the mood for school, this LFP lets him stay home; if the child doesn't like the teacher, the LFP switches him out of that class; if the child isn't tired yet, the LFP lets him stay up. And so on.

CONSEQUENCES OF LAISSEZ-FAIRE PARENTING

As early as 1989, research on laissez-faire parenting established that children raised this way had many developmental difficulties. For instance, they were found to have more behavioral problems, less self-control, greater impulsivity, worse academic performance, and greater dependence on adults. Studies in the past twenty years have confirmed these findings and more, citing increases in narcissistic behavior, low self-esteem, depression, and a generally higher incidence of psychiatric conditions, as well as a higher incidence of risk-taking behaviors, smoking, and drug and alcohol abuse.

LFPs themselves often complain that their children are disobedient, out of control, rude, and even abusive. The LFP may not be setting rules and limitations, but this doesn't stop him or her from feeling helpless and even furious. An LFP may *want* to be nice, but often ends up screaming at the kids because he or she has no other way of dealing with them.

FINDING BALANCE

Each parent needs to apply the 80:20 ratio of love to guidance when raising young children (90:10 for teens). The love side far outweighs the guidance side, but the guidance side *must* exist in order for children to grow up healthy.

Parents have to be able to teach children right from wrong. Yes, a certain amount of learning comes from personal experience and a certain amount comes from living with healthy models. However, a certain amount comes from direct instruction and guidance. Kids are not born knowing that their dishes need to be washed or that it's not okay to yell at your parents.

When parents offer guidance in a respectful but firm way, kids learn that it is safe for them to submit to authority. This attitude is important in the development of their relationship with Hashem, as well as their ability to work well with others in this world.

Moreover, when parents set interpersonal boundaries, teaching kids what they will and will not accept in relationships (e.g., "I only *give* and I only *accept* respectful communications"), they are also showing their children the way to set healthy boundaries in their own relationships. On the other hand, when parents tolerate poor treatment from their children, they are teaching their children how to tolerate bad treatment from others!

Establishing limits is as important as showing love. When done in a healthy way ("the right hand draws near, while the left hand pushes away"), it is the best kind of parenting we can offer our children.

TRIANGULATION

United we stand, divided we fall. But many parents don't realize this. Parents—both mothers and fathers—have a strong protective urge when it comes to their children. When they think that a child is being harmed in any way, powerful forces cause them to rush to the child's assistance. This instinct works well in most cases. They say that a parent can lift a car off her child with the power of child/love–induced adrenaline alone! The trouble occurs when a parent wants to rescue his or her child from his or her spouse. The protective instinct can go haywire, causing a parent to actually harm the child he or she is so desperately trying to protect.

SAVE MY CHILD!

Of course, there are times, unfortunately, when a parent must save a child from a spouse. In some circumstances the other parent is actually a dangerous threat to a child's safety or well-being. To ascertain whether your spouse is in this category, please consider the following criteria for a definition of "dangerous threat":

- **Your spouse physically assaults your child.** Beats the child, uses a belt or other instrument to inflict punishment, leaves bruises or red marks, would be apprehended by your local family service agency if identified.

- **Your spouse torments your child.** Locks him in a dark basement; deprives him of food and water; inflicts cruel punishments such as depriving a child of candy or toys for a year, not permitting the child to see friends for a month, humiliating the child in public by screaming at him or rebuking him loudly in front of guests or strangers; screams in his face even in the privacy of your home; hurls degrading, verbally abusive insults at him (as would be considered harmful by our local family service agency).

A spouse is *not* considered to be a "dangerous threat" if he or she engages in less than perfect parenting: sometimes raises a voice, sometimes offers too much criticism, sometimes threatens or gives a punishment that you don't agree with, asks a child to do something the child doesn't want to do, talks to a child in a tone of voice that you don't approve of, is sometimes sarcastic or otherwise unpleasant to a child, sometimes feeds the child a food you don't think the child should have, sometimes is too strict, sometimes is too lenient, sometimes shows insensitivity or lack of understanding.

HARM THAT COMES FROM "PROTECTION"

Suppose a father is sitting in his chair. He asks his nine-year-old daughter to go outside and bring the mail into the house. The daughter balks; she's not in the mood. Mother, overhearing her husband's request, sides with the daughter. "Why should she have to go?" she asks in front of the child. "You could just as easily go yourself. She's playing right now." Father gets up in a huff and replies, "Fine! I'll just do it myself. There's no point in asking her to do anything."

Mother wants to protect her daughter from unreasonable treatment. In trying to save her the "anguish" of having to do something she doesn't want to do, the mother effectively instills the following messages in her daughter's brain:

- **Children are more important than spouses**.
- **Husbands and wives disrespect each other**.
- **Husbands and wives are insensitive to each other**.
- **It's okay to be rude to your father**.
- **It is not necessary or desirable to fulfill the mitzvah of *kibbud av va'em***.
- **The child is "bad" for causing a dispute between her parents**.

If Mother had said to her noncompliant daughter, "Your father asked you to go get the mail, so please do it right now," the daughter would have learned:

- **Husbands and wives respect and support each other**
- **A child has a mitzvah of *kibbud av va'em***
- **A child cannot come between her parents**

We can see, then, that in the long run the child's mental health is better served by the mother supporting her husband's "unnecessary" or "unreasonable" request. "Unnecessary" or "unreasonable" or otherwise disagreeable is not the same as abusive, as explained above. A parent cannot support a spouse's abusive behavior—the child's mental health will certainly not be served by doing so. However, a parent *can* and *should* support a spouse's substandard parenting behavior—at least in front of the child—because the child will benefit from witnessing the support itself. It is possible to discuss the substandard technique in private, if that seems to be important. Just keep in mind that spouses do things differently and it is not necessary to ensure that your spouse says and does everything *your* way. Excessive criticism is bad for marriage as well as parenting!

So from now on, look at your partner's poor parenting style as an opportunity to show your kids some really important lessons about marriage and family life. You will all benefit!

YOU OWE ME

When you purchase something at the store and don't pay for it right away, you owe the store money. When someone does an act of kindness for you, you owe them gratitude—whether or not they demand it of you. In other words, you owe somebody something to the extent that they have given you something or done something for you. You are indebted to them. The dictionary defines the word "owing" in two ways: "to be under obligation to pay or repay" and "to be indebted (to) as the cause or source of a benefit."

WHO OWES WHO WHAT

Now that we understand our terms, let's discuss who owes who what in family life. We'll begin with the obvious. A parent raises a child, caring for the youngster's physical and emotional needs twenty-four hours a day for years on end. The parent feeds and clothes the child; provides various kinds of formal and informal education; provides stimulation, entertainment, and pleasurable activities; transports the child here and there; pays for every necessity and luxury that he or she can afford to pay for; and, in short, nurtures and supports the child's growth and development in every imaginable way. The parent has been the "cause or source of benefit" as described above and therefore the child is indebted to (owes) the parent. In fact, Rabbi Reiss of Toronto's Mesivta Gedolah gave a talk a few years back in which he quoted the Gemara as saying that a child owes a parent so much just for helping him to survive the first two years of life, that a child could *never* adequately pay the parent back!

But here's the question: what does the parent owe the child?

INDEBTED TO ONE'S CHILDREN

For example, what does a parent owe her fifty-five-year-old son? If the son provides financial assistance, physical care, and emotional support, the parent owes him gratitude. What does a parent owe her ten-year-old daughter? Again, this will depend on what benefit the daughter has provided for the parent. If this youngster willingly helps with child care or household chores, then providing these benefits creates a situation in which the parent is indebted to the daughter and owes her gratitude. (Parents are also responsible for sustaining their *dependent* children—that is, providing them with food, clothing, and shelter.) In a similar fashion, a husband owes his wife gratitude for making him dinner and a wife owes her husband gratitude for providing money with which to purchase ingredients. The fact that everyone is "supposed" to fulfill his responsibilities (i.e., the child is *supposed* to help, the wife is *supposed* to cook, and the husband is *supposed* to provide financially) does not detract from the benefit received. Therefore, the recipient of the benefit owes gratitude.

THE ENTITLEMENT ETHIC

This being the case, how is it that the ten-year-old thinks her mother owes her a designer sweater or a summer at a luxurious camp? Somewhere along the way, we have forgotten the definition of the word "owe." Too many young adult children now believe that their parents "owe" them a large wedding, years of financial support, a house, travel costs, provisions for babies, and much more. They let the parents know that this is their obligation! Of greater concern is that parents themselves feel that they owe their adult children all of these material benefits, as well as Shabbos meals, babysitting, help with errands, and anything else that might be needed. And yet, it was not always this way.

Only a generation or two ago, youngsters were inculcated with the laws and spirit of honoring parents to the extent that there was no question in their minds of who owed who what. Even secular Jews knew full well that it was the *child's* job to pay back the kindness of the parent with regular contact, physical support, and financial support. Moreover, many of these people never took anything from their parents while their parents were alive (or took very little indeed) and enjoyed financial benefit only in the form of an inheritance that grateful parents were happy to leave behind.

Apart from the attitude of some modern children, nothing has changed. Parents don't owe their independent children anything except to the extent that these children have done acts of kindness for them. And then, all they owe them is gratitude.

Kids, on the other hand, owe their parents more than they can ever repay. When children really understand these concepts, they do not get upset when their parents don't choose to buy them expensive games, trips, clothes, cars, or what have you. They really don't feel that their parents owe them these things at all. Instead, children feel grateful for what their parents have *already* given them, and they try as hard as possible to repay at least a little of that kindness.

OVER THE TOP

"Wow, Levi! That's *amazing!* You did that all by yourself? You are the best!"

Fortunately, the last two or three decades have seen a rise in positive, compassionate parenting. Many people whose own parents were critical, punitive, or cold have been able to show healthy affection and positive regard to their own youngsters, thanks to the myriad of new books and classes on parenting. Moreover, parents are more aware than ever that their words and actions can have a lasting impact on their children. As a result, they at least feel guilty, even if they can't always control outbursts of temper or occasions of poor judgment. Healthy remorse helps keep parents on track, trying hard to reduce episodes of verbal abuse, insensitivity, impatience, irritability, and other normal (but harmful) reactions to the inevitable frustrations of child rearing. So, good for all of us! At least we're trying.

GONE TOO FAR

But perhaps we're trying too hard. It seems, in fact, that some of us have gone too far in our efforts to be "nice" to our children. In fact, some of us have become so afraid of hurting our youngsters' feelings that we have become afraid to say no to them, afraid to set limits, or afraid to apply discipline. We don't want them to feel unhappy, even for a short time. The result is sometimes a houseful of out-of-control children. Parents aren't just afraid of hurting them—they're actually afraid *of* them! They don't know what to do to get their kids to behave appropriately. Oddly enough, they often resort to desperate measures, yelling and screaming at them to try to gain some measure of cooperation. Of course, then they feel guilty.

TOLERATING A CHILD'S PAIN

In order to parent well, parents *must* be able to tolerate their child's pain. Being nice to a child does *not* mean saying yes to every request or failing to set appropriate limits. It means being respectful at all times. If the child doesn't like a parent's respectful no, that is just too bad. The parent must not confuse the child's disappointment with the experience of trauma. For instance, no adult has ever come into my counseling office complaining that his mother didn't let him stay up late one night. Of course, at the time of the incident some thirty-five years prior, the scene might have looked like a catastrophe. Mother said no and the youngster threw himself down on the floor, wailing like his world had come to an end. He cried till he was blue in the face, sobbing buckets of heartfelt sorrow as he hurled insults at the meanest mother in the world. It is understandable that a parent might *think* that something terrible was happening to her child, something that she must try to avoid at all costs. However, looks can be deceiving. The child was simply disappointed and had not yet been taught the appropriate way of communicating that feeling.

True trauma, on the other hand, *does* bring people into counseling. When parents use frequent yelling, threats, and excessive punishment, they are very likely traumatizing their kids. Victims of this sort of parenting make up the bulk of a therapist's practice. It is not *saying* no that is the problem; it is *yelling* it.

SICKENINGLY SWEET

There is another error that occurs as a result of fearing children's negative emotions: excessive praise. Now that parents know how important encouragement and positive reinforcement can be, they are eager to use these tools to help their kids feel good about themselves. And yet, excessive praise can actually have the opposite effect, as this thirty-eight-year-old woman explained to me recently:

"My parents praised me nonstop, making me feel stupid, unseen, and uncared for. Everything I did, and still do as an adult, is 'wonderful,' 'amazing,' 'the best.' I made a microwave reheated meal for them the other day and they wouldn't stop going on about how terrific it was. It's as if they were saying to me, 'Wow—you took the wrapper off the package all by yourself? You are so clever!' It doesn't matter if I manage to match my outfit properly or win a Nobel Prize—to them it's all the same."

From this account we can see how important it is to be authentic with children. Say it's "fine" when it's fine. Say it's "good" when it's good. Say it's "amazing" only when it's amazing. Don't worry about crushing your child's spirit because you weren't effusive enough. Worry instead about being so phony that your child ends up feeling invisible and unreal. This is not an invitation to return to excessive criticism; it's truly important to look for the good and encourage it. However, there is no need to go over the top. Your five-year-old may have painted a lovely tree, but it probably *isn't* the best tree ever. Don't lie.

MIND YOUR MANNERS

I have a distinct memory of a lesson my great-grandmother taught me when I was around three or four years old. She was living at my grandmother's house, and my parents had brought us over for our regular weekly visit. I can't tell you much about this great-grandmother, because she passed away a short while after the incident. Here is my one clear memory of this matriarch.

"Bubby-Bubby," as we called her, was sitting on the front veranda. I came outside to play. I don't know what was in my little mind at the time—perhaps I didn't like the way she was looking at me or perhaps I was put off by her ancient appearance. I really don't know. What I *do* know is that I stuck my tongue out at her. And then—*whap!*—the sudden sting of her hand landing hard on my little face. I still recall the shock. And the realization that I had done something very, very wrong.

NOWADAYS

Today, my great-grandmother's educational strategy would likely be called child abuse. Indeed, there are better ways to get the point across, ways that won't cause so much damage. I can't say that I have fond memories of this woman, and I'm not sure that our relationship would have bloomed to the point where she might have become an inspiring role model for me. Nonetheless, her straightforward message, delivered with complete confidence, was clear and correct: *children must show respect to their elders.*

As we mentioned, many modern parents have, to their own detriment, lost the conviction (and hence the ability) to impart this essential message. Busy trying to form healthy emotional bonds with their youngsters, they hesitate to set up barriers such as distinctions between the generations. Rather, they aim to befriend their children and attempt to establish an equal playing field. In fact, some parents are as rude to their children as their children are to them, ensuring that there will be no teacher-student relationship. Others will be very respectful to their kids while failing to demand the same, giving children the false impression that "anything goes." Some will make attempts to teach the basics of respect but often do so in a weak, ambivalent way. "That's not nice. Don't speak like that to Mommy." Such mild reprimands are a far cry from a slap in the face in the sense that they're unlikely to get the child's lifelong attention. And yet, there must be some way to teach children to mind their manners that is truly effective without being emotionally devastating.

THE IMPORTANCE OF MANNERS

A well-behaved child is a more likable child to be around. This helps the child receive the positive attention he needs from parents, teachers, peers, and significant others. Wild, poorly mannered children also get lots of attention of course—mostly negative. This harms their self-concept while it reinforces more obnoxious behavior. A poorly behaved child will have more short- and long-term problems. We do our children a big favor, psychologically speaking, when we manage to teach them how to behave respectfully.

We do them an even bigger favor spiritually speaking, because Hashem wants children to respect their elders. By teaching children how to conduct themselves vis-à-vis parents, teachers, the aged, and other adults, we are helping them to succeed in the performance of important mitzvos. By neglecting their education in this department, we harm them on every level.

STRATEGIES FOR TEACHING MANNERS

The well-mannered child learns much from his well-mannered parents. Adults who speak roughly or too loudly to their own parents train their kids how to do the same to them. Adults who speak rudely to each other train their kids how to do the same to them. Adults who yell or bark at their children train their kids to do the same to them. (Teachers have a similar educational impact through their own conduct.)

In addition to providing an adequate model of manners for a child, parents must also *teach* the child what is permissible and impermissible speech and behavior toward elders. The preferred method of teaching is the CLeaR Method—Comment, Label, and Reward. This strategy uses positive attention to quickly and strongly reinforce the desirable behavior. When a child has spoken nicely to a grandparent, for instance, the parent can Comment ("I like the way you said hello so nicely to Bubby"), Label ("That was so *thoughtful* of you"), and Reward ("I think you should go to the cupboard and get a cookie for you and Bubby to have as a treat").

Unacceptable behavior needs to be firmly addressed. Using appropriate negative consequences, parents can make it very clear that disruptive, rude, or otherwise unpleasant behavior is not fitting for a Jewish child inside or outside the home. Explaining this point is not enough. Children need to feel the ramifications of their behavior. They also need constant, consistent feedback about their behavior. They'll adjust accordingly and reap all the benefits the good manners bring.

HELPING KIDS DECIDE

Not everyone finds it easy to make decisions. In fact, some people suffer terribly over making a commitment to a purchase, a person, or an activity. "What if it's the wrong choice?" "What if other people will laugh at me/think I'm dumb for making this choice?" "What if it turns out to be a very costly error?" These kinds of questions can paralyze decision makers. Exhausting second-guessing, rumination, and intensive research make decision making unpleasant and anxiety provoking for this group.

For decision-challenged folks, the anguish can continue long after the commitment is made. "I shouldn't have bought this one. The other one would have been better. Now I can't take it back and it'll be all wrong forever." "Maybe I can take it back or back out of it and choose what I should have chosen before." Unsure people live in a world of self-recrimination and blame. They can never get it right.

ENCOURAGING CONFIDENCE

Parents can play a role in helping their kids make confident decisions or in fostering decision insecurity. Decision insecurity is fostered by offering frequent negative feedback to the child. "That sweater doesn't go with that skirt," "You should play with so-and-so more often," "I don't understand why you like that author." The child begins to think, "Maybe Mom is right; I don't know how to dress/who to play with/what to read." When an authority figure like a parent decides what is supposed to be appealing and what is not supposed to be appealing, a child can easily lose confidence in his or her ability to make that call. Parents should save criticism for when it *really* matters.

When it comes to matters of personal preference, individual taste should be encouraged rather than discouraged. Personal preference is not halacha; there is no right or wrong. One person may like a particular painting while another despises the same piece of art. One youngster may like ketchup on his peanut butter sandwich while another would gag at the thought. However, a parent who wants to help her child be confident enough to decide matters of personal preference by him or herself will be careful to encourage that confidence. "Why, ketchup on peanut butter is quite original, Yossi! You will probably be a gourmet cook one day who invents all kinds of new delicacies!"

DECISION ANXIETY

Trouble making decisions can be aggravated by critical parents. However, like all forms of anxiety, genes play a role as well. Adults and children with serious difficulties in making decisions are likely to be people whose genetic makeup made them particularly vulnerable to critical parents.

Most families have either a set of depression-type genes or a set of anxiety-type genes or both running through their family trees. Thus, most individuals have a tendency to some degree of negativity or worry. This tendency is reinforced by parents who model negativity and worry by expressing these feelings out loud, including the expression of critical remarks. Parents can be critical because they are anxious. They are worried that their child's perceived poor decision may have serious negative consequences. What will happen if the child goes out in public with the unmatched outfit? What will happen if he continues to put ketchup on peanut butter sandwiches? The parent, so eager to save her child pain, accidentally increases the child's suffering by causing the child to become uncertain.

Sometimes a child's poor choices do end up causing difficulty, embarrassment, financial loss, or other trouble. However, this is true of some of the choices that *anyone of any age* will make. The error itself needs to be welcomed rather than reprimanded. "I told you that wasn't a good idea!" is not a helpful remark to make to a youngster whose poor decision results in a loss of some kind. Rather, parents can offer the more supportive and less traumatic, "You made a choice and sometimes it works out the way you hope it will and sometimes it doesn't—that's just how it goes. It happens to your father and me all the time!" Welcoming errors as part of the decision-making process allows children to continue to take the risk of making a decision. They learn that it is not the end of the world if the decision turns out badly, whereas those children who are made to feel that poor decisions are disastrous may have a lot of angst about making decisions. Similarly, the courage to make a decision is more important than the decision itself. A child who picks out a color for her bedroom wall can be encouraged as an interior-decorator-in-the-making whether or not the parent likes the color in question. Rewarding decision-making behavior can help kids become confident decision makers.

LOOK, MA, NO HANDS!

There's the little guy on his bike, experimenting with holding his hands in the air instead of placing them on the handlebars where they belong. He's so proud of himself that he shouts to Mom to come see his accomplishment. "Look, Ma! No hands!" And while his antics are slightly dangerous, he is truly accomplishing something. He is balancing everything without the benefit of hands—just like his mother had to do during his period of infancy and just like she continues to do with every baby she is blessed with.

MIXED FEELINGS

Precisely because a woman appreciates the gift of motherhood, she is apt to feel guilty when she struggles during the early months of her children's lives. Her gratitude for the opportunity to care for her babies does not, however, translate into boundless energy, four extra hands, and an influx of hired help. Gratitude is one thing, and getting through each day is another. The former is a warm, loving connection to Hashem, while the latter is just plain hard.

It's hard to cook, shop, clean, or tend to toddlers when your hands are full of a baby. It's hard to eat your own breakfast, lunch, or dinner! It's hard to give other family members the time and attention they need, hard to help out community members, hard to daven, hard to get a shower. Everything is much harder. And we haven't even mentioned the other challenges that come with baby care, such as never sleeping for more than a couple of hours at a time and being chronically exhausted.

And yet, many women feel inadequate or just plain bad if they dare to acknowledge that they're finding life with their baby hard. They feel alone, as if they are the only ones who struggle this way. They feel like there must be something wrong with them, since "everyone else" manages to cope. It's so unfortunate that, on top of all the real difficulties that accompany the mothering of an infant, women add to their own suffering by berating themselves in this way.

SELF-SUPPORT

Instead of knocking themselves down, mothers should be applauding themselves for managing to do so much. After all, it is challenging to do everything with one hand! Almost everyone who has had the experience of working outside the home agrees that being at work is far easier than being at home—with or without a new baby on the scene. When there is an infant around, the primary caretaker is particularly challenged. Indeed, when a woman with a baby manages to get through each day even in a minimal way (providing the minimum in the way of meals and household standards) she should be very pleased with herself. When the baby is older, she can make fancier meals and put more effort into household management. During the infancy stage, however, she needs to focus on maintaining her own energy in order to be able to properly attend to the needs of a 24/7 demanding infant.

There's nothing wrong with being kind to oneself—saying nice, encouraging, and appreciative words. A mother can tell herself, "You are amazing! Taking care of an infant is a huge task, and yet you are managing to do that and carry on with the household/ your job/the children/your marriage. Good for you!" Talking to oneself this way is actually very healthy. It can boost energy reserves, reduce stress, and improve functioning. Kindness can also go beyond appreciative words. Give yourself permission to replenish energy reserves regularly: "You're getting tired. Go lie down with the baby for awhile. You can serve cottage cheese and bananas for dinner tonight."

On the other hand, when mothers hear an inner voice scolding them for failing to accomplish enough, they should quickly smother it with an imaginary silencer. The scolding voice receives its fuel from the *yezter hara*, the dark side. It leads a woman to feel so inadequate that she becomes depressed. No longer able to serve Hashem *b'simcha*, the woman enters a cycle of dysfunction in which the normal difficulties of mothering a baby cycle out of control and the entire task becomes so overwhelming that her ability to care for herself and her family is threatened. Self-abuse is real, and it's really destructive. Due to fatigue and overwhelm, mothers of infants are particularly vulnerable to it and need to be vigilant against it. Now is the time to apply "If I am not for myself, who will be?" Lower the bar, increase self-appreciation, and abstain from harsh accusations. Be your own best friend and fan club! It's not narcissistic; it's necessary. If your internal "bank account" is empty, you'll have nothing to give. However, if you make regular deposits of self-appreciation and self-care, you'll be able to continue to give to that baby and to everyone else who is counting on you.

WE'LL DO IT

Naaseh v'nishma—we'll do it, and we'll internalize it, we'll do it and we'll listen, we'll do it and we'll obey, we'll do it and we'll understand. However the phrase is translated, it is completely clear that it starts with "we'll do it!" No questions asked.

Parents would be ever so happy if their kids would adopt the same attitude that the Jews adopted at Har Sinai.

WANTING A REASON

Children of all ages like to have a reason for why they ought to do something. Preschoolers are particularly big on "why" questions. A more sophisticated form of questioning develops as the child matures. Now a straightforward "why" that could be satisfied earlier by a simple one-liner turns into a complex "why" that demands an intelligent response. "Why do I need to eat vegetables if I can get fiber and nutrition from my five daily servings of fruit and grain products, Mom?" Mom might prefer the "just eat it and be quiet" approach to the "let me call my nutritionist and get back to you on that" reply. Nonetheless, the older child often feels entitled to a reasonable, informed, thought-out answer along with full disclosure in every instance; he'll settle for nothing less. Unperturbed by his own lack of worldly experience or maturity, he feels that he knows better than his parents and is willing to take them on in a debate over any issue. He is so convincing that even his parents are intimidated; *maybe he's right.*

SUBMITTING TO AUTHORITY

Whether the child is right or wrong is not the issue. The child needs to learn how to accept parental authority comfortably. The child's insistence on parental justification can be unnerving:

"Our five-year-old daughter Rifky likes a little girl in her class named Ahuva. Rifky wants me to make playdates for her and Ahuva. However, Ahuva's father recently did something terrible to my husband in a business matter—something that hurt us very badly. My husband wants nothing more to do with the family and so I no longer talk to Ahuva's mother. It would be impossible to make playdates at this point. Rifky is constantly asking me why I won't do it—she won't let up. What do I tell her?"

"We are going through a divorce. My husband and I never fought in front of the children and so, in addition to being grief stricken, they are all completely shocked. They want to know why it's happening. My oldest is eleven and the youngest is a baby. There's no way I can explain to them what their father has done. But they are demanding an explanation. What do I tell them?"

"My fourteen-year-old wants to go on a hiking trip with his best friend's family this summer. It would be just the father, their three boys, and my son. I am very against it and I told him he can't go. He is demanding a reason that makes sense to him. Believe me, I have my reasons—but none that he would find satisfactory. Is it okay for me to stick to my guns and say no even if I don't have a reason that he understands?"

PARENTAL PREROGATIVE

Parents *must* establish a track record of being reasonable. Rabbi Samson Raphael Hirsch explains that this is accomplished by frequently offering one brief explanation for parental decisions as a courtesy to the child. "I want you to do your homework before dinner because I like you to have some relaxing time right before bed." There is no need to offer more reasons if the child doesn't like the first one!

Moreover, if the parent conducts himself or herself in a fair and reasonable way, the child will come to experience the parent as a reasonable person. Making too many arbitrary and constricting rules, being emotionally unpredictable, having a bad temper or otherwise showing signs of instability and irrationality definitely erodes trust.

Having done all this, the parent can comfortably decide when *not* to share all thoughts, feelings, and information. As long as this withholding is the exception and not the rule in parenting, it has its appropriate place. Parents can say, "I have my reasons, but I am not free to explain them to you," or "There are good reasons, but you are not at the age where you can understand them—you'll have to wait until you're older," or "I don't feel I need to give you a reason other than this is the way I want it right now."

When a child feels his parents' love and concern and has come to see them as reasonable people, it will be much easier for them to accept an attitude of *naaseh v'nishma* when it is asked of them.

THE
STRONG-WILLED
CHILD

S ome kids are not much of a parenting challenge. They cooperate from day one, quickly establishing civilized eating
and sleeping rhythms, entertaining themselves nicely in their
playpens and later on in the playroom. They generally do what
they're told to. The only discipline they require is a look or sometimes a firm word, although if told to sit on a "thinking chair" for a
few minutes, they will go peacefully and tearfully, already regretting
their misdeed. This is not *your* child.

Your strong-willed child has a mind of his or her own. This child
marches to his own drum. Your wishes are inconsequential. Your

punishment is unimpressive. He punishes you back, trashing his room or lashing out at you physically. He talks as if he is your equal and, often, as if he is your boss. When things don't go his way, the strong-willed child loudly declares his dissatisfaction, wailing intensely for long periods of time. He is not subtle. What he *is* is exhausting.

Parents often worry that they somehow created a monster by making some serious parenting errors. Difficult children are usually not difficult because of poor parenting strategies, although poor parenting strategies can certainly make matters worse. Rather, they are difficult because of genetically inherited characteristics and temperaments. Easy kids inherit the easygoing, flexible, good-mood genes and difficult children inherit a cluster containing inflexibility, moodiness, intensity, irritability, and strong will. Average children have a mixture of both easy and challenging characteristics.

Strong-willed children can also have a mixture of traits, some kids falling out on the easier end of the strong-willed spectrum than others. Strong controlling tendencies may reflect personality differences or underlying mental health conditions, such as oppositional-defiant disorder (ODD), bipolar disorder, attention deficit hyperactivity disorder (ADHD), Tourette's syndrome, depression, or obsessive-compulsive disorder (OCD). Normally children do not receive an early diagnosis of any of these conditions—years go by before assessment is sought or accurately delivered. Meanwhile, parents simply find themselves living with a difficult to manage youngster. Psychiatric diagnosis or not, all parents have to deal with the kind of child they get, or, as *Chazal* say, they must "educate the child according to his way."

LIVING WITH THE STRONG-WILLED CHILD

Parents have to be particularly skilled when raising a strong-willed child. Any tendency that they themselves have to be controlling will have to be seriously curbed. There's nothing worse for a strong-willed child than a parent who won't back down. Think two horns locking. If your child is strong-willed, try to avoid giving instructions. Of course, you'll have to give some instructions ("Time to go to bed!") but if it's at all possible to refrain from giving direct orders, then do so. If you can, give options and choices instead of direct instructions. Intervene less, say less, give more breathing space.

One essential strategy in dealing with opinionated, bossy kids is to carefully select one's battles. The ideal situation is to model flexibility. Don't make every little thing an issue. On the contrary, let the child have it his or her way frequently. When it isn't appropriate for the child to have exactly what he or she wants, try to work out compromises, conditions which are not perfectly to your liking but which are "good enough" for your bottom line standards. The process of negotiation itself helps model and teach compromise to the inflexible child.

However, there will be times when flexibility on your part will not be an option. For example, your child may want to go without a coat on an icy cold day. On those few occasions that you *do* want to hold your ground, ensure that you establish complete authority. If you maintain 80 percent positive, warm, and flexible communication on a daily basis, you can then afford to use intense discipline on the few occasions on which you feel boundary setting, control, or guidance is required.

Effective discipline with this child involves *consistent* action. One explanation is all that is needed regarding any inappropriate behavior (e.g., "Don't leave my sight in the mall, because it isn't safe"). The child should be warned that any similar offense will result in a specific aversive consequence (e.g., "From now on, if you leave my sight, you will have to sit with me for five minutes before we go any further"). A child who doesn't cooperate with punishment will be in line for more intense negative consequences (think "ticket" versus "jail"). Get professional guidance if you need help in asserting your authority or maintaining the ideal love/authority ratio.

Your strong-willed child will require all the skill you have. But take comfort: these kids often grow up to be influential leaders in society. Give it twenty years or so.

PLEASE STOP ME!

I have no control…when I see that tray of chocolate-covered raisins I just eat them till they're all gone…please don't put it out where I can see it!"

"Sure I exercise every day. But when I'm on my own I can barely do ten push-ups. When I'm with my trainer I do twenty, because the trainer doesn't care how much I whine about it—she just makes me do it."

"I used to park here all the time, but the last two times I got a ticket so I don't do it anymore—it's too expensive."

HELP ME STOP MYSELF

We grown-ups don't always have the self-discipline we need. No one is watching, so we misbehave all the time—yelling at our family members and not speaking nicely, eating the wrong things in the wrong quantities, staying up too late, neglecting our paperwork, and on and on. If we experience a nasty consequence here and there, our behavior improves. A ticket, a doctor's warning, a late penalty—it all helps keep us in line. We need outside discipline.

In fact, we *want* outside discipline. We actually pay for the trainer to hold us to our program! We know that we'll be too lenient on ourselves and never achieve our health and beauty goals without someone pushing us, refusing to let us "get away" with our own lazy attitude. We sign up and pay for dieticians or weight loss counselors that force accountability and threaten the punishment of public humiliation for failing to stick to our eating plan. Many people know they cannot function well without structure, the constraints of deadlines, bosses, feedback, and consequences. Left to their own devices, they would flounder and accomplish little.

It's as if we are saying, "Help me control myself in order to achieve my goals. I can't do it on my own."

CHILDREN WANT US TO HELP THEM

If we grown-ups can't do it all on our own, why would we think that children can? They, even more than us, need structured incentives and outside boundary-setters to help them succeed. Schoolwork is no more fun than dieting; kids approach it in much the same way. It is a necessary evil. If no one is looking, maybe they can get away with not doing it. However, like adult dieters, kids want to succeed. They want the thrill of accomplishment and of attaining their goals. When parents take on the role of "trainer"—coach, policeman, or other taskmaster—children have a greater chance of succeeding.

Of course, this reality does not immediately fill a child's heart with overflowing gratitude toward his parents. In fact, the child may feel less sunny emotions, like resentment and even rage. A child benefits from discipline, but the results are not usually immediate.

Being "forced" to go to bed on time for several months on end may lead to a gradual improvement both in grades and daily mood, but the child may never even recognize the connection between the firm parental hand and the positive life outcomes. In fact, the child may take full credit for his success, never even thanking his parents for standing their ground. (In this, he resembles us adults who take credit for our successes without so much as a nod to Hashem.)

Although specific connections may not be made, children usually recognize that parental guidance is necessary and helpful. Even the bar mitzvah boy thanks his parents for all that they've done to help prepare him for the transition into manhood. Had his parents been too busy or distracted to bother with him, the youngster would have felt neglected and even unloved. Children want their parents to step in. They appreciate, even if they do not enjoy, the experience of being called to task. They want someone to pull in the reigns, say no, lay down the law, mete out punishment—so that they do not have to fight their *yetzer hara* alone.

DISCIPLINE WITH LOVE

Children want discipline—and need it. The trick is to deliver it in such a way that it helps them achieve success without acquiring emotional or relationship baggage. Discipline never involves yelling, insulting, diminishing, or hurting a child. It's not emotional; it's businesslike, a pre-warned annoying consequence for unacceptable behavior. When balanced with lots of love and warmth (80 percent good-feeling attention to 20 percent guidance) and delivered in a respectful, nonrejecting manner, discipline is a true gift to one's children, setting them on a path of success.

HE'S NOT MINE

Y ou've seen those parents on the street and in the stores: they're threatening their child, grabbing him roughly, dragging him along while he screams in protest. *What kind of parent is that?* you wonder. *Hasn't he/she ever taken a parenting class? That's no way to treat a precious neshamaleh!*

And you go back to the business of parenting your own kids, applying all that you read and hear, nurturing each one with careful, loving attention. All of them till now have been cooperative. You've complimented yourself on your brilliant parenting techniques. *If only others would do it my way, they'd also have well-behaved children,* you've thought in your heart.

That is, until number 8 (or whoever) was born—the child that broke the mold. Nothing you've done with the others is working with this one. Your patience, your encouragement, your positive feedback—none of it makes a difference. This child laughs in your face as he hangs from the rafters. Going shopping with him is a nightmare. You've become one of "those" parents—if only to save the youngster's life. Without your firm hand upon him, he'd be running off with some stranger or sitting alone in the middle of the parking lot. You're tearing the hairs out of your *sheitel*.

OUT-OF-CONTROL EXPERIENCES

Were you the kind of person who enjoyed amusement park rides? If so, parenting is the job for you. With its ups and downs, sudden curves, dark tunnels, and endless surprises, it offers the ride of a lifetime. And, the feeling of being a helpless passenger just adds to the excitement. There's nothing you can do!

Of course, you're not really totally helpless in parenting. This is because there are some aspects of parenting that are practical and functional—more like a subway ride than a roller coaster. With these parts of the job, you pay for your ticket, get on the train, and go where you want to go. For instance, you sign the child up for school, take him there each day, and let him receive an education. That was in your control. If Hashem wants the rest of the experience to unfold uneventfully for you, it will. But if not, it won't. Perhaps the child will excel or perhaps he will have learning problems or behavioral problems. That's the part that's not in your control; that's the roller-coaster part of child development.

Similarly, you can put your child to bed, but you can't make her go to sleep. You can take her to the birthday party, but you can't make her play with the other children. You can teach her how to use her words, but you can't ensure that she won't slap, grab, or stab the other kids. You can teach your teenager about the evils of substance abuse and yet you can't follow him around to supervise his moment-to-moment activities. In short, you can offer love, guidance, and discipline, but you can't *make* a child benefit from your interventions.

This reality is less obvious with those kids who respond according to the book. Unfortunately, many children haven't read the book. So you do what you can, but ultimately, you learn that can't live in your child's body and control his or her thoughts, feelings, and actions. As in so many other areas of life, you must learn to deal with your helplessness. You pour your heart out to Hashem.

WHEN YOUR CHILD EMBARRASSES YOU

Because you can't ensure that your child will behave appropriately, there will be times when your child's behavior will mortify you. Little kids can cause big embarrassments. And big ones can seriously frighten, humiliate, and dismay their parents. This is true even when the parents themselves are exemplary people. The personal suffering may be intensified when the parents know for a fact that things they've done or said have actually exacerbated the problem. For instance, it's bad enough to know that your child has called the teacher a name, and worse still if you know that the child is only copying what you do at home.

How do parents cope with their children's public displays of bad behavior? Many, of course, want to hide in their houses and never go out again. Others have a philosophy that allows them to hold their heads high despite the shenanigans of their offspring: "Kids are kids—they have to go through all sorts of stages and experiences in order to grow up. It's normal and expected that they will behave badly. As long as *I'm* not the one biting my peers, I don't have to feel ashamed." This sort of philosophy allows parents to tolerate the unacceptable and even outrageous behaviors of their children as part of the normal developmental process. Each child is on his journey, just as we all are.

HANDLING A PARENTING CRISIS

I magine that you embody the trait of honesty. You write to the publisher for permission before photocopying a page of a book, you correct the cashier who makes an error in your favor, you pay all your taxes.

Now imagine your shock, dismay, and grief when you get called into the principal's office regarding your sixteen-year-old-daughter who has been caught cheating on her exam. It turns out that this is not the first incident. Now your participation is required. You listen to the principal as your daughter sits with you, head bowed. You are confused, ashamed, and distraught. Finally, the principal sends your daughter back to class. What are you feeling as you take the long drive home?

PARENTAL SHOCK

Situations like this regularly happen to parents like you. The issue could be discovering that a child cheats, or it could be any other issue: the child steals or lies or abuses younger children. The child is not completely *shomer mitzvos*. The child has a "secret life" with friends you don't know about. The child is taking drugs or abusing alcohol. The child smokes cigarettes. Whatever it is that the child is doing, it is not in accordance with the upbringing you have offered. How could this happen? After all that you instilled! Do you not know your own child? How long has this been going on?

Most parents, learning that their child has disregarded their prime values and educational efforts, feel anger, grief, helplessness, and loss of control. Some parents experience guilt, feeling it is somehow their fault—something they did or did not do all these years. They feel like failures. Depending on what the child has done and how public the action is, the parents may feel varying degrees of humiliation and shame.

.

CONFRONTING THE ISSUE

Despite the overflow of emotions, parents must be practical in the moment. How should the child be handled once the issue is in the open? In our "cheating scenario" above, the mother waits at home for her daughter to return from school. How should she greet her? With the usual cheery welcome? With cold silence? With a snarled order to meet her in the kitchen for a "talk"? And if the mother is seething with emotion, what sort of "talk" will transpire? Many parents, freshly stunned from learning shocking, unpleasant information about a child, lash into the child at the first opportunity: "What were you thinking? Is there something wrong with you? After all these years do you not understand the importance of what we have taught you? I can't believe that a daughter of mine would behave in this way. You are an embarrassment to this family!"

If parents confront a child while their own emotions are still teeming inside, they can cause serious harm to the parent-child bond as well as to the child him or herself. The time for confrontation is always a "teaching moment"—a time in which both the child's emotions and the parents' emotions are settled. This might be *hours* or *days* after an incident occurs. The parent must help him or *herself* before attempting to address the child.

HANDLING THE FEELINGS

Reduce the shock first. Grounding oneself in one's daily routine can be helpful: go shopping, make dinner, go back to work. When you are more settled, think about the incident and notice what is happening physically inside your body (lump in throat, pit in stomach, and so forth). See if you can name your feelings. Naming feelings helps to contain and soothe them. Talk to someone about what's happened: a friend, spouse, or professional. Remember that not everything in parenting is your fault. In fact, the child spends most of his or her day and life away from you, influenced by other people. In addition, the child has his or her own free will, inherited personality traits, and other influences. You are certainly a part of the picture and you do have some influence and input, but you *do not* have any control. Your child is a separate, free human being on his or her own life journey.

Remind yourself that you will be able to best help your child by talking respectfully and caringly about the issue at hand. You are there as a helpful guide through good times and other times. Your job description hasn't changed. You are still your child's educator. Your child needs you now.

HELPING THE CHILD

Once you are calm and settled, you can think about a parenting plan. What do you want to convey to the child? What is your teaching strategy? In confronting the child, be sure to *listen first*; name feelings (the child's and yours) second; and give advice, information, or other forms of guidance third. Discipline, when appropriate, would follow these steps. In this way, you will help, rather than hurt. You can be a positive part of your child's painful learning experiences.

CAN'T RELATE

The school called to tell me that my daughter had been suspended. I, who had never misbehaved in my entire life, had a daughter who could behave so badly that she could be suspended from school! I was dismayed, shocked, and ashamed beyond belief."

How is it possible that our children can be so different from us? Don't we share the same genes? As we said in the previous chapter, parents wonder: How can *my* son be caught shoplifting when *I* am so honest that I return to stores to give them a penny that I owe them? How can *my* child be so lazy when *I'm* such a hard worker? How can *my* child be a bully when *I'm* such a sensitive, kind person?

DON'T IDENTIFY

When the differences are good ones, parents like to take credit for the latent genes that may be at play: "I guess he gets his generosity from my father, who was very much the same way." However, when the differences are not so positive, parents don't want to identify with the child. "No one in our family ever acted like that. This is a total aberration, a one-of-a-kind. Honestly, I can't believe this child is related to us!"

ASHAMED OF OUR CHILD

Parents cannot make their children do, think, or feel anything. At every age—from infancy through adulthood—children are independent beings. Parents can *guide* them and even *influence* them, but they cannot *control* them. Too bad. The inability to control children gives parents a lot of grief.

When a child is different from the parent in a way the parent disapproves of, the parent often feels shame. For instance, when the child lies or steals while the parent is honest and upright, the parent will often feel (along with many other feelings) the feeling of shame. This is an interesting phenomenon. Shame is something that people feel when they know they've done something dishonorable or when they have been exposed as inadequate or lacking. But what did the *parent* do that was dishonorable when it is the *child* who is stealing and lying? What did the parent do wrong when it was the child who got suspended? How is the parent inadequate when the child performs poorly in school?

NACHAS

Parental shame may be more understandable when we look at the phenomenon of *nachas*—pride in our children. People may feel proud when they accomplish something good. Interestingly, parents feel proud when they see their kids succeeding. They have *nachas*.

The more that others recognize the success of the child, the more *nachas* the parent feels. But why should the parent feel pride? What was it that the parent accomplished? If the *child* is doing very well in school, how is the *parent* being successful?

At some level, the parent is accepting control over the child's performance. My child—my flesh and blood—the product of everything that I have done every day in raising him, is now producing admirable results. Ultimately, his success is my success. I am proud of "us."

Similarly, when the child performs poorly, parents feel shame because, at some level, they are accepting control over the child's performance. My child—my flesh and blood—the product of everything that I have done every day in raising him, is performing terribly. Ultimately, his failure is my failure. I am ashamed of "us."

RAISING CHILDREN

The parent's job is to "raise" the child, to bring him to a higher place. We can be proud of ourselves or ashamed of ourselves for the way *we* behave in parenting. However, since the child's success and failure is out of our control, we need to step back. We should not accept credit or blame for the child's performance (except in those areas where we did something that directly impacted positively or negatively on the outcome). When we find that we do have a negative role to play, then *teshuva* (self-improvement) is in order—not guilt and shame. However, in most situations, the parent bears no direct responsibility for the actions of the child. Instead of accepting guilt for the child's behavior, parents need to accept responsibility for helping the child grow through the experience.

When the child has been suspended from school, she needs a parent who can help her get back on her feet. It is Hashem who controls the world, not the parent. Therefore, the parent can assume that

Hashem has sent the suspension issue to the parent to be dealt with in the best possible way. All parents have parenting challenges. Instead of feeling shame for having a poorly performing child, parents can feel proud of the way they choose to handle the situation. And choosing to handle the situation well is the one thing that parents *can* control.

IT'S MY FAULT

"Mommy, where did I sleep when I was a baby?"

"You slept in my bed, sweetie, right beside me."

"I wish you would have put me in a crib like everyone else so I wouldn't be afraid to sleep in my own bed now."

What? After all I did for you? I never wanted you to cry for even a minute! I slept poorly for two and a half years so you wouldn't have to be alone in your own room. I defied my husband, my sisters, my friends, and my entire community in order to do what I knew in my heart was the best thing for you—and now, this? How can you blame me for *your* sleeping disorder?

Sigh. Motherhood is like that sometimes. No matter what a parent does, it can be wrong. "When my three-year-old's tower falls down, he says it's my fault—even if I'm in another room at the time!" "My daughter tells me I ruined her life by moving to another country when she was in sixth grade. She's never forgiven me." "My son blames me for giving birth to him."

Even when children don't openly blame their mothers, the mothers may blame themselves. Some mothers feel guilty for everything. They blame themselves for their children's bad tempers, their insecurities, and their outrageous behavior ("I feel like such a failure when the principal complains that Yossi is bullying the younger children!"). Mothers take it all on. They fail to take into account the enormous role that genes play in determining character traits and behavioral tendencies. They fail to take into account the other factors that affect their children's choices, such as the other parent, the school, the peer group, and the community, and they fail to take into account the child's free will. Instead, they assume that they can actually *cause* their child to behave a certain way. Actually, parents just don't have that much power.

HELPLESS, OUT OF CONTROL AND OVERWHELMED

It doesn't help that mothers, being human, actually do make mistakes. We all say and do things we regret. ("I was so harsh with my older children. Now I've taken parenting courses and I parent my younger ones so differently. I feel so guilty for what I did before. I know I scarred them.") Even after graduating from Parenting U, we make daily errors, some small and others not so small. Later, when the kids have problems, we can always trace them back to our own imperfect moments, our communication blunders, and our poor decisions. We can always blame ourselves.

Indeed, raising a large family invites constant failure. Nobody can smile for thirty or forty years straight, especially when tired, overwhelmed, stressed, unwell, or otherwise in a weakened state. Nobody can say the "right thing" 100 percent of the time. In addition, each parent has her blind spot, the place where she can't see straight due to her own nature or upbringing. She will certainly fall into the abyss on many occasions over the years.

IMPOSSIBLE STANDARDS

The parenting task is destined for failure—if we judge it by its products. Children, after all, are only human—meaning that they have foibles, character flaws, disorders, and issues. Since parents tend to consider themselves "successful" to the extent that each and every one of their children has miraculously overcome the human condition of imperfection, parents are doomed to "failure." And since a mother is only as "successful" as her least "successful" child—at least in her own mind—she can always feel inadequate. Unless, of course, she begins to look at parenting with different eyes.

Suppose, for instance, that she looked at parenting as a journey, a growth process (her own, not her child's). Suppose that, through compassionate eyes, she looked at her progress and development over the decades: moving toward more patience, more *emunah* and *bitachon*, more calm, less anxiety, more maturity, less impulsivity, more understanding, more wisdom. Instead of focusing her attention on what she did wrong, suppose she focused on what she learned. She did what she could do at each parenting moment and of course, what she could do improved with experience and maturity. While there are things that might actually be her fault, she begins to realize that there is no need to accept blame across the board. *Everything* isn't her fault.

In this more compassionate worldview, Mother understands and accepts that Hashem wanted each child to experience the particular "error" she made at the time she made it. Both she and the child were meant to grow from it. She's a successful parent to the extent that she uses the challenges of parenting to examine herself and take the next step forward.

A ROSE
BY ANY OTHER
NAME

You can't tell by looking at someone what is going on inside his mind, heart, and soul. However, you can make a pretty good guess. For instance, if you praise someone, you can assume he'll be feeling pleased and he'll be experiencing a sense of expansion. If you insult him, you can safely imagine that he'll be feeling hurt and he'll be experiencing a sense of constriction. Although there are individual differences in resilience, with some folks having tough skin and some having no skin at all, most children are very thin skinned. All forms of verbal abuse tend to make long-lasting impressions on impressionable minds.

WHAT IS VERBAL ABUSE?

Some people may not recognize that their own style of expression is verbally abusive. "If he's late coming into class, I tell him he's a baby. It makes him pay more attention next time the recess bell rings. Why is that abusive?" asks a first-grade rebbe. Another rebbe agrees: "Humiliation works! I tell a wild boy he has to spend the next hour in kindergarten and he should bring his diapers and pacifier to school. He shapes up. I'm just helping him succeed."

Indeed, many parents follow a similar philosophy. Tell it like it is. "You're impossible!" "You're a lazy good-for-nothing!" "You're driving me crazy!" "You're an animal!" Sometimes parents admit that such words aren't really meant for the well-being of their youngster—they are simply expressions of utter parental exasperation. Whatever their motivation, people who speak like this to their children clearly do not appreciate the severity of their words and the intensity of their negative impact.

Most parents and teachers want the best for the children in their charge. And yet, many will call kids names and assault their characters in order to achieve a particular outcome. "He doesn't listen unless I scream at him, so I scream at him," says one mother, who is surprised to learn that screaming itself is a form of verbal abuse. "I tell him he'll never amount to anything if he keeps shirking his responsibilities—shouldn't I let him know the truth?" asks a father who's struggling with an unmotivated teen. These parents are usually just copying techniques they learned in their own childhood homes. No one sits down and actually *thinks* verbally abusive strategies into place. They just pop up spontaneously to fit the occasion. They can be justified later.

THE COST OF VERBAL ABUSE

Some people feel that the end justifies the means. Do they really understand that verbally abusive communication leaves many scars? Is the final result really worth the cost? The style of parental verbal abuse becomes ingrained in the child's brain. As a result, verbally abused kids often grow up to spew verbal abuse when they are stressed. They speak in hurtful ways to their spouses and children, employees and others. If they are teachers, they abuse their students in the same way that they themselves were abused.

Verbally abusive communication in family life can destroy the family. Without the basics of respect, marriages flounder and parent-child bonds dissolve. Wiring our children's brains for verbal abuse can only ensure them a life of relationship difficulty and resultant pain.

Verbal abuse also harms the child's personality development. The more verbally abusive a parent, the more likely that the child will develop borderline personality disorder, a serious mental health disorder that can lead to an inability to maintain relationships or careers. Verbally abused kids often suffer from low self-esteem, depression, and anxiety. Years of therapy are sometimes required in order to heal from the effects of routine verbal abuse.

Verbal abuse is also a transgression of the mitzvah to refrain from hurting others with speech. Although it is permitted to embarrass a child when necessary for pedagogical reasons, this must be used only if all else has failed, and even then, only in the most minimal manner that will achieve results. We are not to suffer sin on the account of helping others to improve.

ZERO TOLERANCE FOR VERBAL ABUSE

It actually *is* possible to raise and teach kids without using verbal abuse. Parents and educators who want to eradicate verbally abusive communication patterns from their repertoire can do so with a simple bit of "brain surgery." Each time that some form of hurtful speech has slipped out of one's mouth, the person resolves to write out one page of lines (to the effect of "I can find respectful ways to communicate just as powerfully"). The assignment increases to two pages in the second month, three in the third month, and so on. Soon the brain will remember the writing assignment just *before* it begins to produce a strip of verbal abuse and it will change direction. After some months the old pattern may return—at that point the person must take up the writing assignments again. This should be repeated at each relapse throughout one's lifetime. This simple strategy produces amazing benefits for the psychological well-being of families, students, and the entire community.

MISBEHAVIOR OR SOMETHING ELSE?

B oth parents and teachers expect that children will misbehave. Classes for educators are offered on classroom management in order to increase compliance and reduce non-
compliance. Books are written and parenting courses are given to
help accomplish similar goals at home. Misbehavior is normal. Or
is it?

WHAT CAUSES MISBEHAVIOR?

In recent decades parents have accepted the rap for their child's misbehavior—and everyone seems to have endorsed their guilt. Sisters, teachers, doctors, friends, and strangers agree that your poorly behaved, outright rude seven-year-old is the product of parental mishandling. "He needs more discipline." "You need to stop screaming at him." "He needs more love." Your overanxious ten-year-old is a similar fallout of your inadequate strategies. "You've spoiled her—you need to toughen her up." "Don't give in to her." And your troubled teen is obvious evidence of both your troubled marriage and your inadequate parenting skills. In other words, it's all your fault.

At least, this has been the popular perception. Theories about inborn temperament have popped up to give parents some relief. As per the instruction in *Mishlei*, it is necessary to "educate the child according to his [inborn] way." Some children are innately rigid and fearful in temperament, others more flexible and confident. Some are easily startled, some more placid. Inborn traits interact with the environment (including parenting strategies, birth order, culture, personal experiences, and more) to produce the personality that we observe in a child.

Moreover, evidence of the importance of the nature-nurture interaction continues to mount. As recently as this past month, researchers have indicated that very specific genes are responsible for the way a child processes the information he receives. For instance, there is a gene variant that influences whether or not a child easily learns from his mistakes. In the "learning-from-mistakes-challenged-gene" version, children have approximately 30 percent fewer dopamine receptors and less activity in the brain's frontal cortex (where problem solving occurs). In adults this version of the gene has been linked to higher levels of drug addiction, compulsive gambling, and obesity, suggesting that this group fails to note the impact of negative consequences in their lives.

Similarly, it's been discovered that children with a gene called DRD4 are impervious to the experience of having an emotionally distant mother—they suffer no particularly harmful effects. On the other hand, children without this gene version are more likely to become emotionally insecure with the same type of parent. Another interesting discovery is the existence of an MAOA gene that numbs memories of childhood abuse. Children who have this gene version may not acknowledge their early unhappy experiences, or if they do, they might make light of the suffering they endured. However, siblings in the same abusive household who have the active version of MAOA can feel the effects of that abuse so strongly that they turn to unhealthy coping strategies. The role of these and many other specific gene formations on personality development is only recently being explored.

BAD BEHAVIOR LOOK-ALIKES

There are also many less subtle biological factors that can affect a child's behavior. For instance, parents might think that their suddenly unmotivated seventeen-year-old son is having an "attitude problem." Previously a good student, the young man now seems to have trouble getting out of bed, doesn't show up to school consistently, and doesn't even care to groom himself properly. Is it teenage rebellion, a problem at school, signs of a major depressive episode, symptoms of substance abuse, or first indications of schizophrenia? A professional assessment can help determine the cause of the misbehavior and appropriate interventions. An eight-year-old refuses to sleep in her own room at night, even with the light on. Her parents have let her have her way in order to avoid hysterical tantrums and all-night shenanigans. Is she just a spoiled youngster or is she suffering from an anxiety disorder? A ten-year-old boy explodes with rage over "nothing" several times a week. Is it just a case of poor behavior or is this one of the symptoms of ADD? Or perhaps he has intermittent explosive disorder, symptoms of bipolar disorder, or even food sensitivities? What about the child who suddenly becomes intensely preoccupied with details of halacha to the point of constantly supervising the family's standards of observance? Is the child manifesting a burst of spiritual growth, a streak of unpleasant controlling behavior, or a plunge into obsessive-compulsive disorder? It's not obvious, and parents can't be expected to know. Discussing your child's troubling behaviors with a professional can help by providing reassurance or timely, early intervention that can ward off more serious problems.

Although children's behavior and misbehavior is never straightforward, there is one that thing that is becoming increasingly clear: parents are not the simple cause of their child's difficulties. Biology plays both independent and interactive roles that cannot be ignored.

LET'S NOT FIGHT

Everyone has an opinion: the toddler thinks she should stay up late while Mom thinks she should be in bed early. The ten-year-old thinks ketchup belongs on every food while the parents think not. One spouse thinks dishes can dry in the drainer while the other thinks they belong in the cupboard. We just don't agree.

What happens when people disagree with each other? In some households, disagreements bring people to the verge of hysteria (and sometimes beyond). There can be shouting, pushing, throwing, and other aggressive or even violent shows of opinion. In some homes, there is endless argument and debate, a verbal repartee that wears everyone down. In some homes, disagreements melt silently into the atmosphere; they are barely detectable, politely expressed as a difference of opinion. What is it like in *your* home?

FLEE FROM CONFLICT

The Chofetz Chaim urges us to flee from conflict as if fleeing from a fire. The energy of conflict, after all, consumes like fire, wreaking emotional havoc and destruction. It robs us of the greatest blessing of all—peace. However, instead of running when they smell smoke, many people actually throw logs on the fire. They fight fire with fire: they answer back, they argue, they prove their point, they diminish the opponent. The subject of the conflict becomes irrelevant, replaced by the battle to prove oneself right.

WHY WE FIGHT

Conflict of opinion clearly feels dangerous. "What if I am proven wrong? I can't allow myself to be exposed as defective or weak. I will fight to the bitter end to defend *myself.*" Because we feel so threatened, adrenalin is released into our bloodstream. Physical survival takes priority; our philosophical computer goes off-line. We respond automatically, from earlier programming and instincts—which is why we find ourselves saying things we later regret. As the Torah notes, once the words are out, the damage is done.

LEARNING NOT TO FIGHT

Parents can help their children learn to circumvent the adrenalin reaction to interpersonal conflict. They do this in two ways: by their model and by their instruction. Parents who fight with each other or with others teach their children to fight. These kids are likely to grow up to fight with their spouses and their own children. It will not be possible to teach your kids to handle conflict respectfully if you don't do it yourself.

If you are providing a good model of respectful conflict resolution, you still have to *teach* the children how to handle their own negotiations in a respectful way. The combination of the parental model and parental instruction gives the child the best opportunity to acquire this skill. However, the child's nature is also an important factor. Some people are born to argue! Their temperament is rigid and controlling. Other people are flexible and easygoing from birth. Whatever the inborn differences in their children, parents who provide the proper model and education are doing all that is in their power to help their kids enjoy peaceful and loving relationships.

THE "I DON'T ARGUE" RULE

One teaching tool that parents can employ is the "I don't argue" rule. This rule helps prevent escalation of conflict by ending combative conversations quickly. The entire conflict lasts only two rounds. For instance, a child wants to put ketchup on everything but the parent doesn't want him to. The child enters round 1 saying, "Can I put ketchup on my peas?" The parent enters round 1 saying, "No." The child starts round 2 with a variation on the theme (i.e., whining, repeating the request louder, giving logical arguments, or whatever). The parent pauses to think on round 2, then changes his or her mind, *or* repeats the original reply. If the parent repeats the original reply, he or she adds the words, "and that's the end of the conversation." The child does rounds 3, 4, 5, and so on alone. The parent does not continue the discussion in any form, but rather gets involved in some other activity. When this approach is used consistently, children soon learn that they might as well stop talking after round 2 because nothing they say will make a difference. They therefore stop arguing completely.

While using the "I don't argue" rule, parents ignore the unpleasant tactics of their kids. The rule is meant to teach children only one point: *do not go on and on and on*. However, there are certain types of speech that require direct intervention. Kids must be stopped from yelling, insulting, threatening, or otherwise using combative communication strategies. Normal disciplinary strategies can be employed for this purpose.

When parents focus on giving and accepting only respectful communication, they help their children guard their tongues and their happiness. Differences of opinion exist; fighting doesn't have to.

ADDICTED TO YELLING

Many times each week, parents come to my office seeking help "to stop yelling at my children." Such parents already know that yelling is damaging in every way—hurting the parent-child bond, decreasing authority, impacting negatively on *chinuch*, and seriously harming the psychological well-being of the children. Yet, despite this knowledge, these parents cannot help themselves: the loud voice just seems to "happen."

WHY WE YELL AT KIDS

Parents can read books, listen to lectures, and take parenting courses that teach alternative strategies for discipline. Yet, in the moment, they might still shout at their kids. The problem is that yelling "works." The "payoff" for yelling (the child's change in behavior) is what cements the neural pathway in the parent's brain, creating an actual addiction to yelling.

BEHAVIORAL ADDICTION

By definition, addiction is a behavior that feels out of our control. People want to stop eating sugar or drinking caffeinated beverages, but find that they "can't." Those addicted to unhealthy substances or activities would really like to turn over a new leaf, but they find that they just "can't." Parents who want to stop yelling but "can't" are as addicted to that behavior as the smoker is to his.

Usually, the addicted brain is reinforced by the chemistry of pleasure. Rage sends out a chemical response that the brain finds oddly satisfying, and this is one of the factors that keeps the yelling going. Then there is the external payoff we discussed earlier—the child's behavioral shift as he or she finally stops the offensive behavior. To the parent's brain this is much like the gambler's winning deal— something "good" has come of the addiction. Overcoming the addiction to yelling therefore involves addressing both the *internal* chemistry of the act and the *external* payoff.

CHANGING ONE'S MIND

One can alter the sequence of yell/feel good by adding a strong feel-bad feeling to the cycle. The new sequence then becomes yell/ feel good/feel really bad. Altering brain chemistry in this way can help break the addictive cycle. For instances, animals who receive an electric shock after engaging in addictive behaviors will soon stop engaging in those behaviors. Although it's not recommended that parents give themselves electric shocks for yelling, they should definitely give themselves a safe equivalent. If you're serious about stopping your yelling, pick some truly aversive consequence that you are *willing* to give yourself *each time* you raise your voice. You'll experience a rapid cure.

DEALING WITH THE PAYOFF

Children will almost always give parents a payoff for yelling—the change in their behavior. To address this problem, parents must find ways of receiving an even better payoff for *not* yelling. While the reward of having healthier children in the long run is beautiful, it is not the kind of thing that the brain can appreciate in the moment. In order to reinforce the brain, you need a truly rewarding reward that the brain can experience in the short run. Here is one type of reward system you can create for yourself to accomplish this:

Tell yourself that if you make it through the morning without raising your voice, you will give yourself a "star" on your "no-yelling chart." You can earn another star for making it through the afternoon and a third star for making it through the evening. Once you earn a certain number of stars, you can cash in your chart for an extremely desirable reward. You should establish the reward *before* you start collecting stars, so that your brain can anticipate the pleasure. Moreover, cash in your chart within a week of stars for your first reward. Do this by setting the number of stars required at a realistic level—for instance, decide that you need to earn at least 16 stars in order to get your first prize. That means that you can make a few errors in your first week (since there are 21 potential stars in a seven-day period). After you earn your first prize, extend the number of required no-yelling hours so that the day is now divided into two no-yelling periods rather than three. You could potentially earn 28 stars over a two-week period, so set the required stars for your second prize at 21. Give yourself a bigger and better prize when you reach 21 stars. Finally, make each no-yelling period one full day long. You could earn 21 stars in three weeks, so set your requirement at 17 stars. Now give yourself an even *better* payoff once you've earned 17 stars. You should continue your chart in this way, making increasing demands on your performance, for about six weeks in order to firmly establish your new no-yelling habit. Whatever it costs you in personal rewards should be less than the cost of ongoing therapy for you and your children—and it's much more fun as well!

THINK AHEAD

Ruchie simply cannot take her daughter's insolent attitude one more minute. For her part, fourteen-year-old Raizel is equally upset: why does her mother have to scream at her every morning?

The two of them have their daily routine. Ruchie wakes Raizel up. Raizel turns over and goes back to sleep. Ruchie wakes Raizel up again, a little more forcefully. Raizel says, "I'm up." Then she turns over and goes back to sleep. Exasperated, Ruchie comes back yet again and starts a rant, something like, "Why do I have to come in here ten times to get you up? You know you have to be in school soon! You're old enough to get *yourself* up! I'm sick and tired of this, so just get up already." Raizel will rub her eyes, looking slightly dazed and confused. "What?" she'll ask innocently. Ruchie will slam the door on the way out.

Every muscle in Ruchie's body is now tense with aggravation.

It's not even 8 a.m. and she's having a miserable day. Slowly, ever so slowly, Raizel emerges from her room and toddles down the hall to the washroom. Fifteen minutes later the door is still locked, so Ruchie screams, "What are you *doing* in there? We have to leave the house in three minutes!" Raizel opens the door. She's totally composed. Icily, she addresses her mother: "Why do you have a screaming fit every morning?"

WHY, INDEED?

Ironically, Ruchie is screaming at her daughter because she loves her. She wants her to go to school on time because this is what healthy people do. Indeed, many parents get exceedingly upset when their kids aren't behaving in a healthy way. They are prone to express rage when their kids lie, steal, behave badly in school, speak rudely to them, hurt siblings, and so on. The intensity of the parental response corresponds to the parent's feeling of how wrong or otherwise destructive the child's behavior is in their eyes. When a child forgets to say "please," most parents just remind him or her to say it; there's no big emotional outburst on the parent's part. But when a child acts outrageously, parents often respond in kind. Everything inside the parent screams, "You must get the child to stop this terrible behavior right now! It's bad for him or her!" Feelings of concern for the child's development underlie displays of parental rage.

RISK FACTORS

The only problem is that showing concern through expressing anger is a very risky business. While little upsets during the day may seem like they are only little upsets during the day, much more is actually going on. It seems, for example, as if an unpleasant parent-child interaction could start at 8 a.m. on a given Monday and end by

8:06 a.m. on that same Monday. In reality, however, each little upset leaves a residual effect, so that while the bad feeling may start at 8 a.m. on a given Monday, it actually *never* ends. As each little upset is added to the pile of never-ending traces of upsets, the pile grows and grows. Eventually, there is a mountain of dark feelings inside the child. This is why a teenager can come to "hate" her mother or an adult child can decide to permanently avoid her parents.

The risk, in other words, is that the parent-child relationship can be permanently damaged. Parents who are hoping to enjoy a close relationship with their grown children, sons and daughters-in-law, and grandchildren need to lay the groundwork for it two decades ahead of time. They have to realize that every angry outburst leaves its mark and that too many such marks may block the flow of love way down the line.

GETTING BEYOND THE MOMENT

This means that it's important for parents to think *beyond* the present parenting moment. Ruchie's mother in our example above needs to think *beyond* the current need to get Raizel out of bed. She needs to ask herself, "If I continue to display anger every morning to this child, what could happen ten years from now?" This issue is no longer about getting Raizel out of bed. Instead it is about how to preserve a healthy parent-child relationship.

Indeed, each parenting challenge is really about the question, "How can I get the child to do A, B, or C while still building and nurturing a healthy relationship with him or her?" How can I get him to do his homework while still fostering a healthy, long-term relationship? How can I get her to clear the table while still building a healthy, long-term relationship? How can I get them into bed at night while still working toward a loving, healthy, lifelong relationship?

The answer to the question is simple: *when parents are careful to teach every lesson in a respectful, loving way, they will build respectful, loving relationships that they can enjoy for a lifetime.* There are so many effective parenting tools available; anger isn't one of them.

YELL IF YOU WANT TO

One of the really wonderful things about being human is our ability to choose freely. It's up to us. Of course, God gives us some very strong direction, advice, and instructions, but He still leaves it up to us to choose our course of action. Therefore, when it comes to parenting, we can all do exactly as we please.

ALONE IN OUR HOME

Alone with our children, no one can stop us from saying or doing whatever we want to. Thus, if a child isn't "listening" and we're getting frustrated, we can yell at her if we so desire. We can yell at her whenever we want to, as many times a day, week, month, or year as we choose to.

SHORT- AND LONG-TERM CONSEQUENCES

The short-term consequences for children who are yelled at too frequently and/or too intensely may include any of the following:

- **Behavioral problems such as aggression or lack of cooperation.**
- **Academic problems.**
- **Nervous habits.**
- **Moodiness.**
- **Health issues (including headaches and stomachaches).**

The long-term consequences for children who are yelled at too frequently and/or too intensely may include any of the following:

- **Low self-esteem, feelings of inadequacy.**
- **Depression.**
- **Anxiety.**
- **Personality disorders and other psychiatric issues.**
- **Addictions.**
- **Health issues.**
- **Impaired relationship with parents.**
- **Tendency to choose abusive friends and mates.**
- **Troubled marriages due to lack of anger-management skills.**
- **Troubled parenting due to lack of anger-management skills.**
- **Troubled work relationships.**
- **In some cases, criminal behavior.**

SAFE HAVENS

In homes in which parents choose to handle their feelings of frustration, fear, disappointment, rage, resentment, and upset *respectfully*, the entire family enjoys a safe haven, an oasis in an otherwise stressful world. When parents maintain their dignity and respect the dignity of their children during moments of correction, boundary setting, and discipline, their children's brains become wired for self-control, restraint, and sensitivity. In other words, when parents move through the parenting day *quietly, respectfully, and kindly* no matter what they are feeling inside and no matter what their children are doing outside, they provide a powerful model for their children to emulate. Moreover, when they teach their children the skills involved in such self-management, they send an enduring message: Family life is about respect. We do not give or receive verbal abuse *no matter how frustrated, irritated, provoked, or otherwise upset we may be.* The results for children reared in this manner generally include the following:

- **High regard for self and others.**
- **Lifelong positive relationship with parents.**
- **Ability to achieve academic, social, mental, emotional, and physical potentials.**
- **Reduced levels of stress, higher levels of well-being.**
- **A life filled with love: successful marriage and parenting experiences.**
- **A high level of emotional intelligence leading to success in every endeavor.**

IT'S UP TO YOU

If you're tired, stressed, overwhelmed, frustrated with your spouse, annoyed at your relatives, or otherwise challenged, you may feel like yelling at times. Or, if you are feeling helpless and out of control with the kids, unable to get them to do what you want, you may feel like yelling. Yelling "works"—it changes what a child is doing right now. But it comes with a price. The consequences of yelling are real. In the most minor case, where yelling occurs only rarely, it teaches the child about idol worship: "When *I* want something and you are not providing it, then I no longer have to show you basic respect and I no longer have to behave appropriately. When *I* want something and you are not providing it, then I no longer have to care about your feelings—I can just scream in your face." However, frequent or intense yelling does more than teach this one lesson of self-worship—it damages personality.

Nonetheless, if you want to yell, go ahead. Yell if you want to.

FAMILY LIFE

YOU IN FAMILY LIFE

As you build your home, there are so many tasks to keep in mind. There is, for example, the smooth running of the household—making sure there is a supply of food, clean dishes, clean clothing, and all the other necessities of daily living. There is the management of the home economy that allows for the payment of rent or mortgage, the aforementioned supply of food and other necessities, the costs of school and shul, emergency funds and savings. Then there is the family atmosphere that you foster: the mood and attitude that pervades your dwelling, the tone that you set. Finally, there is the impact of *you* within the household—your values, your priorities, your tastes, your routines, and other aspects of your youness that you both express and impose within your family setting.

How do you want it all to be? How do you bring it all about?

MAKING YOURSELF WITHIN YOUR FAMILY

The first step is to bring consciousness to the task. Actually *think* about the home you are building. Analyze its strengths and weaknesses by looking at the different tasks described above. See where improvement is needed and think about what steps you might take in order to bring about that improvement.

When you are thinking about what is happening in your family, you will have to consider the interactions you have with your family members. Spouses and children can be difficult to contend with. If you lived alone, you would make yourself your ideal home—cleaning, shopping, cooking, bill paying, organizing, and so on—in the way you see fit. The few arguments you have with yourself can be quickly and peacefully resolved.

However, because you are living with other people, you can't just do it your way now—at least, not without stepping on someone else's toes. You have your opinions, based both on your personal preferences and on your upbringing, but then so does your spouse. Who decides how it will be? What happens when your spouse wants it one way ("small children need to sleep in their own beds") and you want it another ("small children are welcome in the parental bed")? Indeed, every aspect of family life is arguable—there are just so many different ways to do things, so many different ways to wash dishes, make food, pay bills, discipline kids, spend money.

Will you fight it out with your spouse? Will your children grow up on a steady diet of conflict and stress? Will you lose yourself in exhaustion and defeat or become a person you don't like anymore? Or do you have advanced skills that will help you negotiate even with a worthy opponent? How good are you at compromising, giving in, and giving up? Do you do all that way too little or way too much?

How you negotiate differences will make all the difference. But it is work. One has to learn how to best communicate with one's partner in order to resolve differences in healthy, love-affirming ways. One has to make sure to take care of *oneself* while carefully managing to take care of everyone else as well. The goal is to have everyone come out winning. However, making that happen cannot be someone else's responsibility. One has to concentrate on one's *own* behavior, doing the best one can to bring out the best in the others. It requires skill, determination, and emotional fortitude. Yet, it is this very struggle that brings about growth in the one who perseveres.

Who do you want to be? As you build your home, keep checking the mirror. See if your ideal self is smiling back at you.

COMPLEXITY OF FAMILY RELATIONSHIPS

Anyone who lives in a family has to negotiate sharing space, possessions, time, and resources with the other family members. Many people feel overwhelmed with the job of taking care of so many needs and wants. In larger families there are larger needs, just by virtue of the numbers. However, one special-needs child in a family of any size can severely tax the emotional and physical strength of parents. In fact, a special-needs child can tax the marital relationship as well. Even without an official diagnosis, of course, every child is "special" in his or her "needs" and requires all sorts of time and attention from parents. In addition, there are some children who are just excessively demanding, taking more than their share of parental input. How do parents take care of themselves and each other while properly tending to the needs of everyone else? How much energy does one person have?

It's easier to reduce sibling rivalry, competition, and other un-pleasantries in children when one has a plentitude of parenting skills and ideas. It's easier to work with each child in the family when one has lots of options. Those who read books, take courses, and seek counseling usually have more tips at their fingertips. Ditto for those who take the "learning" approach to marriage, studying up and seeking outside support. Being more skilled brings about better results in a less stressful way.

DYSFUNCTIONAL FAMILIES

Building a healthy home life is quite the challenge. Our emotions often seem to get in the way. Impatience, intolerance, and even over-sensitivity can wreak havoc with the home environment. Dysfunctional families exhibit way too much drama and negative emotion. Parents can frighten their children by their inability to calmly and rationally handle the stress of family living. Children can fail to learn healthy ways to feel, think, and behave in the home environment when the grown-ups are not showing them how it is done.

Of course, there are different ways for families to be dysfunctional. Instead of being overly emotional, they may be chaotic, unable to smoothly manage the normal routines of life. In such a home, dishes may clutter the sinks, tables, and counters all the time, except when they are quickly cleared for Shabbos and special occasions. Clothes may never see a hanger, making their journey from the floor to the washing machine and dryer and back to the floor again (perhaps in a basket now) without being sorted and put away. The whole house may be a mess of clutter and disorganization, creating stress for all its inhabitants. Children may not want to bring friends home. They fail to learn the routines for organization and structure because no one is teaching them.

In some homes, dysfunction is expressed in the financial realm.

Perhaps money never stretches through the whole month and there is much doing without and last-minute panics to make things happen—it's not predictable, safe, and stable. Sometimes husband and wife fight constantly about how to utilize the funds that are available or about how to bring more money in. The children not only feel the tension but also become anxious, worrying about how their needs will be met.

Dysfunction can occur in many other ways as well. No one sets out to establish a dysfunctional family, and people who have created one do not necessarily recognize that their home is lacking. Instead, they may feel that their spouse has issues or that the situation they find themselves in is too challenging. In fact, many adults have themselves come from dysfunctional families and lack the skills they need because they, too, have been deprived of healthy teachers and good models. Those who have been challenged in this way know that Hashem expects them to pick up the pieces now that they are building their own homes. There is much work to be done, the very work that causes growth through family living.

GROWING INTO IT

As you grow along with your family, you may want to consider the following tips:

- **All of the experiences of family life happen for your benefit, to help you become the best person you can be.**
- **Hashem is with you every step of the way.**
- **It is *supposed* to be challenging.**
- **Permanently smiling faces exist only in photo albums.**
- **When the going gets tough, the tough get help! You're not supposed to do it all alone.**

- **Every challenge you are facing has been and is being faced by others**. If possible, draw on their experience and wisdom.

- **The happier you are as an individual, the easier it will be for you to build a happy home**. Be sure to tend to your *own* needs so that you can tend to the needs of everyone else.

- **Because of the stress inherent in family life, having good stress-management skills is a must**. Take time to build your relationship with Hashem, exercise, eat properly, laugh, relax, socialize, and do whatever else helps to keep you *under-whelmed*.

- **Mistakes are a necessary part of the growing process**. Just learn from them.

- **Remember to acknowledge yourself with regular positive feedback and encouragement**.

Add your own tips to keep in mind to help you negotiate family life:

_____

_____

_____

_____

_____

_____

_____

_____

_____

_____

_____

_____

_____

_____

_____

_____

_____

_____

_____

_____

_____

THE PERFECT FAMILY

Human perfection doesn't exist. But that doesn't stop people from trying to pretend that it does. People sometimes feel that if they dress perfectly, behave well, and do what they're supposed to do (at least as far as anyone can tell), they can pass off themselves or their families as pretty perfect. They are trying to create a still-life snapshot of themselves, the picture of okayness, the image of well done. The trouble is, it is very hard to hold that pose. People are complex. Children are immature. We're all fallible. Things change.

EXPERIENCING A FALL

A couple came to see me recently. They were shaken to the core.

Their eleven-year-old daughter had been expelled from camp for deviant behavior. The details don't matter here—whether she had been stealing from the camp office or bullying a young camper or engaging in other illegal, immoral, or dangerous behaviors. Suffice it to say that the parents were shocked that their daughter had done what she did. It changed their image of her and of themselves as a family.

The father trembled as he spoke, obviously close to tears. "People are talking about us; there are rumors flying at camp, and tomorrow is visiting day. Then, everyone in the city will also know. They'll look at us differently. Our family, our good name, is ruined. My daughter's future is jeopardized. I want this not to have happened. I want this to be a nightmare that I wake up from very soon. I want my family back."

The mother, too, was deeply disturbed. Like many mothers, she blamed herself. "I should have reminded her before she left that she needs to use good judgment and watch out for her reputation. Why didn't I tell her to be careful and responsible? How could I have just let her go off like that? Of course, everyone will be pointing fingers at me: 'What kind of mother are you? Why does your daughter behave like that?' I've done it myself. When I hear that someone has been expelled from school or camp, I assume that the child is horrible and the parents are at fault. Why shouldn't others think the same of me?"

This family's image of themselves had been shattered. Till now they thought of themselves as a "good family." They believed they were "good parents." They felt they had "good kids." In a flash, all of that changed. They didn't know who they were anymore.

PARENTING ISN'T FOR THE FAINT OF HEART

In fact, the couple was experiencing more of a shattering of their assumptions about family life than a shattering of their actual family. They had believed that a good family was one without any issues—no problems to solve. Now, faced with a real problem, they had no frame of reference. Can a family be a "good family" and the parents be "good parents" if a child gets into serious trouble or has serious problems? It had never occurred to these people that a really good family is a group of people who support each other well. In fact, a "perfect family" is one in which parents expect their kids to make lots of mistakes (including some serious ones) or have lots of problems (including some serious ones) and who see their job as being loving, respectful helpers, guides, teachers, and resources. It is a family that is fluid, rather than static. It changes. It's a family that is flexible, rather than rigid. It rolls with the punches. It is a family that sticks together rather than falls apart. It's close and caring.

Kids do all sorts of crazy things as they grow up. Some are just developmental experiments like trying to see what happens if you take fish out of a tank. Some are the result of immaturity, impulsivity, and poor judgment—the traits that define teenagers in particular. Some are the result of inherited mental health disorders. While some kids get into less mischief than others, giving birth to them may be "the luck of the draw" (a gift from Hashem). Many kids get into major trouble before they leave home, and many continue to get into trouble even after that. Parents need nerves of steel to do their jobs well. They need maturity, compassion, skill, and lots of outside support. The going can sometimes get rough.

We know that a person cannot, according to the Torah, be appointed as a judge unless he is a parent. Being a parent is a humbling experience, facilitating the recognition that we are all vulnerable, that errors are truly human, that we all require second chances. Imperfection in family life is not about people having problems; that's just the human condition. Imperfection occurs when parents set the bar inhumanly high, requiring of themselves and their children a seamless path to faultless performance. The perfect family, on the other hand, is one that loves each other through trials and tribulations, accepts each other's imperfections and learns and grows together. That's the perfect family.

THE CHALLENGE OF FAMILY LIFE

E veryone has hopes and dreams for their children. Right from the beginning, parents hope that their baby will be healthy, cooperative, and content. Later, they hope that their toddler will make an easy, positive transition to playgroup. Over the next two decades they hope their child will succeed academically and develop excellent *middos*. As the child becomes a young adult, parents hope that he or she will set up a beautiful *bayis ne'eman b'Yisrael* and raise perfect grandchildren.

What happens when things don't go quite as expected? What happens when the baby is neither cooperative nor content? How do the parents manage when the toddler fails to make a smooth transition to playgroup or when the child's behavioral problems create difficulties in every school setting? How do parents cope when their children have academic challenges, when they have trouble making friends, when their physical health is challenged, or when they develop mental health problems? In other words, how do parents deal with the *real* job of parenting as opposed to the rosy ideal of their dreams?

FAMILY LIFE IS COMPLICATED

The real job of parenting involves lots of laughter, pleasure, and joy; lots of stress, worry, disappointment, and pain. Like life itself, family life is complex. Constantly happy faces are picture-book images, not real-life images. In real homes, children don't always get along with each other—they fight, argue, insult each other, and hurt each other's feelings. Children don't always feel close to their parents, and many parents have trouble relating well to each one of their kids. Husbands and wives do not always live in constant harmony. The number of people in a house is constantly changing as the family adds and subtracts members, and the dynamics of the house follow suit. There are calmer times and more chaotic times. There are "mixed" times as well: for instance, when there are lots of children in the family, many can be doing very well during the same period of time that one or more are floundering. Nothing about family life is black and white (except the Shabbos suits).

Parents usually try their hardest to provide their children with every opportunity and every form of support, but their efforts cannot always prevent a child from experiencing emotional distress, trauma, and suffering. Every child is on his own spiritual journey, and Hashem individualizes each one's path, just as He does with all of us. We cannot save our children from pain; this fact itself is a major source of parenting pain.

However, once we understand the value of struggle—our struggle as well as our children's struggle—we can cope with difficulties much better. Struggle is an excellent tutor in the school of personal development. It can bring forth wisdom, maturity, strength, and beauty. Valuing struggle while keeping an eye on the future, imagining and working toward positive outcomes, is a strategy that can help one survive and thrive in difficult times.

WE'RE IN THIS TOGETHER

In dealing positively with the vicissitudes of family life, another helpful strategy for parents is to acknowledge that family struggles are actually *normal*. Although it may *appear* that someone else is having an easier time, wise parents aren't fooled. What we see when we bump into others at the supermarket or sit with them at a *simcha* is not the same as what we would see if we were a fly on the wall in their homes. Fortunately, most people know how to behave in public. In their hearts and homes, however, there is always a jumble of emotion. Even the perfectly normal trials and tribulations of parenting and marriage cause plenty of stress.

Those who cope best remember King Solomon's famous ring with the inscription "This, too, shall pass." No matter what is going wrong at the moment in family life, it will change for the better again. Family life is all about ups and downs, good hours and "bad" hours, good weeks and "bad" weeks, good years and "bad" years, and even good decades and not so good ones.

Adjusting our unrealistic expectations of family life can make the reality easier to handle. Clients often tell me, "I didn't sign up for this," referring to some serious family problem they are experiencing. Actually, when we build a family, we *are* signing up for the challenge. We're signing up for the growth experience of a lifetime. Fortunately, we can access Hashem's support every inch of the way.

Getting human support for the hard issues is also advisable, whether it comes from rabbis, family, friends, or professionals. With *emunah*, patience, and practical efforts, we can negotiate the challenges of family life successfully.

SELF-GROWTH

Everyone has relationship problems at some point or other. The most common relationship difficulties occur within the nuclear family: between spouses, between siblings, between parents and children. Most people have the same idea as to how all these relationship problems should be solved—the "difficult" person should improve his or her ways. The unhappy wife wants her husband to improve. The disgruntled child wants his parent to change. The irritated sister knows just what her brother needs to do.

WHY RELATIONSHIP PROBLEMS OCCUR

Many people think that relationship difficulties occur because the people they are dealing with have various faults. In fact, the human imperfections of our loved ones have nothing to do with why relationship problems occur. Relationship problems happen for the same reason that poverty, illness, unemployment, natural disasters, and war happen: Hashem wants to send us challenges. All of the difficulties we encounter in life are for our own benefit.

Suppose the car in front of us suddenly slowed down, forcing us to come to a sudden, jolting stop. It would be silly for us to get mad at the car, wouldn't it? Cars have no free will. Obviously the *driver* of the car is at fault rather than the car itself. And yet, those in the know wouldn't bother getting mad at the driver either. The driver is only an instrument in Hashem's hand. *Hashem* made the car slow down in front of us—*zol zein a kapporah* (the aggravation should atone for our sins).

And so it is in family life. Our spouse, mother, father, sister, brother, child, in-laws, and all the rest of the cast of characters who are in our lives are there to prod and provoke us into *our own growth*.

SEIZE THE OPPORTUNITY

When we put all our effort into trying to change these people, we are actually giving away the opportunity of a lifetime. Hashem sends us interpersonal aggravation in order to change *ourselves*. By focusing on something else entirely (like trying to get others to change), we miss the opportunity to change ourselves. Since the entire purpose of our life is to grow and elevate ourselves, missing this opportunity is no small thing.

Of course, it seems to us that the "problem person" in our relationship difficulty is the one who needs to change. While this may be true, that person is the one who will have to realize that on her own and get to work. Meanwhile, Hashem let the aggravation fall into our laps as an opportunity for *us* to change. If the relationship difficulty isn't your fault (in your humble opinion), what sort of changes should you be contemplating? Here are some suggestions:

- Become more accepting of other people's flaws.
- Become more patient, tolerant, and nonjudgmental.
- Become less critical.
- Develop new skills on how to bring out the best in others.
- Learn how to make peace even in difficult situations.
- Learn how to motivate and inspire others in positive ways.
- Learn how to ask for and get what you need, in healthy, relationship-building ways.
- Learn how to access outside help.
- Learn how to pour out your heart to Hashem.
- Learn where and how to acquire more effective relationship solutions.
- Learn how to think more positively.
- Learn how to radiate more positive energy.
- Learn how to set healthy boundaries in healthy ways.

And this is only the beginning of the possibilities for growth through painful relationship issues.

ASKING FOR CHANGE

As you can see from the list above, one of the areas of personal growth that may be relevant for certain people is learning how to bring out the best in others (particularly family members). Before you get all excited about this being your "in" for working on changing someone, make sure that this is a problem that *you* have. You may have this problem if you are very negative, critical, passive, passive-aggressive, angry, abusive, poor at communication, codependent, controlling, emotional, or unable to express yourself appropriately. If you *do* have one of these problems, then you *do* need to learn how to help others change their behavior using healthy, constructive, appropriate communication skills.

Keep in mind that you shouldn't be handing someone a page in a book or article to read about a flaw that you think they have. You shouldn't be offering negative feedback or criticism that exceeds the minute allotment for not-so-good-feeling communications in the parent-child relationship (20 percent of all communication) and marriage relationship (5 percent of all communication). You shouldn't be asking for apologies or engaging in lengthy discussions about what is wrong with the person or the relationship. If you need to learn how to help others change, start with the Torah precepts that require sensitivity and kindness above all else.

And when you've mastered these traits, you'll notice that Hashem is sending you far fewer relationship difficulties to help you grow.

SEEING YOURSELF THROUGH YOUR RELATIONSHIPS

Hashem arranges the details of our days to help us develop spiritually. This means that He sends us all sorts of experiences—some pleasant and some not so—to provoke our development. Anything that happens to us, including the things that others say and do to us, comes directly from Hashem. All interpersonal events are sent to help us learn about ourselves and improve ourselves. However, in order to reap the benefits of these events, we must be willing to utilize them for this higher purpose. There are two main areas we can examine: we can look carefully at how others respond to us, and we can look carefully at how we respond to others.

HOW PEOPLE RESPOND TO US

When a spouse, parent, child, sister-in-law, friend, neighbor, or perfect stranger treats us badly, we naturally feel upset. We might feel irritated, angry, or hurt. The most natural next step is to direct this upset toward the offending person, judging them, rejecting them, or otherwise concentrating our attention on *them*.

For instance, suppose you are driving somewhere with your spouse. You are the passenger. Your spouse is taking Avenue A, which is moving rather slowly. You offer, "Why don't you take Avenue B? I think it will be faster." Your spouse replies testily, "Why don't you just let me drive?"

Your feelings are hurt. You start thinking to yourself, *Do I really deserve this type of treatment? My spouse is horrible. Why did I marry this person? He/she is so abusive.* Pain may trigger this barrage of negative thinking, but the more you think this way, the more pain you feel. The supposed-to-be-pleasant drive with your spouse has turned sour and you are now miserable.

The hurt that a person feels when insulted is understandable. However, in order to grow through the experience that Hashem sent, more is needed than just being mad at someone. A few small questions to ourselves can turn a meaningless, painful incident into a superhighway to spiritual growth. "What is there about my behavior that could have triggered irritation in my partner? In which way or ways can I improve, moving forward?" Just because we are well-intentioned and good-hearted doesn't mean we are perfect human beings. There is always room for improvement in specific areas. In this example, you accidentally hurt your spouse in the innocent process of trying to be helpful. No one is saying you are a bad person because of this. What you *can* do, however, is learn from the interpersonal experience, *learn* from the reaction of the person you are dealing with. In this particular scenario, you might discover that your error lies in one or more realms. For instance,

- **I tend to criticize unnecessarily.**
- **I am a controlling person.**
- **I am not careful to stay in the 95:5 positive-to-negative communication ratio with my partner.**
- **I give advice when it's not asked for or wanted.**
- **I'm not sensitive.**
- **I don't let people breathe or do things their way.**

Suppose you have a different problem. Your daughter-in-law, sister-in-law, brother, or some other relative has stopped calling you. In fact, this person has stopped visiting and pretty well stopped having a relationship with you. This person has withdrawn. Again, you might be tempted to start assessing and judging that person: he/she is rude, selfish, arrogant, inconsiderate, two-faced, and so on. Or, using the reaction as a catalyst for your own growth, you ask yourself, "Is there anything I might have done or said to trigger that person's withdrawal? What do I need to improve in?"

Perhaps, upon reflection, you will realize that in your past interactions with this person you have been

- **Critical.**
- **Self-focused.**
- **Impatient.**
- **Angry.**
- **Unavailable.**
- **Taking more than giving.**
- **Demanding too much.**

- **Unpleasant.**
- **Improperly behaved (e.g., gossiping).**
- **Something else.**

Here is another example. Your teenager has been dishonest lately, neglecting to tell you things or outright lying when confronted. Yes, you will want to think about the child and about what you need to do to help the youngster with this behavioral pattern, but you might also ask *yourself*, "What might I be doing that encourages dishonesty? What do I need to improve?" You might come up with a list of possibilities:

- **Maybe I set the bar too high for this child.**
- **Maybe I give the impression that I will be disappointed.**
- **Maybe I display rejection.**
- **Maybe I am very critical.**
- **Maybe I am explosive.**
- **Maybe I make the child feel uncomfortable or unsafe to tell me the truth.**
- **Maybe I am too punitive.**
- **Maybe I lack compassion.**
- **Maybe I am too harsh.**

Finally, let's look at the example of being taken advantage of. In this scenario, you feel that others use and abuse you. They expect you to do things for them, but do little for you. In fact, you feel that you give more than you get in return in almost all your relationships. While it is possible that you pick obnoxious, demanding people as your friends, it is also possible that *you* are doing something to provoke this imbalanced dynamic. When you sit down to think about it, questioning your own role in the problem and where you might make changes, you come up with the following list:

- **I say yes when I mean no.**
- **I don't respect my own limits.**
- **I don't ask for what I need.**
- **I don't put myself forward. I give mixed messages.**
- **I don't communicate assertively.**
- **I give more than I want to and then feel resentful.**

While we are never responsible for other people's bad behavior (i.e., we do not cause anyone to be rude, abusive, cruel, selfish, and so forth), we certainly may play a role in any difficult interaction we are having or in any dysfunctional relationship we are participating in. Even if the other person has the greatest role in generating and maintaining the problem, we can still learn and grow from our own small relationship deficits or personal flaws. The other person will have to work on him or herself; *we* can work on ourselves, keeping in mind that Hashem put the other person in our life for this very reason.

HOW WE RESPOND TO OTHERS

The second way in which we can learn about ourselves from looking into our relationships is through analyzing our response to others. We might find, for instance, that we often feel hurt or rejected. If so, this would point to a vulnerability that we have, an area within ourselves that requires strengthening. After all, we live in an imperfect world with imperfect people. Others can't say and do everything "just right" all the time. When we are healthy enough, we are able to give others the benefit of the doubt and enjoy positive relationships despite inevitable communication errors. Excessive sensitivity on our part—too much or too chronic an experience of social pain—points to a need for healing.

Fortunately, there are so many ways to heal and so many helpers available. Therapists, rabbis, classes, books, self-help, and more are resources that Hashem has provided for us to enable us to remove emotional blocks. Spiritual elevation and emotional clearing go hand in hand. The evolved Torah personality is essentially a healthy personality, the kind of personality that most closely emulates the qualities of Hashem. The more peaceful, compassionate, generous, loving, optimistic, and patient we are, the closer we are to the balanced Torah ideal. Our emotional suffering points to the areas that we need to work on.

Another example: Suppose we find that our relationships trigger frequent feelings of anger or judgment on our part. We hold resentment in our hearts. Again, these emotions point us down the road to healing. Whether it is anger, fear, or sadness, negativity harms us on every level and impedes our spiritual growth. Instead of focusing our attention on the people who trigger us, we can again look in the mirror. We want to find what it is exactly that is being triggered; we want to heal it. If we do the work, we will be rewarded with greater peace and health.

THE PURPOSE OF INTERPERSONAL STRUGGLES

Our dealings with people, especially family members, are complex. They react to us and we react to them—it's only natural. However, when we use our relationships as a mirror, a reflection of who we are, where we're at, and where we need to go, we can achieve tremendous growth. Humility and courage will enable us to view our relationship difficulties as royal roads to spiritual development.

THE RELATIONSHIP RULE

"D on't you ever speak to me like that! Do you hear me? I won't stand for any chutzpah in this house!"

We parents are a funny group. We often expect our children to be more mature than we are! We want them to remain calm and polite even when they're feeling frustrated. We expect them (and rightly so) to speak respectfully even when they're upset. And yet, so often, we ourselves lose control. We speak too loudly. We say insulting things. Even if we justify our actions ("He deserved much worse than that—I was holding myself back!"), we know in our hearts that there is no excuse for our own rudeness. In fact, when we're on the receiving end of someone else's verbal abuse, it becomes obvious that excuses are irrelevant. Once the words are out, the damage is done.

WHAT IT SAYS

The relationship rule states: "I only give, and I only accept, respectful communication. I do not give, nor do I accept, disrespectful communication" (or, to put it more bluntly: "I do not give, nor do I accept, any form of abuse"). The relationship rule refers to both verbal and nonverbal communication. People who want to teach this rule to their kids (and spouses) need to be able to follow it. They need to be able to convey:

- **I don't roll my eyeballs at you; please don't roll your eyeballs at me.**
- **I don't shout at you; please don't shout at me.**
- **I don't hang up on you; please don't hang up on me.**
- **I don't call you names; please don't call me names.**
- **I don't mock you; please don't mock me.**

In other words, those who wish to set healthy boundaries using the relationship rule ("...*nor do I accept* disrespectful communication") will only be able to do so if they follow the first part of that rule ("*I only give*...respectful communication").

HEALTHY, HAPPY, AND WHOLE

The relationship rule leaves every member of the family intact, protecting our most precious commodity: love. It does so by ensuring that we always maintain our dignity while communicating (we don't lower ourselves to a crude, rude level of behavior), we protect our dignity while receiving communications (by refusing to allow others to show disrespect toward us), and we respect the dignity of each person we are addressing.

By following the relationship rule, we teach others how to treat us well. This protects them as well as us, because by setting this boundary, we've ensured that they'll continue to be likable and lovable. In other words, *we'll* be able to like and love them because they are nice. On the other hand, if we allow others to hurt or diminish us, *we* harm our relationship with them; we allow them to become unlikable and unlovable. In the case of children, this is particularly dangerous, not only because they *need* us to like and love them, but because they are being allowed to practice the kind of behavior that may lead others to dislike them as well. For instance, a child who is allowed to be rude to his parents for twenty developmental years will be all too likely to be rude to his wife when he's stressed by the normal challenges of marriage. His well-entrenched habit of verbal abuse may cost him dearly throughout his life. His parents do him no favor by allowing him to practice hurtful behaviors.

ENFORCING THE RULE

The more closely we can follow the relationship rule, the happier we'll be. Therefore, it will be worth the trouble to train our brain and the brains of our family members to be able to follow it.

We can train our own brain by setting a negative consequence for ourselves—any annoying punishment will be sufficient to interrupt the neural pathway that runs our rudeness program. Was I sarcastic just then? I'll make myself write out a page of lines. Did I raise my voice or bark or snap? Lines, lines, and more lines. After the first week, the cost will go up to two pages per offense. The third week, it will be three. If I really make myself follow through and write, all of my rudeness will be gone within a week or two. If I don't, I (and my family) will probably have to live with it for a lifetime.

Training the brain of family members is equally simple. Work out an agreement with your spouse about what should happen when one of you has shown disrespect. With the kids, set out consequences as you've done for yourself. You might want to give them a couple of weeks' practice first that are consequence free. During this learning period, simply name the disrespect. Let them know that the consequences will start on a particular date on the calendar.

That's all there is to it. Enjoy your peaceful, loving home.

GETTING WHAT YOU WANT

There are many disappointments and frustrations in family life. Kids just don't listen. Spouses just don't understand. Parents don't get it. The same frustrating communications happen again and again and again. Eventually, someone blows up: "I just can't get through to you! You never listen to what I'm saying! You tune me out. This always happens. You're not even trying!"

VERBAL COMPLAINTS

A frustrated parent, spouse, or child issues the complaint. "I can't stand this. It's never going to change!" Said in loud, angry, even hysterical tones, the message is clearly a cry for help. However, it usually serves to alienate the one who needs to hear it. It comes across as a major attack, an assault, a criticism. As such, it gets people's back up. It fails to elicit the sympathy and compassion that it so badly requires. In fact, it usually leads to more intense interpersonal conflict. "Oh, yeah? Well, I can't stand it either! (so there)"

FRAME IT POSITIVELY

The secret to getting what you want in relationships is to ask for it. "Mom, can you please just repeat back what I'm saying to you— then I'll know that you heard it." "Spouse, I really want you to help me out more; I'm too tired to carry the burden alone." "Child, I want you to clean your room as you promised you would and I want it done by Sunday at four."

Instead of telling family members what you don't want, what you don't like, and what you can't stand, tell them what you do want, what you would like, and what would make you happy. People want to succeed. When you tell them how they can do this, you help yourself and them at the same time.

FROM FEELINGS TO NEEDS

Is your child aggravating you by forgetting to take out the garbage? Beware of the tirade: "I can't count on you for one simple task around here and I am sick of having to take out the garbage myself every week!" This unfriendly speech elicits defensiveness rather than cooperation. Instead, name your feelings and then your needs or desires: "I find it really frustrating to have to take out the garbage every week. I need you to be more reliable about this job. I want you to remember to take it out each week."

Is a spouse letting you down? Skip the criticism "Why do I always have to come home to such a mess? I can't stand walking in this door!" Instead, say what you want: "You know what would make such a positive difference in my life? Coming into an orderly house. I'd be so happy if you could tidy things up before I walk in the door. It would mean a lot to me if you could do that for me."

ASK FOR WHAT YOU WANT

Is your child being too noisy? Instead of complaining, "You're too noisy," just ask him to please quiet down. Is your teenager mumbling again? Forget the accusation "Why do you always mumble like that?" Instead, ask for what you want: "Can you speak more clearly, dear?" Is your spouse too critical? Instead of criticizing the criticism ("Would you stop picking on me for once?"), just ask for what you want: "Darling, I could really use some positive feedback—could you tell me you think I'm beautiful/handsome?"

When you get what you ask for, don't discount it as fake ("They don't really mean it—they're just doing/saying what I ask them to"). Rather, understand that you've helped your family members succeed at doing what they want to do: please you! Be sure to thank them for their efforts. Let them know it means a lot to you that they care enough to do what you ask them to do. You'll find them trying harder to please you of their own accord, once they see how easy it is to do what you want them to do.

People don't really want to alienate each other or cause conflict. By learning how to ask for exactly what you want while refraining from hurtful accusations ("You always do this to me!"), words of hopelessness ("I give up already"), and negative programming ("You'll never understand"), you can make your family life more pleasant, more loving, and more successful. Send out positive hypnotic statements: "I know you can do it," "I know you care about this, too," "It makes me so happy when you put in the effort." Think good, talk good, and it will be good!

SIBLINGS: BEST FRIENDS FOR LIFE?

Not necessarily. But maybe. You just never know. Siblings are like any other two people that might find themselves living next door to each other: they may have a lot in common (after all, they moved into the same neighborhood), or they may be very different from each other—even incompatible.

Parents usually hope that their first child will have at least one sibling. It doesn't always work out that way, but the reasons parents hope it will often include the following considerations:

- **A sibling will be a companion.**

- **A sibling will help the child be less self-centered.**

- **A sibling will help a child learn to share and get along with people.**

- **Siblings create a fuller and therefore happier family life.**

- **A sibling will share the burden of eldercare later on in life's journey.**

Let's look at each of these reasons more closely.

THE COMPANION THEORY

Sometimes siblings truly keep each other good company. This is the hope of every parent. The reality in many families, however, is that siblings spend more time tormenting each other than playing nicely together. Siblings can be hurtful, insulting, unkind, and otherwise unpleasant. Their communications can be so destructive as to constitute "sibling abuse."

Many parents are completely frustrated by the conflict that occurs between their kids. In a large family, it may be just one pair of children who can't get along, or it may be groups of children who are hostile toward each other. Whoever and whatever the number of combatants, parents are usually very distressed by the constant, unpleasant, and unnerving conflict. Just as children do not enjoy living in a household in which their parents fight, parents do not enjoy living in a battleground built by their youngsters.

A common tactic for parents is to join in the fray. *"Stop fighting already!"* they scream at the top of their lungs. In fact, parents must keep their cool when their kids fight, if only to show them how to respond to provocation. A parent who steps in quietly and calmly can reset the tone. "Gosh, guys. What's going on here?" the parent can softly inquire. "I hate him!" one youngster declares. "I hate him more!" the other rejoins. Mom *refrains from the temptation to preach:* "Now boys, *never* talk like that. You two will be friends for life. So shake hands and make up." Instead, Mom acknowledges their feelings of upset: "You two are clearly *very* upset with each other! Let's sit down and you can tell me what's happening here." As each child unburdens his woes, Mom continues to acknowledge their anger, frustration, and upset and possibly the hurt as well. Only after the feelings are welcomed, does she begin to teach and encourage problem solving. "So now I know why you are both so upset. When we're not happy about something, we need to talk about it to each other clearly and calmly—that's the only way a problem can get solved. So let's think together now about what solutions might work for this problem."

THE "EXPANDED PERSONALITY" THEORY

Parents hope that having siblings will encourage less selfish, self-centered behavior in a child. In reality, many children are challenged by intense jealousy of their siblings. "You love them more than you love me," "You always give him more." This gnawing insecurity can last a lifetime. Had the youngster been an only child, she might actually have been more secure in her parents' love! Although the generosity of spirit may not pan out, the insecurity brought on by siblings is not always a bad thing. This insecurity can prompt a lifetime of sibling competition, causing a person to strive higher and higher only for the purpose of outshining his sibling(s). This *lo lishma* behavior may lead to actual greatness in the end. Competition and insecurity can be a good thing when it is about being truly better.

THE "HAPPIER FAMILY LIFE" THEORY

Only if they get along. Otherwise, a houseful of fighting kids is a "fuller family life" but not necessarily a happier one. Sibling rivalry is common and normal. Parents may have to spend the full two or four decades of child rearing helping their kids learn to speak nicely to each other and refrain from hurting each other. As a result of the opportunity to fight with a sibling, a youngster will receive instruction as to how to properly manage anger and frustration. This will serve the child well throughout life. Therefore, it's good to have a sibling to fight with.

THE "SHARED ELDERCARE" THEORY

This may not work out either, for a variety of reasons. However, as you can see by now, it really doesn't matter if siblings work well together or don't. The struggle itself has merit for personal development. So, look on with contentment as you watch your youngsters pummel each other to the ground. It may not be good for *you,* but it will be good for them.

STATUTE OF LIMITATIONS

Rachel's mother-in-law asked Rachel's husband (the new *chasan*) to do an errand for her just two days after the wedding. Twelve years later, Rachel still refers to the incident whenever she perceives similar insensitivities occurring. The pain is surprisingly fresh.

Mendel's wife "abused" her cell phone privileges badly, accumulating a bill that took them half a year to pay down. Although it happened seven years ago and never again since that time, Mendel still mentions it regularly

Chaya cut her little sister's hair off—pretty well all of it—when she was six and Shevy was just three. Although Chaya is now fifteen, she is still routinely reminded about her faux pas, especially when guests and relatives are visiting. What was once a humorous family anecdote has become a tiresome and irritating tale from her point of view. She wishes her parents would put it to rest already.

STUCK IN THE PAST

Sometimes it feels like family members don't want to let each other off the hook. Instead of letting bygones be bygones, they drag the past forward into the present where it can serve as a constant reminder of unacceptable behavior. There are three primary reasons why people tend to do this:

- **Even though an offense occurred many years previously, the offended party hasn't healed from the pain.** The past is very present—active and alive—in his or her psyche. Professional counseling may be required in order to place the offense in the past.

- **The offended person believes that constant reminders will prevent a recurrence of the offense.** He or she fears that the minute he or she forgives and forgets, the offender will repeat the offense. The offended person needs a better way of exerting an effective boundary.

- **The offended person likes to use reminders of past crimes as a way to gain power or control in a situation.** Since the offender is helpless to undo the past, the offended person can use it on any occasion to help support a current complaint or to validate a reaction ("Your mother hasn't liked me from day one when she asked me where my grandparents came from. What she said this afternoon is just one more example of her prejudice against me. I don't want to have anything to do with her"). Power attained in this fashion causes relationship problems; better strategies are needed.

TRAPPED BY PAST MISDEEDS

Each and every human being makes mistakes. If our loved ones freeze us in our errors, neither they nor we can ever recover. Indeed, hopelessness and despair can settle into our relationships. It is demoralizing to find that even after we have acknowledged our wrongdoings, apologized, and improved our ways, we will still be reminded of the "bad old days." Healthy relationships, on the other hand, leave room for recovery, focusing on today rather than on the past, and moving optimistically into the future. Like spouses, parents must be careful to create a forgiving atmosphere. "I never told my parents when I got in trouble at school. It would just be an excuse for them to remind me of everything I ever did wrong. They could never deal with just the one issue."

TAKING IT OFF THE RECORD

Creating a family statute of limitations can help foster a healthy atmosphere in which everyone is allowed to err and move on. The statute consists of an agreed-upon time period for reminding someone of an offense. For children, a shorter period is most appropriate, since they make frequent errors by virtue of their youth and inexperience. Two weeks, for example, may be a fair time in which an error can be referred to for a young child, six weeks may be fair for a teenager. However, once the period is over, that error goes off the record, never to be referred to again (except where absolutely necessary in order to address a *current* situation—for example, a teenager's current refusal to drive a car is linked to a severe accident he caused when he first got his license three years earlier. This information must obviously be relayed to the mental health professional treating the current phobia. However, it should never be mentioned just to "rub it in," even if he gets into an accident again). For adult misdemeanors, a period of three months might be offered, after which the misbehavior goes off the record (with the same exception as above).

In order to apply a family statute of limitations, all parties must be willing to acknowledge, apologize, and repent after erring. Failure to do so makes it very hard for offended parties to heal and move on. Getting into the habit of focusing on present issues without reference to the past keeps family life fluid and growth oriented.

MISUNDERSTOOD

Ⓦe all know the feeling of being misunderstood: it's lonely. It's a sad, dark, all-by-myself type of feeling where others "don't get it." We feel unheard, as if there is a large, impenetrable barrier between ourselves and our listener; we can't get through. It is the feeling that alienates children from their parents and married people from their spouses. It is the feeling that nurtures depression, withdrawal, and escapism. It is an awful place to be.

IT CAN BE HARD TO UNDERSTAND

Although we hate being misunderstood, we seem to enjoy misunderstanding others—particularly those closest to us. Misunderstanding them helps *us* feel safer and more comfortable. After all, who *really* wants to understand a teenager who feels we haven't done enough for her? The notion is ridiculous, and understanding it is tantamount to accepting it (at least in our minds). Therefore, it is better for us if we refuse to understand it.

Similarly, understanding that a spouse has serious complaints against us is painful. It's easier, and far more pleasant, to refuse to understand (accept) those complaints by showing him or her just how ill-founded they actually are. Even when the issues that others bring to us for understanding have nothing whatsoever to do with us, they can still be threatening and therefore uncomfortable. A young child who talks about wanting to die can really upset a parent. Better not to understand his point of view—try to talk him out of it as quickly as possible.

HOW TO MISUNDERSTAND OTHERS

Since truly understanding can be so excruciating, we have become experts at *not* understanding. Here are some of our favorite tactics:

- **Explain how the other person is wrong.** This is our basic not-understanding technique. It involves arguing with the speaker. Our goal is to talk the speaker out of his or her feelings, since we find those feelings somehow upsetting or repugnant. A classic example of this strategy sounds like this: Spouse A says, "We don't have enough money for a vacation this summer." Spouse B—the misunderstander—says, "That's *ridiculous*! You have enough money for whatever you want all year long."

- **Discount the other person.** This technique involves minimizing what the person is saying. It sounds like this: Child says, "I hate going to camp!" Parent says, "It's not that bad." The discounting tactic acknowledges that the speaker has an issue but is, essentially, making a mountain out of a molehill.

Here's another example of discounting: Spouse A says, "We don't have enough money for a vacation this summer." Spouse B replies, "You worry too much about money. You need to learn to calm down."

- **Explain how the other person doesn't know what he or she is talking about.** This is similar to explaining how the other person is wrong except that it focuses more on the other person's *viewpoint* and less on objective facts. In action, this technique sounds like this: Spouse A says, "We don't have enough money for a vacation this summer." Spouse B says, "You're looking at it the wrong way. You have to consider the big picture and our values, like the importance of giving the kids fond childhood memories."

THE RESULTS OF FAILING TO UNDERSTAND

When we fail to understand our loved ones, they feel unimportant, invisible, and uncared for. Our brilliant arguments only serve to push the significant people in our lives further away from us. Indeed, when we consistently prove our spouse and children wrong, they stop opening up to us.

HOW TO UNDERSTAND OTHERS

Understanding is easy. In fact, it requires much less work than not-understanding does. No need to think, conjure up fancy arguments, debate, or otherwise exhaust yourself. Instead, simply summarize in your own words what the speaker just said. Summarize the *overt* and *covert* messages—what was *said*, and also, what was *conveyed* by tone of voice, facial expression, and body language. That's all you have to do. Do it for each sentence until the speaker has finished speaking. It sounds like this: Spouse A says, "We don't have enough money for a vacation this summer." Spouse B says, "Really? You feel we can't afford the cost of a family vacation this year?" Spouse B will continue in this way for each sentence that Spouse A speaks and only then begin to offer his or her own thoughts on the subject. Similarly, for the child who says, "I hate camp!" the understanding parent simply reflects back that message: "Oh. So you really don't like camp at all. You hate it!" See how simple this is? And yet, it is precisely the accurate reflection of the message that causes a person to feel understood by his or her listener. Yes, it slows down the conversation a bit but it's well worth it. Being understood is priceless.

WHO IS
RESPONSIBLE?

R ead the following scenarios and carefully consider your answers:

- **Nine-year-old Naftali forgot his lunch at home again.** Should Mom bring it to school for him? (yes or no)

- **Twelve-year-old Shoshana really struggles to wake up in the morning.** How many times should Mom come into her room to help her get out of bed? (choose one: zero times, two times, three times, as many times as necessary)

- **Sixteen-year-old Masha needs to make a doctor's appointment.** Assuming they both have time to make the call, who should do it—Mom or Masha?

- **Four-year-old Yudi has trouble getting his snow pants on**. Should Mom help him or let him struggle on his own?

- **Twenty-eight-year-old Yechiel constantly loses his keys**. When he is in a rush in the morning, should his wife interrupt her morning responsibilities with the children to help him find his keys so he can leave on time? (yes or no)

- **Thirty-six-year-old Ruthie doesn't like to attend medical appointments on her own**. Should her husband interrupt his daily schedule to go with her? (yes or no)

TO HELP OR NOT TO HELP?

It is often hard to know when to help, how much to help, and when not to help at all. When is a person being kind to herself and when is she being kind to the one who needs her help?

Let's imagine that Naftali's mother's name is Shifra. Shifra is a "helper." When Naftali forgets his lunch, Shifra is happy to bring it to him. She has chosen to be a stay-at-home mother for just this sort of reason: to be available when her kids need her.

Let's imagine another scenario. In this one, Naftali's mother's name is Adina. Adina is a worrier. When Naftali forgets his lunch, Adina worries that he'll be hungry and then she worries that he won't be able to learn well in the afternoon. She interrupts her schedule during the day to bring him his lunch. It's worth it for her—she's afraid of the consequences of letting him go without food.

Now let's imagine that Naftali's mother's name is Ilana. Ilana's middle name is "guilt." She brings Naftali his lunch not because she *wants* to, but because she would feel like a bad mother if she didn't. She knows that good mothers don't let their children starve. She resents Naftali for constantly forgetting to take his lunch, but she feels she has no choice but to save him from himself. Even if it means making her feel stressed, overwhelmed, or exhausted, she just can't say no.

Then there is a mom named Sari. Sari hates conflict. She knows that Naftali will have a fit later on if she doesn't bring him his lunch. She's not in the mood for that today. It's just simpler if she brings him his lunch.

Finally, let's imagine that Naftali's mother's name is Deena. Deena recognizes that Naftali has two lunch problems: (1) what will he eat for lunch today, and (2) how will he learn to remember to bring his lunch to school every single day. She asks herself the question, "What does *Naftali* need?" Shifra, Adina, Ilana, and Sari solved the lunch bag dilemma by addressing *their own* needs, not Naftali's. Bringing the lunch makes Shifra feel helpful. Bringing the lunch eases Adina's anxiety. Bringing the lunch soothes Ilana's pangs of guilt. Bringing the lunch helps Sari avoids unpleasant conflict. Only Deena solves the problem by addressing Naftali's needs rather than her own. Naftali needs two things: something to eat today and an educational plan that will help him remember to bring his lunch.

Deena calls the school and asks the teacher to provide Naftali with a few crackers if possible—not enough to fill him up but just enough to help him concentrate through the long afternoon ahead. Although she feels badly for her son, she absolutely refuses to bring his lunch this time and every other time that he forgets it. She knows that the disappointment and hunger will help him re-member it in the future. When Naftali comes home that night, she helps him develop a strategy for getting his lunch into his school-bag daily (e.g., he makes himself a big reminder picture and tapes it to the front door so he'll see it as he leaves each morning).

PROMOTING HEALTH AND HEALTHY RELATIONSHIPS

Overfunctioning (doing things for others that they need to be doing for or by themselves) hurts in three ways: the overfunctioning person may get burned-out or become resentful, the underfunctioning person may remain dysfunctional, the relationship between the two parties may become strained due to the inevitable resentment of the overfunctioning party.

Although it's sometimes easier to just step in and rescue someone, it's often kinder in the long run to stand back.

MY STRESS,
YOUR PROBLEM

What do you do when you discover that you forgot an important appointment? Do you say "oops" and reschedule the appointment? Or do you beat yourself up out loud (*"I can't believe I did that! Why am I so stupid? This will cost me money...I just can't believe I did this..."*)? What do you do when you drop a glass on the floor (because you were rushing, because you were late, because the kids wouldn't cooperate) and it smashes to bits? Do you explode? Or do you just sigh deeply?

What do you do when your spouse does or says something provocative? Do you react immediately with a stabbing retort? Do you stay silent and think about how you will handle this later on? What if your child ruins the pile of laundry you just so carefully folded? Do you shriek? Do you laugh? Do you apply the "two times rule" (a respectful form of discipline)?

All of these situations are stressful. Waiting in long lines, discovering an overdrawn account, trying to do too may errands in too little time—these examples of daily-hassle stress take a toll on everyone. In fact, daily-hassle stress can be harder on the body than single-major-event stressors. Daily-hassle stress occurs *daily*. When people experience this kind of stress in the moment, they respond by doing *something*. Very often, the thing they do helps to release the stress they feel. Making loud noises, wringing hands, slamming doors—these transfers of energy help to move stress out of the body. But where does it go?

MOVING STRESS

Research shows that unexpressed stress can harm a person physically and emotionally. Keeping stress responses *inside* the body creates a time bomb. Eventually the accumulated stress explodes. The explosion can take the form of a fit of rage or a flooding of tears or a physical illness. It can lead to emotional collapse (so-called "nervous breakdown"). So it's not a good idea to keep stress bottled up.

However, letting stress out can create its own set of problems. Expressed stress can ruin relationships, destroy family life, and lead to physical illness. (The literature shows that disease stems equally from stifled stress and from expressed stress.) Fortunately, there are some safe and healthy venues for moving stress out of the body and mind. Clear communication helps release interpersonal stress. Personal stress is reduced with many different techniques. One is regular (preferably daily) exercise. Another is regular personal counseling sessions. Another is daily pouring out of one's soul to Hashem. Another is taking daily private time to examine one's feelings and experiences of the day, to pay attention to the accompanying thoughts, emotions, and even physical sensations, and address the needs that arise out of all this information. Relaxation techniques do not remove stress per se, but they help the body handle stress more efficiently by keeping one's physical and emotional "thermostat" at a lower, calmer overall level of functioning. Therefore, relaxation techniques can be used as part of a stress-reduction program as well.

EXPRESSED STRESS IS CONTAGIOUS

Although there are many healthy ways to remove stress from the system, a lot of people don't use any of them. Many people simply express their stress in the moment it occurs. Often, such people are products of homes in which proper stress management wasn't taught or even more likely, homes in which the parents routinely expressed their momentary stress in dysfunctional ways. When people release their stress by raising their voices, shouting at themselves, shouting at family members, or doing something physical (like throwing something, slamming something, or pounding something), stress flows out of them and into their homes. Every family member will breathe and absorb the stress that's been dumped into the kitchen or living room. It isn't pleasant, comfortable, or emotionally safe to live in such environments.

PRIVATE STRESS, PUBLIC HOME

Unless someone lives alone, their expressed stress is not a private affair. The home must be considered a public place. The way you react to your personal stress can affect all members of the household. Knowing this is step 1. Caring enough about the people you live with to *act* on this knowledge is step 2. This means that you consciously choose how you will express your stress (or not express it), keeping the welfare of loved ones in mind. Step 3 is adopting some of the stress-management strategies listed above so that your actual stress level will be minimized.

A stress-reduced home does not occur by accident. It is the product of hard work and love.

MIXED MESSAGES

Aaron is confused. Does his wife love him or hate him? He just doesn't know. And yet, considering the extremes of the two possibilities, how is it possible that the man doesn't know what his wife is feeling? Love is a warm, fuzzy emotion filled with tender care, while hate is an aggressive and destructive energy. One ought to be able to sort out the two.

GOOD TIMES AND BAD TIMES

There is a simple explanation, however, for Aaron's confusion, and it is this: Aaron's wife Shoshy behaves in radically different ways in different situations. When things are going her way and she is not particularly stressed, Shoshy is a friendly, bubbly person. Often, she'll turn to Aaron and express her heartfelt appreciation for all that he is and does. "You are the best husband ever!" she'll exclaim.

"No one has a better husband than you!"

On these kinds of days, Aaron knows exactly how much his wife loves him. He feels respected, acknowledged, and cared for. But then, there are the other days—days when Shoshy is tense or overwhelmed. It can happen when the kids are out of school for too many days or when she has a big project to do for her business. It's perfectly understandable that she should be on edge—anyone might feel the same. However, if Aaron happens to do or say something the wrong way on such a day, then *pow*: Shoshy number 2 appears:

"I can't count on you for anything! I have no idea why I married you in the first place! You're absolutely useless!" she'll scream at the top of her lungs (regardless of how many kids are around to hear her). Maybe Aaron forgot to do an errand or maybe he had trouble putting one of the little ones to bed. Whatever it was, Shoshy's response is a deep, personal attack on him and their relationship. She feels relieved after discharging her negative energy. However, Aaron, now smothering in the discharge of his wife's toxic energy, feels sick in every cell of his body.

Aaron has been living with his on-and-off wife for eight years now. In the first years he was sure that Shoshy loved him; he explained her outbursts to himself as episodes of stress in which "she didn't know what she was saying." After a while, however, he began to wonder about that. Maybe the *real* message wasn't the loving message after all. Maybe it was that she really did hate him. The more times she hurled hurtful insults at him, the less trusting he felt of her loving comments. Eventually, he became dead inside. Neither her praises nor her insults could touch him. He withdrew from her emotionally, to protect himself. And that's where he is today. He can't say for sure what his wife feels about him. But he can say for sure that he no longer trusts her—or cares for her very much.

CONFUSED CHILDREN

Adults aren't the only ones who get confused about their relationships. Children can also become uncertain, and for the very same reasons. Little Dini, for instance, can't figure out whether her father loves her or hates her. At times, she receives gentle, approving, even adoring attention from him. At other times, however, Dini experiences her father's "other side." For no reason that she can decipher, he can be short-tempered and irritable, even explosive at times. Dini is only seven and knows nothing of the adult world and its stresses. She just knows that sometimes her father is warm and loving, and other times he is rageful and terrifying. She feels loved and adored and hated and despised. She's not sure if she's a good girl or a bad girl. Experiencing the love-hate dynamic as "normal," she grows up internalizing the lesson that "love hurts." When she marries, her ability to establish healthy boundaries will be compromised. She never learned that people who love each other treat each other well *always*, even when they are stressed or tired. It might take her fifteen years of living in an adult abusive relationship—or more—before she begins to realize that bad treatment isn't acceptable in relationships. And only *after* that realization will she be able to change what's happening in her life.

CONSISTENCY

Rageful, hurtful, destructive communication has *no* place in any kind of *loving* relationship. Sure, people will feel irritated, hurt, and angry at their loved ones from time to time. And yes, they are allowed to express their emotions—but always with sensitivity to the person being spoken to. Being able and willing to put the brakes on one's mouth is an essential skill for building and preserving the feeling of love in any important relationship. Use whatever resources you can—Torah study, self-help or professional help—in order to acquire it. You owe it to yourself and your family.

CRAZY-MAKING

Family life is challenging, and all the more so when a particular family member makes you "crazy." *"My mother drives me crazy!" "My son makes me insane!" "My wife makes me nuts!"* What do all these people mean? How do their loved ones drive them over the brink?

NOW YOU SEE IT, NOW YOU DON'T

In fact, there are some very popular communication tools that have the effect of inducing neurosis in family members. The purpose of this article is not to teach you these tools so that you can use them at home against your loved ones (sorry). Rather, the purpose is to help you identify when these tools are being used on *you*. By recognizing what is going on, you will be able to better maintain your sanity. You will also be less likely to fall into the trap of arguing and fighting. In a few cases, you will even be able to get the crazy-maker to stop doing what he or she is doing.

You may also be able to recognize that you, yourself, use crazy-making communications on occasion. Some people use only one or two of these destructive techniques, while others use many. Some people use them only rarely, while others use them constantly. However, the more a person employs any of the following crazy-making communication techniques, the more they harm their relationships with spouse and children. This sort of communication tends to break trust and alienate family members, preventing close, loving relationships.

Many people use these techniques accidentally, having picked them up in their own childhood homes. Some have developed them as protective interpersonal strategies along the way. However, since their short-term benefit—whatever they accomplish in the moment—is far overshadowed by their destructive effects, they are worth identifying and losing as soon as possible.

Crazy-makers cause people to feel disoriented, confused, upset, and uncomfortable. Recognizing crazy-making communications helps us to protect ourselves when they're used on us and helps us to avoid using them ourselves.

- **Punishing a person for doing what you asked them to do.** A wife tells her husband, "I won't get upset as long as you call me to tell me you'll be late for dinner." Husband calls to say he'll be late, and his wife *screams* at him, "You know we're having fish tonight! Why do you pick tonight of all nights to come home late?" She asked him to call and then yelled at him when he did.

- **Being impossible to please.** A husband asks his wife to serve meat and chicken less frequently for dinner. She starts to supplement the menu with dairy and vegetarian dishes. He complains, "This doesn't taste like food!" A wife asks her husband to please tidy up the cutlery drawer when he has a moment. He does it that same day. She looks it over and says, "You call *this* tidy?" In both cases, the spouse ignores the positive efforts of the partner to comply with requests and concentrates instead on the flaws and imperfections of performance.

- **Denying something that has been discussed and agreed upon.** Wife reminds husband that he promised (a couple of months ago) to bring her mom along on their next vacation. He responds, "I wouldn't have said something like that! I never would have agreed to that. You're making that up to suit yourself!" Some people chronically deny that they said things or agreed to things. In this way, they destroy any sense of collaborative partnership in their marriage. They become untrustworthy.

- **Unclear communication.** Mom says to daughter, "Your room is a mess! Make sure you clean it up before you do anything else!" A while later, Mom enters the room to find Daughter hanging up clothes. She asks, "Don't you have a report to do for class tomorrow?" Daughter replies, "Yes, but you said I should clean my room before anything else." Mother says, "You knew exactly what I meant! I didn't mean before your schoolwork obviously! I meant before you read your books!" This technique is related to expecting others to read one's mind. Instead of saying exactly what one means, one expects others to read between the lines and blames *them* when they don't.

- **Refusing to accept one's part in an agreement.** A mother agrees to allow a child to choose his new glasses and then criticizes his choice ("Why would you pick frames in *that* color?"). A wife lets herself be "talked into" buying a certain vehicle and then blames her husband repeatedly for its various flaws ("*You* were the one who wanted this car"). These people refuse to acknowledge that they freely, of their own volition, worked out a compromise or an agreement. They act as if they had no choice. The most intense version of this is saying to one's spouse, "Well, *you* were the one who wanted to get married. I didn't think it was such a good idea."

- **Building up hopes and then dashing them without a satisfactory reason.** Mom tells the kids that she will take them to an amusement park on Sunday. The kids are excited. When Sunday comes along, they start begging her to go. "I've changed my mind—it's not a good day for it," Mom says. The children ask her why they can't go. Mom gets irritated: "I *told* you it's not a good day for it and that should be enough. Now go play!" Making no sense in a communication initiates a severe breakdown of trust.

- **Sticking to exact words rather than their generally accepted meaning.** Wife is very upset that Husband stopped in for thirty minutes to visit his ailing mother on the way home from work. Husband defends his behavior, exclaiming, "But you yourself told me to check in on her on the way home from work!" Wife retorts, "Yes, I said *check in on her*. I didn't say to stay there for half an hour!" If a family member feels they need to have a lawyer on twenty-four-hour call in order to protect themselves from your letter-of-the-law style of communication, your style is crazy-making.

- **Acting as if the other person said something they didn't say (putting words in their mouth).** Wife to husband: "Did you see my keys? I thought I left them right here on the counter." Husband to wife: "No, I didn't see them." Wife: "That's funny—they were here a minute ago." Husband to wife: "Are you calling me a liar?" Attributing hurtful words to another person is unfair and confusing. It puts the speaker in a position of having to defend behavior they didn't engage in.

- **Accusing another person of sinister motives.** At the Shabbos table, Father is expounding a point of halacha. Son happened to hear things a little differently from his rebbe and asks, "Is it possible that there's another answer?" Father slams the table and shouts, "You just want to provoke me!" Unless the son has a reputation for being provocative, the father's accusation is more than hurtful. Being so disconnected from factual reality, it becomes crazy-making. Similarly, Wife says to Husband, "You suddenly have all this work to do because you don't want to go out with me." Again, unless there is evidence that the husband is trying to avoid the wife, the attribution of bad motives is crazy-making.

- **Blaming another person for one's own bad behavior or mistakes.** "You made me drop the cup. You shouldn't be talking to me when I'm making coffee." "You made me slam the door. You just don't know when to stop." Although other people can provoke us or trigger us or distract us, *we* are ultimately responsible for coping with all these things in a productive way. For instance, if we're prone to drop things when someone is talking to us, we can stop what we're doing while they're talking and listen to them, continuing our activity only when the conversation ends. Other people don't "make" us behave badly or carelessly. When someone says it's *your* fault that they messed up, they are engaging in crazy-making communication.

- **Consistently ignoring the wishes of a family member.** If a family member wants something unreasonable, it may be necessary to ignore his or her wishes. For instance, if a wife wants a husband to have twelve hours of sleep each night, he doesn't have to comply with her wish (especially if he gets by just fine on seven hours). They may need some marriage counseling to take up the issue, though. However, when a family member expresses a normal wish, consistently ignoring it is not only unkind, it is a troubling communication as well. For instance, if a husband asks a wife to include bananas on the shopping list because he enjoys them and they can afford to purchase them, and she consistently "forgets" or just plain doesn't do it, claiming the whole time that it is an "accident" (week after week, month after month, year after year), this is a crazy-making tactic.

Crazy-making behavior is very difficult to correct without third-party assistance. It is almost impossible to get someone to acknowledge and correct their crazy-making communication. Although small doses of crazy-making communications may be tolerable, larger doses are destructive. When this kind of communication is so pervasive that family relationships are suffering or so intense that one's own mental health is affected, it is time to access professional help.

WHEN IS
A MOTHER NOT
A MOTHER?

I s a mother always a mother or is she sometimes her own person? Let's see:

WHEN SHE'S A WIFE

When a woman is being a wife—talking to her husband, taking care of his needs, buying him a birthday present, assisting him in life, sharing responsibilities with him—she is showing her children how a wife loves, respects, partners with, and cares for her spouse. In this way, she is not only modeling spousal behavior for her kids, but she is in fact deeply ingraining patterns of emotion, attitude, and behavior into their developing brains. In other words, as a wife, she is very much a mother.

WHEN SHE'S A DAUGHTER

How does Mommy talk to Bubby? The children are listening and absorbing. Does Mommy speak kindly, caringly, and with respect? Or is there impatience and irritability? Does it ever erupt into a screaming match? Does Mommy reach out enthusiastically to help or does she do so resentfully? Is she close to Bubby or distant? The mother/daughter is teaching her children what it means to be part of a family and how that should be lived out. As a daughter, she is still very much a mother.

WHEN SHE'S A SIBLING

Of course, similar lessons are bestowed through Mommy's dealings with her siblings. Do they coexist in harmony and friendship? Or are there decades when someone isn't talking to another? Are there frequent flare-ups? Children can learn from watching Mom deal with her siblings how one should handle conflict. Sibling relationships are "forced" relationships (forced by Hashem). Siblings aren't friends that we choose—they're people we're put with on life's journey. Because of this, there may be more stress and conflict than we experience in other, more freely chosen relationships. Sibling-in-law relationships are an even more intense case of the imposed relative and present numerous interpersonal challenges. How does Mom handle it all? She's teaching her children to do likewise. Even as a sister, she's still very much a mother.

WHEN SHE'S A FRIEND

Does Mommy make time for personal friends? If she does, she

teaches that it's important to develop a social network. If she doesn't, she teaches that family is all one really needs. If Mommy has some friends, how does she fit them into her life? Do they take priority over the children at times, the housework, or even over the marriage? Is she out every evening with them or constantly on the phone with them? Or does she squeeze them into small corners of her life between spouse, children, extended family, work, home, and community? However Mother manages her social life, she is showing her children how it is done. If they feel she gave friends too much attention at their expense, they may react by consciously limiting their out-of-house activities when they raise their own children. If they feel that she never allowed herself the fulfillment of satisfying friendships, they may react by carefully carving out more social time for themselves. There will be an impact of Mother's interpersonal life. Even as a friend, she's still very much a mother.

WHEN SHE'S OCCUPIED IN HER CAREER

When Mom goes off to work, is she happy about it? Can she manage her other responsibilities with competence and grace, or is she overwhelmed, exhausted, harried, and resentful? Is work something that "you have to do and that's just the way it is" or is it something that "you want to do in order to fulfill your highest potential?" Or is it something that women don't do at all? What Mom says about her work and how she carries herself off to work teaches her children just what work is for a woman. They live through it with her and absorb the lessons into their growing bones. Mother the worker is still very much a mother.

WHEN SHE'S ENJOYING
HER OWN FREE TIME

Does Mom actually have free time? (Are mothers allowed to have free time?) If so, what does she do with it? Does she chat on the phone? Does she paint pictures or engage in scrapbooking? Does she attend *shiurim*? Does she say more *Tehillim*? Does she volunteer? (Does one do "frivolous" and fun things or does one engage in spiritually elevating endeavors?) However Mom lives out her free time, she is conveying important messages about life itself and how it should be lived. As usual, the children are watching and learning. Even when Mom is at the very end of her day, finished with all of her responsibilities, the choices she makes about how to spend that last hour (or the "free" hours on Shabbos and *yom tov*) teach her children how to utilize the commodity of time. Even when she's off duty, Mother is still very much a mother.

So when is a mother not a mother?

Never.

Part Four

EXTENDING
THE FAMILY

YOU IN THE EXTENDED FAMILY

The nuclear family consists of parents and their children. But as we all know, family life consists of a whole lot more than this small cast of characters. The extended family—consisting of siblings, in-laws, cousins, aunts, uncles, and others—is right in there with us, often impacting our lives in dramatic ways.

The only person that we "choose" to be relatives with is our spouse. While we may or may not be pleased with that choice as time passes, it is at least a choice. Everyone else comes with the package. We inherit our own relatives at birth, and we inherit our spouse's relatives upon marriage. We inherit our sons and daughters directly from Hashem, and we inherit our children's spouses (and parts of their families and extended families) upon our children's marriages. Then we must find ways to enjoy, tolerate, or work with each one of these people. Sometimes we must find ways to protect ourselves from them. Sometimes we must find ways to protect our marriages from them as well. Hashem, in His wisdom, puts each one of these people in our lives for our own greatest benefit—whether we like it or not!

NUCLEAR CHILDREN BECOMING EXTENDED FAMILY

A particular challenge that every parent faces is the transition of one's own child into a sort of extended family member. When the child is young, he or she is clearly part of the nuclear family structure. The home that parents make for him or her is called the child's "family of origin." However, as the child becomes older, he or she psychologically, and then physically, separates from the parent. This happens in gradual stages, beginning with schooling that requires boarding elsewhere and most often ending with marriage. Sometimes a child lives independently either temporarily or permanently. In all cases, the child is no longer living at home, and although still technically considered a member of the nuclear family, he or she is rapidly becoming part of the extended family.

This transition is often very challenging for parents. In fact, many parents never successfully complete the transition, continuing to treat their forty-year-old kids as if they are still schoolchildren living under their jurisdiction. They find it hard to see their kids as independent adults who must make their own decisions and their own mistakes in order to develop their own soul potentials. But even when parents do manage to let go, even when they are *thrilled* to see their children moving forward into a good life with a good future, they often experience different types of painful emotions alongside their joy: grief, loss, worry, emptiness, and more. Of course, in some cases, there are other feelings like relief, guilt, remorse, and so on. A parent could feel everything and anything as his or her children move beyond the family.

IN-LAWS EVERYWHERE

At first, there is usually a small group of parents-in-law to contend with—generally four or less people unless divorce has created various doublings. While some people have beautiful, supportive relationships with their in-laws, some people have enormous in-law challenges that sometimes threaten to strain a marriage to its breaking point. Siblings-in-law sometimes prove to be wonderful friends, and other times a constant, pricking thorn in one's side. Later, when the children marry, more in-laws appear. Sons- and daughters-in-law sometimes become ideal children who don't carry the baggage of one's earlier parenting faux pas, while sometimes they appear to become clear agents of the Satan, snatching one's child and grandchildren away. In a large family, parents may have in-laws of all kinds. Again, one must remember that Hashem knows what He is doing. Every in-law offers a spiritual benefit, even if it is not immediately clear what that benefit could be! The fact that in-law relationships often create struggle is a hint, however, that within that struggle, as within all big tests, is the potential to find one's own greatness.

As you negotiate the world of your extended and extending family, you might want to consider the following tips:

- **Shalom is one of the names of Hashem.**

- **Each of us is required to pursue shalom, rather than wait for it to come to us.**

- **Our children are always watching our dealings with**

extended family members and learning from them.

- **If things are difficult with extended family members, seek professional help as soon as you can.** There is no point in suffering for twenty-five years before getting help.

- **The interpersonal mitzvos (such as being respectful, kind, loving, compassionate, judging favorably, guarding our tongue, and so on) apply to relatives as well as to everyone else.**

- **Extended family members are people who want and need your love and positive regard; when you give it to them, they'll almost always respond in kind.**

- **Be prepared to take the lead in all extended-family relationships.** Your kindness will most likely be reciprocated over time. Even if it's not, Hashem will reimburse you for your efforts.

- **Love your spouse's relatives as a favor to your spouse.** When your spouse sees that his/her relatives love *you*, it will make your spouse love you even more.

- **When extended family members hurt your feelings, try to let them know about it, but be sure to do so without causing them pain, aggravation, or embarrassment.** Focus the discussion on what can be done to improve things for the future. Causing a small amount of temporary distress may be worth it if the outcome is improved relationships. However, if you can't avoid causing *significant* distress or if no positive outcome will occur in any event, it's best *not* to take it up with them (you must *try* a few times before you conclude that no positive outcome will be forthcoming). Instead, take it up with Hashem.

- **Your job as a child-in-law is to be really nice to your parents-in-law, within the normal limits of your strength and energy**. You don't have to do anything crazy in order to earn anyone's acceptance or love. Call your parents-in-law by the most affectionate names that you can, bring them gifts, and contact them just to say hi. A little goes a long way.

- **Your job as a parent-in-law is to love your child's new spouse no matter what**. You don't have to fix the newcomer in any way. That kind of work will be up to your child. You are there to encourage and strengthen your child in the difficult journey of marriage. Only speak well of your child-in-law to your child, helping your child to see the good as well. Never try to talk your child out of his or her marriage in the hopes of seeing him or her happy (unless your child is being *physically* assaulted; your child can handle emotional abuse on his or her own). If your child decides to end a marriage for whatever reason, the original thought or any subsequent thought or action should never be traceable back to *you*. Marriage and divorce are responsibilities of the individual—not his or her parents.

- **Your child's spouse is the gatekeeper of your grandchildren**. Keep the gate open with your positive regard.

- **Remember that your grown child is twenty or thirty or forty years younger than you and still developing**. Always picture best-case scenarios and best outcomes. Your thoughts and images can have powerful, positive effects.

Add your own tips to help you remember your priorities and strategies for successful relationships within your extended family:

_____

_____

_____

_____

_____

_____

_____

_____

_____

_____

_____

_____

_____

_____

_____

_____

_____

_____

_____

_____

LETTING GO

We normally think of children as the ones who suffer from "separation anxiety"—the panic that occurs when one is left by another. However, this phenomenon happens to parents as well as to children.

Moms who have to return to work after the birth of their babies may feel the pain of separation even more than the infants. Sometimes parents stay home with their infants and toddlers so that the first separations occur when the child is the one to leave for camp, playgroup, or school. Little kids may cry and cling to their parents on these first excursions from home. However, parents may inwardly be doing much the same. After the child boards the bus or enters the building, Mom may find a private spot to shed her own tears. Many mothers find it hard to let their children attend out-of-town seminaries and yeshivos. Giving up their ability to nurture their youngster on a daily basis can be hard. However, the hardest separation for parents to bear is often the one that occurs when a grown child leaves home for good.

SAYING GOOD-BYE

It is, of course, a good thing that children grow up and leave home. No one wants their child to stay at home forever. However, the fact that it is healthy and appropriate does nothing to lessen the upset for parents. Many mothers have very positive, close relationships with their older teenage children of both genders. When the child moves out, he or she will have adventures and experiences. If the child is moving out into a marriage, then he or she will have a new intimate companion and a new life. It is the parent who is left behind.

Marriage being what it is, it sometimes happens that the relationship one has with a grown child is closer, less conflicted, and happier than the one that a person has with her own spouse. When this happens, the grief of "losing" a child is all the more intense. In fact, this is one reason that couples should always nurture their relationship to the utmost—to ensure that they *have* a relationship when their youngsters move out to form their own. However, even if the marriage is fine, some women will enjoy a mother-child relationship that is quite different from the marital relationship; it may be fulfilling, satisfying, and gratifying in a completely different way. When the tight bond is severed by travel, school, or marriage, the mother can experience deep grief.

It is not uncommon for people to anticipate the loss months in advance. Some women literally lose sleep over the thought of the loss of their child. Intense anxiety can occur in those who have been prone to anxiety in their lives. Depression can affect those who are prone to depression. Losing a child—even to good causes—triggers the old vulnerabilities and unfinished business of adults.

COPING WITH LOSS

The first task in coping well with loss is to allow oneself to feel the pain. Becoming hyperbusy and distracted only prolongs the suffering. There will be time for extra projects later. When painful emotions are acknowledged and allowed, they float away. Just as a good cry clears up blocked emotions, listening to one's own heart allows the heart to heal. There are many ways to begin this process. Talking to friends about grief is not the best way, since most people will want to talk you out of your feelings ("Don't worry—soon you won't want her back"). Instead, keep a temporary journal. In it, write down—very quickly—your thoughts and feelings about your child leaving home. Do this for just a few minutes each day. The quick writing helps to get to your deeper feelings instead of staying on the calculated surface of the mind. Another exercise you can do is visit a counselor. The departure of a child can trigger many other issues—why not clean them all up now? Learning and using the Emotional Freedom Technique can be a very fast way to relieve the grief. Look for a local practitioner, book, or course on this subject.

Being compassionate toward yourself is essential. Of course this hurts. You've put your heart and soul into raising this child, and you spent endless minutes and hours invested in his or her well-being. Why wouldn't it be monumental for the young person to walk out of your life now? Of course, many children don't walk too far—their parents will talk to them daily and see them often. And yet, it will never be the same. Honor the parenting voyage by allowing yourself to feel those feelings at the end. You'll free yourself up to feel the joy of the next stage of this awesome journey.

PARENTING ADULT CHILDREN

D o we really continue to parent our adult children and their spouses? Yes. Not because we want to, but because we are parents. Our relationship to our children is always one of teacher and guide. We teach both with our conscious efforts and strategies and with our unconscious behavior. We impact them by our very existence, our model of how to think, feel, and act in this world.

There are many areas where parents impact on their adult children. One important parenting issue for young adults is called "boundary setting." Boundary setting lets others know how to treat you. Failure to set boundaries lets them know they can *mistreat* you and get away with it. Boundary setting both establishes and teaches healthy relationship skills. In parenting younger children, we also set boundaries all the time. We often use negative consequences to do so. For example, we might say to a child, "If you continue to shout at me, you'll have to go to your room." To an adult we might say, "If you continue to shout at me, *I'll* have to leave the room." Boundary setting occurs with spouses, colleagues, and any other person with whom one has dealings. Therefore, we do not specifically call it "parenting." Nonetheless, when we actually engage in boundary setting with adults who happen to be our children or our children-in-law, it retains a parenting "flavor," if only because the young people will certainly perceive it that way.

In addition to boundary setting, parents continue to parent their adult children and children-in-law through their personal model. A young couple looks at their parents and in-laws and makes life decisions based on what they see. "I don't like the way your father treats your mother—I don't want you to treat me that way," "I hope that we can have a marriage as wonderful as your parents' marriage," "I love the way your mother entertains—we never had that in my house growing up. I'd like to make it part of our home," "I don't like the way your folks handle money. We need to work out something different."

But there is more. Young couples are always children to their parents and parents-in-law. This means that the older generation still wants to nurture and protect the younger generation, and the younger generation still looks to the older generation for approval and support. The words a parent speaks to his or her child impact on that child as no other words ever will, as they hold a psychic force that deeply pierces the subconscious mind. There is a similar (though not identical) impact of the words and actions of in-laws. They can hurt more than the words and actions of other people, and they can also heal more powerfully. Kind, encouraging speech and action from parents to their children and children-in-law are more powerful than those from any other source. Thoughtless or neglectful parental speech or action can unintentionally cause enormous pain. In other words, parents are never just "normal" people (no pun intended). They are always bigger than life both to their children and their children-in law. Parents of married children need to be aware of their ongoing power. This relationship is not one of two couples on a level playing field. Between parents and children there is *always* a hierarchy. Parents must wield this power carefully in order to avoid causing serious harm.

One of the most important parenting jobs for parents of young married couples is to support their marriages. As more experienced people know, marriage can be challenging. Young people—especially in today's quick-divorce culture—need all the support they can get. The parental task is not to minimize or discount a child's pain, frustration, or fear but to help him or her find the resources to cope with all challenges. Parents can help de-escalate conflict by normalizing marital struggle and growth. Except during marital crisis, they can sing the praises of the child-in-law. They can encourage their children to seek rabbinical advice or professional counseling. However, if parents bad-mouth the child-in-law or weaken the child's resolve to work things out, their input can be highly destructive, harming the child's life as well as his or her confidence. (The exceptions to this supportive strategy are those endorsed by Torah as expounded by one's rabbi, such as cases of untreatable abuse, incurable true mental illness, and so forth.)

As we can see, although parents may wish to retire, that option is out of the question. Even in death, parents continue to influence their adult children's behavior. The best solution is to be cognizant of one's importance and impact and consciously endeavor to be a worthy model and teacher all the days of one's life.

PARENTS-IN-LAW

G etting along with relatives requires a different skill set than getting along with friends. After all, you carefully *choose* your friends, while Hashem chooses your relatives. While members of our own extended family can sometimes be hard for us to deal with, members of our spouse's family can often be even harder. Let me issue a disclaimer at the outset: Many people have been fortunate enough to be surrounded with loving family members, both blood relatives and in-laws. However, having nothing but excellent relationships with family members of all kinds is rare—something akin to winning the lottery. Most often, people find some of their relatives challenging. Commonly, people find their in-law relatives particularly challenging. And commonly to the point of being completely normal, people find their parents-in-law to be somewhat challenging (or even very challenging). Let's see why and what can be done to improve the situation.

PARENTS

To begin with, parents-in-law are parents. That in itself poses a problem. As you may know, adults don't want parents. Young adults, particularly, have finally gotten away from parental control and are more than ready to spread their independent wings. While they may be delighted to accept gifts (money, babysitting, or whatever), they are no longer delighted to be told what to do or how to do it. And this is from *their own parents.* They certainly don't want this sort of information from someone else's parents (i.e., their spouse's parents).

Which brings us to a second issue with parents-in-law: they are strangers with strange ways. They are unlike one's own parents, with whom one often identifies, feels at home with, and even copies. They are *different* and perhaps even *wrong.* "My parents don't do that," "My parents would never say that," "My parents don't believe that." In other words, *"I can't relate to your parents at all."* While feeling uncomfortable with one's parents-in-law isn't the end of the world, it *is* uncomfortable.

Then there's personality. A parent-in-law is often very present in one's life. While some people live so far away from their parents-in-law that they rarely have to deal with them in person, many live within minutes by car or foot. Others who don't live nearby end up living with them (in their house or in their own) for several weeks of the year. Contact with parents-in-law can be strained when you don't actually *like* one or both of them. Some people discover that a minor flaw they tolerate in their spouse exists in gigantic proportions in the spouse's parents. For instance, a husband is mildly irritated by his wife's tendency to get nervous and overwhelmed under pressure. However, when spending the holidays with his parents-in-law he now sees where this tendency comes from: his wife's mother is *completely* overwhelmed by every small household task and preparation. This is a trait he doesn't like even in small proportions, and now, twice a year, every year, he has to live with it for extended periods of time in Technicolor.

Finally, there is the issue of competition. One's parents-in-law have a claim on one's spouse: they raised that human being who you now claim belongs to *you*. Parents don't let go that easily. Your spouse will always be their little girl or boy who they poured their heart and soul and physical strength into for two unbelievably intense decades. Some parents-in-law make this all too clear by continuing to act as if *your* spouse is *their* child. They may have private conversations with him or her, give him or her private gifts, practically ignore *you*, or do other things that convey property rights. Unless you are extremely secure in yourself and in your marriage, these parental behaviors can be a bit unnerving.

EASY SOLUTIONS TO PARENT-IN-LAW STRESS

As we have just seen, parents-in-law love to help, have their own ways of doing things, have their own personalities, and still love their child intensely. Addressing each of these factors can help solve parent-in-law stress. Accept help graciously, but remember you are free to live your own life and make your own decisions. Just say, "Thank you so much for that idea. We'll look into it." As for their own ways and personalities, when you are very pleasant to your parents-in-law, all differences and personality issues become less relevant, and ample space is made for peace. Finally, the love that your in-laws have for your spouse is natural. You're going to love your babies forever, too. Remember that your in-laws can only have their love fulfilled in small minutes here and there, because you now live full-time with their child. There is no real competition between you and your in-laws—you win. Knowing the truth of that can restore balance.

CHILD-IN-LAW CHALLENGES

O f course, for every child dealing with such in-law challenges, there are one or two parents-in-law who are dealing with the challenges of getting along with in-law children. What are some common hurdles and how do people cope?

POSSESSIVE CHILD-IN-LAW

Raising a child for twenty years is an intense project. Parents put heart and soul into this activity. They sometimes love their children more than they love each other and often more than they love themselves. Parents often *live* for their kids. So, at the end of the parenting journey, when some youngster comes along and seemingly scoops up their beloved child, taking him or her far away (virtually anyplace that is not the family home), they are often heartbroken. Of course, they have other feelings as well—joy, relief, *nachas*, and more—but a special kind of grief and mourning is equally common. Their child is gone.

The pain of the loss is assuaged somewhat when the new child-in-law is generous with his or her spouse's parents' "visitation rights." "Go ahead and call your mom as often as you want—I'm glad you two get along so well!" "Sure we can go to your folks every Shabbos. Why not?" "I'm happy to spend *yom tov* with your parents—I know how much you miss them."

However, a child-in-law is not always so openhearted. "I don't want you running errands for your mother—I need you here at home," "Please don't call your parents when I'm in the house—I need your attention," "I don't want to go to your parents' house so often," "I don't want you running over there all the time." Parents can find that their child is increasingly inaccessible. *Shalom bayis* obviously takes priority, and one's child may have to make unpleasant choices ("Sorry, Mom, but Yerachmiel gets so agitated if he knows I'm coming over—I just have to cut back"). A parent sometimes feels as if his or her child has been kidnapped.

This scenario is a deep challenge for any parent. As with all challenges, there are better and worse ways to respond to the situation. Here are some strategies and ideas to consider:

- **Don't speak badly about your child's spouse to your child.** If your frustration and pain is intense, speak to a mental health professional.

- **Don't blame your child's spouse.** *Your child* is a grown person who is making his or her own choices. Unless some sort of abuse is going on, your child has many healthy options for dealing with the in-law issue within marriage. If your child chooses to abandon you, that has more to do with your child than your child's partner.

- **Avoid conflict with your son- or daughter-in-law.** Instead, put your best self forward. The easier and more pleasant you are to be with, the less "problem" your child and child-in-law will have in spending time with you.

- **Consider the possibility that your child-in-law may have some personal issues or even mental health issues that make relationships with relatives threatening or difficult.** Be prepared to build trust over a long, slow period. Your patience and perseverance can pay off in increased closeness over the long run.

DIFFERENT PERSONALITIES

A completely different problem that many parents-in-law face is dealing with the personality of their child-in-law. This newcomer to the family has his or her own ways—both an inborn personality and characteristics learned within his or her own family of origin. Parents carefully raise their own kids to reflect their own cherished values. "I insisted that my kids make their own beds every day despite the fact that we always had hired help. I think kids need to learn independence, as well as respect for the effort that goes into running a home." Meanwhile, New Child-in-Law was "spoiled" and never had to lift a finger at home. This young person now sits at the Shabbos table waiting for Mother-in-Law to serve and clear, never considering for a moment that Mother-in-Law may appreciate—and expect—help from all able-bodied diners. Or, Mother-in-Law never fed her kids candy and now has to watch as her grandchildren *live* on junk food. Or, Mother-in-Law made sure her babies learned to sleep on their own by seven months of age and now has to stand back silently while Daughter-in-Law lets them sleep in her bed till age five!

All such differences in ways of thinking and being can challenge parents-in-law. While issues that impact on them directly (like helping out in the kitchen) might be sensitively dealt with, most differences must be accepted, if not embraced. The strategy that helps the most is to focus attention not on differences, but on all the beauty and goodness that this new child brings into the family.

MOTHER-IN-LAW TRAUMA

There are two types of trauma: "big *t* trauma" and "small *t* trauma." The former term refers to life-threatening events such as surviving a severe car crash, experiencing assault, witnessing violence, or living through the ravages of war. Such events can unravel the nervous system, leaving a person riddled with nightmares, panic attacks, intrusive memories, depression, and other debilitating symptoms. "Small *t* traumas" are the common stuff of life—common, but very painful—such as humiliating oneself in public by wearing a very "wrong" outfit at a certain gathering or by mumbling pitifully through one's oral presentation, being bullied or rejected by a group of popular kids at school or by a group of ladies on the block, being harshly reprimanded by a principal—or by a mother-in-law. These traumatic events are only called traumatic events when they harm the brain, as evidenced by a trail of traumatic responses: an "allergy" to situations or people that are similar to those involved in the original trauma (resulting in a very strong desire to avoid all such situations or people), an inability to "get over it" even with the passage of decades, easily evoked upset upon recalling the original trauma, "exaggerated" or "unreasonable" responses (including panic) to having to reexperience situations or people associated with the original trauma, and associated changes in behavior or lifestyle in order to accommodate avoidance of such situations or people.

WHAT IS MOTHER-IN-LAW TRAUMA?

Mother-in-law trauma is one type of "small *t* trauma." The triggering event usually occurs early in a woman's marriage—often sometime within the first year. A young bride enters her husband's home hoping to be received with loving, open arms. She hopes that her new in-laws will approve of her and be pleased with her. However, due to her youth and inexperience, she doesn't always know how to increase the likelihood that this will be the case. Unlike her mother-in-law, she is not yet a mother. Nor is she forty-five or fifty-five years old. She is simply a young girl with a young girl's mind. She may not be able to relate well to her husband's mother; apart from the young man, the two may share nothing in common. She may not know how to bridge that gap and she may not know that she needs to find a way. When she and her new husband are invited to her in-laws for a Shabbos meal, she may forget to compliment the cook. She may not realize that she could offer to bring a contribution to the meal. She may not yet be in the habit of rushing to her mother-in-law's side with offers of help to prepare, serve, or clear. In fact, she may sit shyly by her new husband, too intimidated to leave his presence. Since she meant no harm, it may come as a shock to her that her mother-in-law feels irritated or resentful because of her lack of communication or lack of helpfulness. A bigger shock will come if her mother-in-law is not mature enough to handle those feelings of frustration in a sensitive, caring manner. If her mother-in-law sits her down to vent her feelings toward her, the young woman may suffer psychic damage that lingers throughout her marriage. Particularly if her new husband doesn't defend her (which he, in his youth and inexperience—still clinging to his premarital version of *kibbud av va'em*—may not), she may never fully recover from the shame, pain, and humiliation suffered at the hands of her mother-in-law.

Mother-in-law trauma is often caused by criticism, complaints, and perceived rejection. However, there are other causes as well. For instance, the trauma may occur through omission; a mother-in-law may simply favor her daughters or other daughters-in-law more than the newcomer. Relegated to the "odd man out" position, the daughter-in-law nurses her wounds privately and forever. It causes incredible pain to be cast aside or rendered insignificant.

Mother-in-law trauma may also be caused by intrusion. Husbands who are very close to their mothers may neglect to make their new wives feel secure. Their mothers may inadvertently or purposely exploit this maternal bond to make excessive demands on the son's time and energy. This can cause new wives to feel threatened and eventually to resent the source of that threat. Unending jealousy, hurt, and anger may plague the young woman all the years of her marriage.

PREVENTING MOTHER-IN-LAW TRAUMA

Preventing mother-in-law trauma is the job of every mother-in-law. It is easily accomplished. Simply apply the principles of good parenting—show plenty of warmth and avoid negativity. Ask for what you want or need in a gentle, respectful, and kind way. Mothers-in-law—being mature, experienced mothers—must take the lead in building and nurturing a healthy, loving relationship with their new daughters. Doing so will magnify family love—between the son and his wife, between the couple and their parents, between the grandparents and the grandchildren. *The wisdom of a woman builds her home.*

PARENTING IN THE THIRD DECADE

A little girl becomes a teenager and then a young woman. There are changes that mothers must make throughout all the stages of development. Mom may be able to tell her eight-year-old when to go to bed, but won't get far with her eighteen-year-old on the same issue. If the adolescent needs guidance, Mom might have to learn to stand back and let natural consequences take their course. It's hard for mothers to take those steps backward after decades of standing close. Just because their daughters are taller doesn't mean that mothers can stop caring, worrying, or wanting to help. Moms are still twenty or thirty or forty or so years older than their youngsters and really do have so much to offer in terms of knowledge, information, and life experience. They want to be involved. Why should they have to stand on the sidelines when they can so easily step in and continue to mother their child?

THE RIGHT TO FAIL

Everyone has the right to fail. It's all part of the learning process. If you aren't allowed to make mistakes, you can't learn to type or knit or write or read or, well, anything. Failure experiences provide feedback that allows us to succeed. Although someone can save us trouble by just telling us everything we need to know, the learning process itself has value. Toddlers know this instinctively. They'll grab the shoe out of Mommy's hand, screaming "*Me* do it!" meaning that they want to find their *own* way to put it on and build their own neural pathways. They seem to know that personal experience is necessary in order to wire their little brains.

Grown-up children (young adults) fail all the time. They spend too much money and find they don't have enough left for the things they want and need. They prepare for a trip too late and don't have time to arrange for necessary documents. They make too much food for too few guests, wasting time, effort, and money. They take a job for which they are poorly suited by temperament or ability. All of these "failure" experiences provide important information, helping the young person do better in the future, make important adjustments, and move forward. Hashem, who runs the world, could easily save all of us from failure experiences by ensuring that everything turns out right the first time around. However, Hashem Himself stands back to let us fail. Out of love for us, He does what is hard for all parents—He lets us live our own lives and face our own challenges.

WHEN DAUGHTERS MARRY

When a daughter gets married, she faces many new challenges. Her first task is to leave home to bond with her new husband and form a new home of her own. However, she can't *leave* if Mommy comes with her. She can't begin to create her own life without the necessary space to do so. This space includes time, privacy, physical distance, and other boundaries. In her own space, the married daughter can learn how to interact with her spouse, manage her time, run her house, and live her new married life. In her own space, she can experiment, fail, adjust, and move forward. When she becomes a mother, this process will continue as she enjoys the space to grow and develop as a parent. Although she can certainly reach out for advice and support, she no longer needs to be told what to do. She needs to find her own way.

While it is easy to understand how a married daughter may need her space, it is also easy to understand how hard it can be for mothers to give it. Mothers not only want to help, as explained earlier, but they are also attached to their daughters at a very primal level. While a daughter may be thrilled to move forward, a mother may be devastated to be abandoned. And yet, mothers *have to* step aside, eagerly or not. Failure to do so will hurt their daughters' development and quite possibly their marriages. What can help mothers give the necessary space with the minimal amount of personal suffering?

MOTHERS AFTER MARRIAGE

As their daughters start on a new journey, mothers can do the same. Developing new hobbies, interests, careers, or activities not only fills time but also fills the mind and soul. If a mother is busy learning—trying, failing, adjusting—she'll be much more content to let her daughter do the same. Moreover, a mother who looks forward to her own day has lots to share with her married daughter; her interest in her own life frees her daughter to pursue hers. Mom may be too busy to *parent* a grown-up child, but she'll have just the right amount of time to enjoy her.

Part Five

WORKING WITH EMOTIONS

STEP INSIDE

We don't actually live in our homes; we live inside *ourselves*. Oh, sure—our bodies stand in our kitchens and prepare buckets of food, just as surely as they run through every other room straightening and tidying and organizing all of our material possessions. But whatever happens inside those walls, whatever conversations take place, whatever dramas unfold, whatever pictures decorate the fridge—it is all experienced *inside* of us. It comforts us or frightens us, maddens us or gladdens us. It is our reaction to it all that constitutes our lives.

FAMILY LIFE TRIGGERS US

In fact, family life is meant to trigger the full array of human emotions. Hashem gave us emotions to light the way for our growth. Each emotion provides a signal, an alert that the next step is needed.

Sadness, for instance, signals loss, telling us that we need to get to work to fill the void or find a replacement. Fear signals danger, warning us to be cautious and more vigilant. We appreciate its assistance when walking down a dark, deserted alleyway. Anger alerts us to a boundary violation. We need to make a correction, to establish our place. It happens all the time in parenting. Feelings of confusion push us to gain clarity. We need more information, direction, or support.

And sometimes these negative emotions signal the need for more spiritual work. Unfounded sadness, fear, anger, and confusion can be so uncomfortable that we relentlessly seek relief. So often we discover it beneath the wings of Hashem.

NEGOTIATING EMOTIONS

Sometimes our emotions, or the emotions of our family members, frighten us. We want to be, and we want others to be, calm, pleasant, and rational. Too much of any emotion—even happiness—disturbs us. It seems (and probably is) out of balance. Often, we don't know how to help ourselves or our family members. Is this emotion normal, or is it a sign of illness? How do we find out? Is there a pill to take? Or perhaps a special therapy? What can we do to calm our child's terror—or our own? How can we get a spouse to stop raging? How can we motivate a child to *want* to study? How can we lift ourselves out of despair?

Of course we daven. We do this, too, when we or someone we care about is sick. But we also take action, find doctors, take medicine and treatments. Emotional imbalances are imbalances of the soul. When we're off-balance, we need strategies that can help us regain equilibrium. Do we know any? Are we teaching them to our children?

A SIMPLE MAP

Oddly enough, few people even know how their inner world is constructed. It's difficult to stop the pain in the center of your body if you don't know that you have a stomach. Once you know that you have a stomach and that it digests the food you eat, you can begin to experiment with changes in your diet. Now, you might discover by omitting this food and that one, what makes the center of your body hurt more or less. Similarly, when you learn that your psyche—the seat of your emotions—is made up of many different parts, you can begin to use strong, healthy parts to help heal vulnerable, wounded parts. You can learn how to hold, comfort, and ultimately transform your own emotional pain. Your inner therapist can help you to negotiate the turmoil wrought by your experiences in your family life. You grow through them, becoming stronger and wiser than you were before. And as you learn how to meet and greet yourself, you are increasingly able to help your family members as well. You are the voice of emotional guidance that your children will hear in their own heads, decades after they have left your home. "It's okay; we all make mistakes," "Please don't be perfect—it's not the human way," "Your own taste in clothing is what matters—not anyone else's," "Of course you're upset—anyone would be in this situation," "It's okay to be sad; it really hurts," "Feel the fear and do it anyway!" As you learn more about yourself and the workings of your own inner world, you have so much more to offer them.

EMOTIONAL EDUCATION

Emotional intelligence can be fostered in many ways. Listening to ourselves compassionately is an excellent starting point. Less judgment, more acceptance, helps negative emotions float away. We can talk to the part of ourselves who agrees to listen to and acknowledge what we're saying. It's an odd little dialogue with powerful results. Try it in two chairs, one for the part that wants to talk about its problems and the other chair for the part that is willing to say them back and validate them. "I'm sick and tired of all this housework!" you say to the empty chair. Then you hop into the empty chair and say back to the first chair, "Of course you are. You're just so sick and tired of doing this day in and day out. I understand." Keep hopping back and forth, expressing the angst, acknowledging and accepting it, expressing some more and accepting that, too. Go ahead and ask yourself for some practical help—you'll be surprised to find how one part of you sitting in one chair is so full of clever ideas and good advice.

There are lots of books, as well as teachers and therapists, available today that can help guide us through the inner labyrinth. There is no reason to suffer alone for long periods of time. There are new, quick cures for emotional pain—gifts from Hashem. Avail yourself of them so that you can subdue the *yetzer hara*, the force of spiritual impurity that wants to drown you in your own negativity. Hashem has many helpers; help yourself out of an emotional quagmire only when you can, and when you can't, then reach out. Hashem answers on the day we call.

When you feel overwhelmed, discouraged, exhausted, or frightened; furious, depressed, traumatized, or terrified; bored, dissatisfied, resentful, or lost—or when you hear an inner cry of any kind—consider the following tips:

- **You are never alone.** Call out to Hashem along with David Hamelech—set your conscious mind and its objections aside, while you allow your aching soul to be bathed in the healing and cleansing waters of *Tehillim*.

- **As Shlomo Hamelech said, "There is nothing new under the sun."** You are not the first or last person to feel the way you do. Your feelings are normal.

- **Feelings are just feelings.** Watch them without acting on them. This allows them to clear safely out of your system.

- **No one to talk to about those issues lurking in the recesses of your heart? Try journaling.** Write your feelings down quickly—some like to use their nondominant hand to more easily access material below the level of consciousness. It doesn't matter if it's legible or not. Don't keep this material—tear it up afterwards, having in mind that you have released the pain from your soul and are discarding its remnants.

- **Don't want to bother writing it out? Try imagery.** Sit back with your eyes closed and feel whatever it is that you are feeling. Then you can try lots of things: imagine packing the feelings into a suitcase, dropping the suitcase into a hot air balloon and sending it to outer space. Or, imagine filling a clear glass bowl with all of those feelings and then add detergent and hot water and swish them around until they're all clean and refreshed. Or, while the feelings are still inside your chest and your belly, imagine that you are in a shower of silver light, the light penetrating your skin, your bones, and your soul to give a deep clean to all the negative energy inside. Or, ask your feelings what they need from you and then follow through to fulfill their request. Use your intuition and imagination to heal emotions, keeping in mind that these are the right tools for the job.

- **Accepting the feelings of your family members is as important as accepting your own feelings.** Don't rush to fix them. Just let them sit a bit. It's funny how this kind of patience is itself very healing.

- **All feelings—even anger and rage—need to be accepted**

before they can be healed. You can't just tell yourself, or anyone else, not to feel a certain way. However, once the feeling is acknowledged, the healing process immediately begins.

- **As long as emotions are not overwhelming, try self-help first.** When self-help isn't working as well as you'd like it to, try natural aids for emotional support. When this is not working either, seek professional assistance. Even a short course of therapy can make a big difference to the way one feels for the rest of one's life.

- **When feelings are intense and unremitting, and particularly when they are interfering with functioning at school, work, or home (whether they belong to you or to anyone else in your family), seek professional assessment and treatment.** This is the fastest and most effective way to achieve balance and emotional well-being.

Add your own tips for regaining and maintaining emotional balance while negotiating family life:

_____

_____

_____

_____

_____

_____

_____

_____

_____

_____

_____

_____

_____

_____

_____

_____

_____

_____

_____

GROWN-UP
CHILDREN

The human face is the only part of the body that reveals the inner self. If you look at someone's arm or neck, you can't tell anything about what that person is thinking or feeling. The same is true for every part of the body except the face. The face opens the door to the inner world. In Hebrew, the word for "face" reflects this reality: *panim* shares the root of the word *penim*—inner. Moreover, *panim* is a word that is plural, not singular. It reflects the plurality of faces we have—the many parts of our psyche.

This explains how it is that we have so many facets to our personality, how we can be so mature at times and immature at other times, so calm and then so anxious. Indeed, our personality consists of many different parts, representing many different states of mind and degrees of maturity. The little child in a grown person is always there, an important part of a complete "inner family." At ninety years of age, a woman has parts of her personality that are ninety; parts that are—believe it or not—older and wiser; and parts that are much younger, including helpless baby parts, rebellious teenage parts, and young woman parts. Different parts are triggered in different circumstances, so that the part we call "I" is simply the part that is in the driver's seat in a given situation.

TRIGGERED STATES

Our current adult self is usually in the driver's seat when we are performing a grown-up activity that is not particularly emotionally charged. At the supermarket, provided we have enough funds for the excursion, our current self may pick out good cuts of meat, fresh vegetables, and assorted other items. It can add two and two to get four. In the candy aisle, however, a child state may zip into the driver's seat, grabbing some unhealthy, overpriced, but delicious comfort food. This part can't add dollars or calories—it's too young!

At home at four thirty in the afternoon, an adult, nurturing part may serve cookies and milk to the kids. Later that night (around ten o'clock), a child part may stamp his or her foot and scream at the kids when the grown-up part was unsuccessful at getting them into bed. When visiting Mom and Dad, another child part may slip into the driver's seat, feeling all safe and secure again in the warm embrace of home. In other cases, being in the presence of parents triggers the desperate, lifelong search for approval ("Please love me") or the routine of a long-standing battle ("Could you stop criticizing me for once?"). Indeed, at thirty or forty-five years of age, a grown man or woman may still struggle daily with his or her mother, trying to get her to understand, validate, and celebrate. Although the grown person no longer needs these things from the older woman, the unhealed inner child remains young and vulnerable. This is the part that is still hurting and is still trying to get unmet needs fulfilled.

MOTHERS OF GROWN CHILDREN

Mothers of grown-ups also have many parts of their personality. Now in their fifties, sixties, or beyond, these women still have a mothering part—an inner young woman who is raising her babies. This part is triggered when she sees her adult children. "Mommy" slips into the driver's seat, ready to guide, advise, and even reprimand her young brood (who are now middle-aged). "Mommy" may not realize that her children are no longer children. She may fail to respect their adult boundaries and she may have difficulty releasing them into their own lives. It may be hard for her to step back, step aside, or step out of her grown children's lives. "Mommy" needs to step aside *inside* first, making room for a new "childless" adult to enjoy the privileges and opportunities of maturity.

While past-due mothering can be frustrating, other scenarios can also arise out of inner-family dynamics. For instance, a child part may be triggered in the mother of grown children when it sees that there are new "grown-ups" that might take care of her. In this case, an able-bodied older person seems not to be able to think for herself, make decisions, carry through on tasks, or otherwise act like the mature person she is (at least in years). Sounding and behaving very much like a small child, this child-parent now turns to her children to mother *her*. While role reversal happens naturally in the truly elderly and physically dependent, premature dependence creates unnecessary burdens for grown children.

Mother and child—and a multitude of inner family members—

engage in a lifelong process of adaptation and change. Drawing on the wisdom of one's oldest and wisest parts can make this process easier and more comfortable. The main thing is not to let the inner children fight.

SELF-ACCEPTANCE

I went to my neighbor's house for Shabbos and I was blown away: her table was beautifully set with an original centerpiece she designed herself. The napkins contrasted with the tablecloth in a way I wouldn't have dared to try, but it looked fantastic. Her salads contained foods I've never seen before! It was really amazing. But I'm never having her over to my house. My salad consists of lettuce, cucumbers, and tomatoes, and while my table is set with plates and cutlery, that's about all I can say for it. I can't compete with her."

"Whenever I have a challenge, I discuss it with my sister. She can come up with a creative solution within minutes. For some reason, she can turn the problem on its head, look at it from a new angle, and see a solution I never could have produced. I wish I had her skill. My mind is so black and white. I can't think outside the box at all."

GIFTED WITH CREATIVITY

We all admire creative people. They boggle our minds and delight our senses. We feel in awe and often wish that we had their talent. And since they often get such positive attention for their efforts, we may even feel a bit jealous, wishing that we ourselves could garner some of that recognition. Somehow our old-fashioned chocolate chip cookies just don't earn the accolades generated by our sister-inlaw's plum butter Linzer torte with its unique lattice topping. We fail to impress others, but worst of all, we fail to impress ourselves. We beat ourselves up for not being creative enough, as if creativity were somehow a mitzva or a measure of our personal worth.

In fact, creativity is a gift from Hashem, a trait that exists on a continuum in human beings. In this way it is not unlike the trait of intelligence. All people have intelligence, but they have different kinds and different amounts of each kind. For instance, someone may have "school" intelligence—the kind of smarts that earns top grades in academic settings. However, that same person may have a much smaller amount of "people" smarts, resulting in poor communication skills, lack of empathy, and other social deficits. People vary in their mechanical intelligence (how "smart" they are with their hands), their artistic intelligence, their musical intelligence, their technological intelligence, and so on. Humor is another trait that varies in individuals. Some people are naturally quick-witted, able to make rapid-fire comebacks and plays on words. Others may specialize in subtle, ironic humor. Others are good at getting jokes but not making them. And so on.

So it should come as no surprise that we all have different types and levels of creativity. If we need to be creative in our work, our relationships, or our kitchen in order to fulfill our life's mission, Hashem will see to it that we will be creative that way.

THE COMPETITION

Suppose that Hashem gifted your child with social intelligence but low creativity. Your child is sensitive to everyone's feelings, has great interpersonal skills, and is virtually a walking ray of sunshine. However, she can't fold a napkin in half nicely, let alone make fancy, fanning fabric designs wrapped in hand-painted, contrasting ribbon. Is she any less a person for her creative deficit? Obviously not. Someone else will bring joy to the world through innovative napkin designs, and she will bring joy in her own charming way.

What should you say to this youngster when she complains that she is so untalented compared to Shoshi, Shani, and Shaindy, the creative stars of her class? Should you sign her up for creativity lessons to help improve her skills? Should you apologize for not modeling more creativity in the home? Should you encourage her to try harder? No, no, and no. You should use emotional coaching—the technique of naming her feelings—and provide important information. For instance, "I know it's frustrating to see other people finding it so easy to be creative when you yourself can't do the same sorts of things. I know you sometimes wish you could be like them and get all the lovely attention they get for their efforts. I guess if Hashem would have wanted everyone to be the same, with the same talents and skills, He would have made us all that way. You know, if He only wanted roses in His garden, then He would have made only one kind of flower! But Hashem loves variety—all sorts of beautiful flowers—and so he gives *you* a beautiful big heart and He gives others the special gifts that they have."

And after you give this speech to your child, turn around and give it to *yourself.* Accept and use the gifts that Hashem gave you and *enjoy* the talents of those around you.

THE TURNAROUND

L ife being what it is, most people get discouraged at one time or another. Anything can be a trigger: dissatisfying work; marital conflict; disappointing, frustrating, or frightening behavior in a child. Whatever starts it going, the downhill slide soon takes on a life of its own. It's bad-mood time.

DARK GLASSES

In this constricted state, things start to look black and bleak. The doors and windows of the mind are shut; there is no way out. Nothing will ever get better. Nothing has worked. Nothing makes a difference. Nobody cares. Nobody can help. Even Hashem appears to have turned away. Exhaustion. Despair. Emptiness. Boredom. Why bother?

Sometimes the feelings whisper in the background while life seems to go on as normal. At other times, their deafening roar brings a halt to all constructive activity. Often, they linger somewhere in between, slowly and quietly draining the life force, the joie d'vivre. One feels like a helpless victim. There is nothing to be done but wait it out.

PRIVATE BATTLES, PUBLIC CONSEQUENCES

Perhaps one could justify the decision to wait until the dark cloud lifts if one lived all alone in an unresponsive universe. However, it's not like that. As the *Nefesh Hachaim* explains, a person's thoughts, words, and deeds impact on all the worlds. Our private joy brings blessing everywhere. Our private despair is equally potent. Our moods translate into spiritual consequences for good or for bad. We each have a social responsibility to lift ourselves out of the pit that we fell into.

On a more obvious level, one's less than joyful demeanor has immediate effects upon one's loved ones. Whether one's sadness is expressed behaviorally as withdrawal, or increased irritability, or observable unhappiness, one's family members are sure to be negatively affected. Not only is it unpleasant to spend time around moody or miserable people, but it is also unhealthy. Moods of all kinds are "catchy." We bring others along on whatever ride we're on. Moreover, loved ones are worried and stressed by the unhappy campers in their midst. All in all, it is clear that those who live in families have a responsibility to help themselves reach their best emotional states—if only for the sake of those they love.

THE SLIPPERY SLOPE

Even though a specific external event or internal thought or internal physiological process might trigger a drop in mood, it is the subsequent events that determine how far and how fast this drop will be. Let's say, for example, that a person received some disappointing news. Upon hearing or reading the news, the person starts thinking negatively ("Oh, no. This isn't good."). The negative thoughts release a cascade of negative emotions, which in turn release a cascade of stress chemistry into every cell of the body (see Dr. Candice Pert, *Molecules of Emotion*). The stress chemistry leads to more negative thinking, which leads to more negative emotions, which leads to more stress chemistry—all causing a deep and rapid descent of mood. It is up to each person to take specific action in order to prevent this natural decline from occurring.

TAKING ACTION

Action begins with identifying the thoughts, feelings, and actions that signal "bad mood about to take hold." These differ in each person. One person might notice that her mind is filled with negative thoughts. Another person might notice that she is feeling tense, mad, or sad. Another might notice that she doesn't want to talk to anyone. Another might find herself snapping at family members. It's a good idea to familiarize yourself with your own unique warning signals so that you can take *early* action.

Once you realize that your mood is dropping, you can take any or all of the following steps in order to reverse the chemistry of low moods:

- **Ask Hashem to help you get into a better mood and meditate on the reminder inscribed on the ring of Shlomo Hamelech—"This too shall pass"—or any other encouraging thoughts.**

- **Exercise (whether you are in the mood to do so or not).**

- **Do some activity that you normally enjoy when you're in a better mood, even though you aren't in the mood to do it now.**

- **Do something that makes you feel a sense of accomplishment (clean a drawer, pay some bills, take care of a task that's been waiting).**

- **Even though you're not in the mood to deal with people, have social contact of some kind with at least one person.**

- **Have some good food and some rest or sleep.**

- **If your mood has already slipped significantly or has been low for a while, then be sure to address your feelings directly using self-help strategies or the assistance of a professional.**

- **Employ stress-reduction strategies that you have already learned** (e.g., meditate, listen to music, take remedies, and so on).

Taking action to restore positive mood is something we can and should do for ourselves, our family members, and the world. Even if we find it hard or unpleasant—even if it doesn't work right away—we want to remember that our positive efforts have huge positive ramifications. May they hasten the day when none of us will ever suffer from low moods again.

EVERYTHING IS
NOT OKAY

CHILD (SHOUTING). You don't love me! You only love (fill in name of sister two years older).

MOTHER. That's not true—I love you very much.

CHILD (PRACTICALLY CRYING). Everyone says I'm fat!

MOTHER. You're not fat. You're just right for your height!

Nothing can be more natural than reassurance. Every parent wants to help his or her child's bad feelings go away. "Here, let me clear that up for you...you don't have to feel bad anymore, see?" Although reassuring parents are trying their best to be helpful, they are in fact being *unhelpful*—possibly even harmful.

"No matter how many times I reassure Devora that she is smart, she keeps saying she is stupid!" In fact, this parent is inadvertently reinforcing Devora's concept that she is stupid. When Devora is struggling with her homework she feels anxious, frustrated, and miserable. She expresses her agitation by complaining to her mother, "I'm so stupid!" Her mother makes her feel better with reassurance. The sequence in Devora's brain is now something like this: insult yourself, get rewarded with a *compliment* ("you're very smart"). It's as if every time Devora says, "I'm so stupid," her mom gives her a ten dollar bill! If the child is rewarded every time she insults herself, the tendency to negative self-assessment is strengthened. Moreover, Devora can develop an addiction to reassurance, since this is the "drug" that eases her emotional pain.

FINDING FEELINGS

Devora needs a way to make herself feel better. The uncomfortable feelings triggered by her homework experience—anxiety, frustration, and unhappiness—are inside her body and mind. She needs to learn how to "self-soothe"—that is, release her negative feelings from her body and mind and restore herself to a calmer, happier state. The more skilled a person is at doing this, the happier and healthier he or she will be throughout life.

Releasing negative emotions requires locating them. Do you want to throw out the garbage from your kitchen? Then you first have to go to the kitchen and *get* the garbage. Only then can you throw it out! Similarly, if you want to remove stressful emotions like sadness, worry, frustration, and irritation, you have to first go *get* them. This is accomplished by naming them ("I feel bad"). Afterwards, more accurate naming ("I feel worried, angry, and upset") dissolves the feelings, releasing them from body and mind. When Devora complains that she's stupid, she is failing to notice her feelings. She *says* she's stupid, but she *feels* anxious, frustrated, and miserable. Until she *recognizes* her own feelings, she can't begin the process of letting them go. She needs someone to help her learn to identify those feelings.

CONFRONTING ONE'S OWN FEELINGS

Instead of guiding Devora quickly *away* from her feelings with reassurance about her intelligence, Mother can actually lead the child directly *to* her bad feelings. She can do this by responding to Devora's "I'm so stupid" with "You sound upset." This is the first step of going to find feelings in order to release them. When Devora goes on to say that she can't do "the stupid homework," Mom can begin naming the feelings more accurately: "That sounds very frustrating" or "It's maddening when the homework is so hard" and so on. Mom's continued naming of Devora's bad feelings helps Devora to identify what she is experiencing *inside,* allowing the feelings to begin to dissolve.

Eventually, Devora will be able to internalize her mother's approach to stress, learning to name and release her own emotional pain. Instead of seeking constant reassurance, she'll recognize her troubled feelings, name them, and let them go. She'll bring herself back to balance.

THE COURAGE TO NAME FEELINGS

Naming difficult feelings teaches children that the world of feelings is safe to experience and explore. It removes the need for escapist solutions to emotional pain—like addictions, self-harm, and other avoidance strategies. Instead, it introduces a "meet and greet" philosophy to the inner world. It's challenging, but possible for parents to do the following:

CHILD (SHOUTING). You don't love me! You only love (name sister two years older).

PARENT. You're feeling really sad and mad.

The child will get sadder as this conversation unfolds, but it's okay. She is hurting inside and she is finding her pain. By naming it, she will be able to cry it out of her system. When she's done, she's likely to turn to Mom and say, "I didn't mean that. I know you love me, too." *The way out of feelings is through them.* Help your child learn to let go of painful feelings by teaching him or her how to find those feelings in the first place.

Now see if *you* can fill in the parent's response to this child's statement (remember to name the child's feelings):

CHILD (PRACTICALLY CRYING). Everyone says I'm fat!

YOU. _____

_____

SENSITIVITY
TRAINING

We measure our lives in feelings. "How was Shabbos?" That depends on how it felt. "Did you have a good vacation?" Let me check my feelings and I'll let you know. "Should I invite the Golds over for lunch?" No, I'm not in the mood for them this week.

Every moment of every day is experienced through our feelings. Perhaps that's why the Torah emphasizes sensitivity to the feelings of others. "That which is hateful to you, do not do to your fellow. That is the whole Torah; the rest is the explanation," as Hillel the Sage so succinctly put it.

What can parents do to help their children develop sensitivity?

THE WISDOM OF TORAH

Hashem gives us a sensitivity-training tool in the form of the halachos pertaining to the mitzvah of *kibbud av va'em*. A child's obligations to his parents train him, day after day, every day, for the first twenty years of life, in the art and skill of sensitive behavior. For instance, there is an obligation for a child to refrain from eating his meal until his parents have started to eat theirs. The child must put aside his own ravenous appetite to wait until the parents lift their forks. Often, the father will wait for the mother to finish serving and begin to eat before he starts to eat. After all, is it nice to start eating when the host and hostess have not yet begun? (Indeed, other Torah laws require a guest to wait for their hosts to eat before they start their own meal.) Have you ever shopped for a meal, cooked the meal, and served the meal only to discover by the time you sat down that everyone at the table had already finished eating? Although some women are "used" to this, others will feel taken for granted, unappreciated, as if they are nothing more than servants. The Torah requires that parents be treated like king and queen. The child must wait in order to show respect, honor, and sensitivity to these most important people who have taken the time and trouble to put food before him.

When a child comes to the table for twenty years, each time waiting for her parent to begin to eat, what does this do to the child's character? It helps her to realize that she is not the center of the universe. There are other people and these other people have *feelings*. By waiting for Mother to start to eat, the youngster shows appreciation for her efforts. Thus, the halacha instills patience, sensitivity, appreciation, self-control, and humility. What a treasure trove of traits for one small and simple behavior!

But there are other halachos as well. For instance, a child is not allowed to interrupt her parents. Why not? Because the child is not the only one who matters or whose needs are important at any given moment. Her parents are having a conversation and would not like to be interrupted. Her parents' feelings are as urgent and as important as her own. A child is not allowed to wake up a parent who wants to sleep. Why not? Because this would cause upset to the parent. The child must learn to consider the parents' feelings. A child is not allowed to agree with one parent when the two parents are in disagreement. Why not? Because the other parent would feel hurt.

PARENTAL GUIDANCE

Another way that parents can increase their children's sensitivity to feelings is by using the skill of emotional coaching—naming their children's feelings. For instance, if a child wants a gift because a sibling received a birthday present, a parent can name the youngster's feelings: "Gifts are fun to get. Shalom got one and you want one, too. You're disappointed that no one got you a gift today." Naming feelings has been shown in numerous research studies to increase a child's sensitivity to *other people's* feelings.

Moreover, when a child causes pain to a sibling, a parent can help the child tune into the feelings of the wounded victim: "Look at his face? Do you see him crying now? He is very sad because you grabbed his toy."

By paying attention to feelings, parents can help to raise children who will have less "feeling accidents" as adults. Accidental insensitivity occurs all the time. Walking very quickly past an elderly person who is toddling along can be insensitive. On the other hand, walking slowly with the older person, exclaiming about how lovely it is to take a leisurely stroll, can be the height of sensitivity.

Sensitivity involves thinking about how others will feel and taking care to protect those feelings. Will the mistress of the house feel better or worse if you compliment her hired help on the wonderful meal that was prepared? Could it make someone uncomfortable to ask about the activities of their relatives or children? Maybe just comment on the weather instead. Teaching kids to think about the impact of their words and actions on the feelings of others gives them the opportunity to perform innumerable acts of kindness throughout their lifetimes.

DON'T BE SHY

I stand by the fence and peek into the schoolyard. My heart breaks to see Yossi standing by himself. He doesn't know how to make friends."

"My daughter Estie is seriously shy. I keep trying to encourage her to pick up the phone, invite friends over, or at least accept the invitations she gets. But she refuses to even try. She has her one good friend and she sticks to her like glue. I'm really worried about her."

"My husband is very good one-on-one. But he is really bad in groups of people – even at our own Shabbos table. He'll give a short *devar Torah* and then say virtually nothing for the remainder of the meal. *I'm* the one who has to keep the conversation going. It's very uncomfortable."

SOCIALLY CHALLENGED

Some of us are socially challenged. That's just the way it is. Socially challenged people don't *choose* to be this way; it's much more fun to be socially comfortable. They are, for the most part, born into this condition. Shyness, awkwardness, self-consciousness—they're all manifestations of a certain type of anxiety. Socially anxious people may feel inhibited, judged, inadequate, or uncomfortable around people they don't know. In some cases, they may even feel this way around people they've known for a long time. Certain treatments and therapies can sometimes help increase social competence and social ease. However, many socially challenged people will retain at least some of their discomfort throughout their lives. Still, most people will eventually find ways to cope and work around their social issues, if not completely cure them. The challenge is for family members of socially anxious people to find a way to do the same.

DEALING WITH SOCIALLY CHALLENGED FAMILY MEMBERS

A common error is to reprimand a socially anxious family member. "Just smile, for goodness' sake! Make people feel comfortable!" "Helpful suggestions" do not really help socially uncomfortable people, and they may even do damage to the truly socially anxious group. Instructions are often experienced as criticisms, further eroding confidence. Those whose discomfort is minimal can benefit from learning and practicing a social-skill set but, depending on age and ability, this set may be best learned from books, social skills classes, or behavioral therapists. Those whose discomfort is intense will benefit much more from psychological and perhaps pharmaceutical treatment than from "helpful tips."

Social discomfort ranges on a scale from "personality style" (a way of being that doesn't significantly interfere with functioning in the world) to "social phobia and/or anxiety" (disorders that cause significant distress and do interfere with ability to function). When a person is socially uncomfortable rather than truly anxious, the best treatment may be no formal treatment at all. Instead, a person can learn specific techniques and strategies to reduce social discomfort, to be used on a per need basis. For instance, using EFT (Emotional Freedom Technique) before a *simcha* or a performance can increase confidence and relaxation. The technique can be employed hours, days, weeks, or even longer before an event to help eradicate nervousness. Used consistently over time, this tool can eliminate many types of social nervousness. For instance, many people have overcome their fear of public speaking or making Kiddush and other public *berachos* by using EFT. Bach flower remedies can also be helpful for those who feel stressed in social scenes – especially Mimulus, Cerato, or Rescue Remedy. A person can also consult a Bach flower practitioner for a specially made mixture of remedies.

INTRODUCTED, SHY, OR SOCIAL PHOBIC

Introverts—those who prefer their own company and the company of a small group of trusted friends—should be allowed to be themselves. It is not that introverts are incapable of socializing; rather, introverts are drained by social interactions while extroverts are energized by them. Often introverts become deeply involved in their own projects and activities, devoting "social time" to these personal and/or professional pursuits. As a result, introverts often make great contributions to humanity.

Shy kids and adults—those who wish they could be more outgoing but simply can't—can be offered help to reduce their discomfort (see above), but should also be accepted as they are. Shy people can lead full, normal, healthy lives spending time with a smaller group of people.

True social phobics are suffering. These people experience panic and painful anxiety in social situations. Parents and spouses cannot cure their family member's social phobia. This condition requires professional help.

People who live with socially anxious children or spouses want to help them be happy. The best help that they can give is to be accepting and supportive and to refrain from criticism. Pointing toward appropriate tools or professionals can also be helpful, but after that, it is important to step back. Socially anxious people will find their own way.

DOWNTIME

The pressure is on. Both adults and children face full, packed schedules every day. Even Shabbos is highly structured and typically offers true respite only in the form of a brief nap. When one is awake, one is davening, learning, entertaining, looking after children, serving, cleaning up—some people actually find Shabbos one of the busiest days of all.

DIFFERENT WAYS OF BEING

Some people (children, teens, and adults) thrive on tight schedules. Their motors are running from dawn till midnight on full blast. They love the constant stimulation and are nourished by it. Every moment is productively occupied with mitzvos of various kinds; they are always on-task. They are, of course, in the minority.

Most people push themselves hard—they try to do what they're supposed to do as much as possible. However, they feel the strain. They experience physical, mental, and/or emotional fatigue off and on throughout the day. Some of these children and adults will get minor illnesses that force them to rest; some will carry on indefinitely but with irritability, anxiety, or low mood.

Then there are the people who feel truly squeezed. The demanding, sometimes relentless, schedule of the *frum* lifestyle is hard on them. Children with school days that never end, adults with financial burdens that boggle the mind, parents with children peeping out of every crack and crevice—many people find it hard to manage, not so much because of personal weakness as the simple fact that it *is* hard to manage. Unlike those who can force themselves to plod on despite the pressure, this group may be more sensitive to the effects of sustained stress. Perhaps their own natures and nervous systems crave more space, rest, or variety. Perhaps they naturally move more slowly, need more time. Or perhaps they get more intensely overwhelmed when the to-do list is running off the page. Whatever it is that makes it especially hard for them, the struggle to keep up eventually knocks them down. In one way or another, they just stop trying.

TAKE TIME OUT

We don't live in a one-size-fits-all world. While some people need very little or no downtime at all, others need regular breaks in order to refresh and reenergize. If this latter group cannot get off the roller coaster they find themselves on, they will eventually suffer in the form of unexplained chronic illness, disorders of anxiety and depression, interpersonal conflict, challenges with religious observance, inability to serve Hashem *b'simcha* and other, sometimes devastating, reactions to intense stress.

Yet many people feel that the need for downtime suggests a major personal failing. They might consider it a "waste of time," not realizing that a few minutes of relaxation, distraction, or variety might fuel them for many more hours of serious work. Refusing to indulge in this "waste of time" may, in some cases, lead to a much larger loss of productive activity in the end.

Teens particularly need to be directed to appropriate activities for downtime. Leaving them without any acceptable form of refreshment can result in the development of unhealthy stress-reduction habits like smoking during the weekdays, enjoying too much Kiddush on Shabbos, or searching out inappropriate pastimes. The question all parents must be able to answer is "What *can* a child or teen do for a healthy break?" What can anyone do who feels the need for brief diversions?

ALL FOR THE GOOD

Hashem implants talents, interests, and abilities in everyone. A young man who loves to learn all of his waking hours has a special gift that he will no doubt utilize. However, another young man may find that he needs to take learning breaks in order to maintain long hours of concentration. What should he do in that time? Leaving him to smoke or sleep is irresponsible. He needs to be shown how to find kosher activities that are appropriate, enjoyable, and energizing, activities that he can use throughout his life. His parents and his *rav* need to help him in this regard. Similarly, adults need to direct their downtime in positive ways—ways that enhance and strengthen their *Yiddishkeit*, while contributing to increased energy and joy in living.

For some, a few daily minutes of physical activity (exercise, dancing, juggling) may be all that's needed. For others, a few minutes of mental stimulation (reading, Sudoku) will do the trick. But while personal interests and hobbies may provide the basis for personal stress relief, they can also become venues for contributing to the community. An avid reader might become a popular writer. A talented baker might take her products into the community. A gifted musician may become a valuable contributor to local *simchas* and events. Those who do crafts may donate their wares to *gemachim* and charities.

Being proactive in establishing healthy downtime activities can help people of every age prevent the destructive effects of poorly managed stress.

REJECTED

All people get rejected. A newborn can be rejected by her siblings or, in some cases, even by a parent. A toddler can be rejected by older children who don't want to play with him or by the kids at playgroup. Children and teenagers face rejection by peers, cousins, teachers, and temporarily angry parents. Adults routinely experience rejection, including the experience of job rejection, social rejection (unfriendly faces on the street, at shul, at a *simcha*, or at a "tea") and personal rejection (as when one or one's child is not considered for a particular *shidduch* or when one is not invited to a gathering or one's help is not wanted on a particular committee).

Although rejection is a normal, common experience, it still hurts. Getting a paper cut is also a normal, common experience, but this does nothing to soften the individual sting. The hurt of rejection is far from imaginary. The brain actually responds to rejection in the exact same way it responds to pain from physical injury or assault:

social rejection causes increased activity in the anterior cingulate cortex, which is linked to the pain response. Brain researchers conclude that the brain considers social rejection to be an injury. Human experience verifies that rejection does indeed *hurt*.

THE COSTS OF REJECTION

Rejection is so painful, in fact, that it can dramatically affect life decisions and choices. When children experience constant rejection at school from teachers or peers, they make decisions that will help them prevent that kind of pain in the future. For example, they may permanently avoid the type of people who once rejected them. In Jewish schools, this sometimes means that students who feel rejected by their rebbe'im will try as soon as they can to avoid anyone who looks like a rebbe. This means that when these children leave school, they may also leave the community. Rebbe'im may have good intentions in offering harsh reprimands to offending students, but they also run the serious risk of making the youngster feel so rejected that the child will work hard to avoid future contact with anything that reminds him of the pain of that rejection. Similarly, a rejecting peer group acts naively and innocently in selecting out like-minded companions for pleasant socializing; students generally have no idea that they can negatively affect their peers for a lifetime just because they were—in their immature youth—socially unkind. Sometimes children and teens select "bad" friends because these are the only people who show them warmth and acceptance. When "good" kids reject others, they can inadvertently be the stimulus for a child's emotional and spiritual decline.

Adults, too, experience the cost of rejection. They, too, will adjust their life courses according to the level of social acceptance or rejection they experience. People will move out of shuls and neighborhoods where they feel they have been snubbed, ignored, or otherwise rejected. When the rejecters are clearly "religious" people, they may turn off or turn away other Jews in this fashion. Whether or not religion is involved, rejection can aggravate other preexisting vulnerabilities. For example, people may become depressed, anxious, or physically ill as a result of the rejection they feel.

LIVING WITH REJECTION

The destructive consequences of rejection should not be minimized. Rather, they should be acknowledged and addressed at home and at school. Parents and teachers are the ones to instruct youngsters on correct social behavior and to discipline rejecting behaviors in the same way they would discipline a child who physically attacks another. After all, the consequences of a "social attack" are just as serious, and sometimes more serious, than those of a physical assault.

At the same time, we must all remind ourselves that we impact on everyone we deal with. This is hard because we are all wrapped up in our own lives, our own circle of friends, and our own worries. However, heightening our awareness that we are strongly connected to the life journey of others may help us to work on developing and maintaining warm social skills (e.g., a welcoming smile, a pleasant greeting to strangers, and so on).

When we experience rejection ourselves, we can help clear the feeling most rapidly by accepting it without judgment. This is something we can do to help our children with feelings of rejection as well. Instead of trying to talk ourselves or them out of feelings, we acknowledge to ourselves (or to our children) that indeed, rejection hurts. Just as we need to rest a sore ankle after we have twisted it, we need to rest an aching heart before we go on with our day. Treating *ourselves* with kindness, warmth, and loving care (and showing our children how to do the same) helps to rapidly heal the wounds of rejection.

OVER AND OVER
AGAIN

Why do people do things over and over again that just don't work? Take Zvi Cohen for example. He is astonished by his wife's way of keeping a schedule. Batya Cohen uses an enormous wall calendar to keep track of all of her appointments. The calendar hangs on the kitchen wall where she can see it. Zvi finds the system ridiculous: "What if you're in the car and you need to check the address or telephone number for the appointment? All the information is on the wall in the kitchen! How is that going to help you?" Batya finds that this is never an issue for her. Once she has written the information on the calendar, she is good to go.

The scheduling process is not a problem. What *is* a problem is the conversation that Mr. and Mrs. Cohen have with each other several times a week, every week of the year for decades on end whenever Mrs. Cohen is marking an entry on the calendar. It goes like this:

ZVI. I can't believe you're doing that again! Why don't you use a device or at least a notebook?

BATYA. Don't tell me how to run my life—I'm a grown woman!

And a few days later,

ZVI. I can't believe what you're doing!

BATYA. I can do what I want—leave me alone.

And the next week,

ZVI. I don't understand how this can work for you!

BATYA. I'm not telling you what to do; don't tell me what to do!

And on and on and on. If you found this annoying to read, just imagine what it feels like to *do* over and over again for twenty years straight!

REPETITION COMPULSION

In psychology there is a concept called the repetition compulsion. It refers to a human tendency to keep doing the same thing over and over again in order to make it end better than it did before. Trying to fix something by repeating it might seem odd, but really it's very much the way we normally learn. For instance, if we're learning how to write the alphabet, we keep writing the letters over and over again until we perfect them. Our natural learning process tells us "practice makes perfect." If so, why not continue to try to be heard and acknowledged by our spouse or child? Perhaps, if we keep saying the same thing repeatedly, they'll finally get it and the communication will end "correctly."

The problem here is that the "practice makes perfect" experience refers only to our own, individual behavior. Once we involve another person, an entirely new process is required. This is because our repeated behavior does *not* trigger a new response in our spouse or child. In fact, it triggers the *exact same response* that it triggered on previous occasions. When you want another person to change his or her response to you, *you must change your own communication or behavior.*

GETTING OUT OF THE LOOP

Let's say that Mrs. Cohen is finally getting tired of the calendar ritual (after twenty-two years or so). She can be the one to break the cycle by changing *her* response to her husband. Instead of giving him her usual retort, she can say nothing at all when he complains about her method. Although this isn't a fast way to extinguish someone's behavior, it is a fairly successful way. It isn't going to be nearly as rewarding for Zvi to comment on his wife's habit if she offers absolutely no response. And, after twenty-two years or so, what more is there to say really?

The only problem with this solution is that it can be very difficult to do. Whenever Mr. Cohen comments on the calendar issue, Mrs. Cohen's brain is triggered into its automatic retort. To break the very real, very physical brain circuit that connects his comment to her response, Batya Cohen can enlist the help of a simple acupressure maneuver: She can firmly touch the area between her two eyebrows (at the bridge of her nose) with three fingers, while replaying her husband's annoying remarks in her imagination. She should notice how agitated the replay makes her feel and rate its intensity between one and ten. She should then keep imagining the scene over and over again, continuing to notice how strong her agitation feels—until she rates it at zero intensity. The whole process usually takes just a few minutes and can be repeated as often as necessary to completely stop a triggered response. Once there is no emotional charge, it will be very easy not to respond in real time to a real provocation. After repeated experiences of no retort, Zvi's behavior will eventually diminish (it's no fun fighting with oneself) and the dysfunctional interaction can be put to rest once and for all.

MY RIGHT
TO RANT

Joshua K. doesn't buy it. His wife piles the parenting books high on his desk, beseeching him to read just one. "You've already told me what's in them," Josh complains, "and I just don't agree. I know how *I* was raised and I know what the Torah has to say about it and I don't need your books." "But you scare the kids with your yelling," his wife presses on, "and you shout at me as well! Clearly, something is wrong here!" "Who says I can't yell?" Josh replies, "People get mad and they express themselves. It's healthy and completely normal. And I don't want my kids living in some glass bubble where they can't deal with the real world. Their teachers are going to yell and their spouses are going to yell—they need to get used to it!"

BEING REAL

Joshua is not alone in his sentiments. Many people feel that it is not only permissible to openly express anger, but that it is actually the *right* course of action. Let's look at their line of reasoning more closely. Here are some of their common beliefs along with considered responses:

"I should be able to express my feelings."

Yes, this is true. A person needs to be able to express his or her feelings. However, the Torah asks us not to hurt people with our words (*Vayikra* 17:20). Since angry words are inevitably hurtful—they tend to be too loud, often contain insults, and may convey unpleasant or frightening threats of various kinds—they are prohibited.

"I should be able to be my authentic self."

Every personality has its authentic "shadow" side and its authentic animalistic side. The Torah restrains our exposure of these parts of our personality. Every expression of our true selves is not appropriate for public exposure. We have doors on our washrooms. We need to censor ourselves so that it is our "best" selves rather than our authentic selves who interact with our spouses and children. Authenticity is not an excuse for hurting our loved ones.

"I should be able to be passionate rather than a robot without emotions."

Sure—but be passionate in positive ways. Have a passion for life and for love. Throw yourself into worthy projects and activities. Dream at night about great things you want to accomplish. Talk to your spouse about your current interests and your future ambitions. Be passionate—but not in anger. The Rambam cautions us to take the middle path in our character traits, with the exception of the trait of anger. This one cannot be balanced. It must be totally eradicated.

"I need to be able to convey how serious the matter is. No one listens unless I scream."

Hysteria reduces the impact of your message as the listener concentrates only on your emotion and its impact on him or her. You will be heard better when you learn effective tools of communication that will help you get your message across calmly but firmly. Professional guidance may be helpful.

"I can't control myself—I just lose it."

Yes some people cannot control themselves. Fortunately, there are effective solutions that can help, including psychotropic medication, alternative medicine, anger management classes, and intensive psychotherapy.

"It's normal and natural to express anger. It's not normal to have to be so careful about every word and how it's said."

Our Jewish goal is to go beyond "normal." It's normal for people to have marital conflict, but that is not a norm that we want to be part of. Rather, we'd like to be in the group of people who manage to enjoy a peaceful and loving relationship—no matter how small or "abnormal" that group may be.

"There was lots of screaming in my childhood home, but we all know how much we love each other and we're all very well adjusted."

It's great that it turned out well for you. However, with large groups of people we find that the more anger is expressed in the home, the more mental health problems, relationship problems, and health problems will be found there. The more anger is expressed in a marriage, the less happy and stable that marriage will be. The more anger is expressed in parenting, the more problems the kids will tend to have lifelong and the more problems the parent-child relationship will tend to suffer as well. However, it is true that some people will emerge unscathed from a home in which anger was expressed liberally (as long as they have hardy genes and as long as love was also expressed liberally). Nonetheless, I don't know how many people would want to expose their children to generous amounts of anger in order to test which group they will end up in: the damaged group or the very well adjusted group.

Remember: Anger is an *emotion*. It is not a marriage or parenting tool.

WORRYING

Parents tend to worry. Before the baby is born, parents worry about its birth, its health, its future and their own. After it's born and from then on, parents worry about every aspect of the child's well-being: his or her physical health, emotional state, spiritual state, academic and social functioning, marriage prospects, marriage, work, community life, and whatever else can be worried about. For parents of one child, worrying can be a full-time job. For parents of many children, it's the same; there are, after all, only so many hours in a day (and night).

WHY WORRY?

Worrying helps give parents the illusion of control. By ruminating, people can delude themselves that they are preventing something bad from happening—for them, worrying is better and somehow more powerful than just sitting around helplessly doing "nothing" about the possible pitfalls and dangers that lie ahead. Of course, worrying is not exactly the same as planning or problem solving. Indeed, focusing on an area of concern can be helpful at times, especially when it involves problem solving. For example, when a parent sees that her child does not like to study, she can think about this for a bit and try to come up with some helpful strategies. The worrier, on the other hand, worries about the problem (thinks about it over and over and over again) with or without problem solving.

In a funny way, worrying soothes anxiety. Thinking about a problem is a sort of distraction from the emotional consequences of that problem. Instead of paying attention to underlying feelings of sadness, despair, hopelessness, helplessness, and pain, worriers get to stay on the surface of an issue, wringing hands, thinking and talking constantly, always "busy" with the problem rather than experiencing its emotional consequences. Oddly enough, feeling the pain is a fast way to end worrying and restore peace of mind.

WHO WORRIES?

Everyone worries sometimes. While waiting for a potentially serious doctor's report, for example, most people will worry. While waiting for exam results that have important implications, many people will worry. Before embarking on an intense, first-time experience (like giving birth for the first time), many people tend to worry.

However, there is also a group of "professional worriers" who will worry about issues that regular people do not fret about. Professional worriers go into full gear when a loved one is a little late in arriving home. Professional worriers get overwhelmed when a child comes home with a low grade as they anticipate dire consequences such as a ruined adulthood. These people worry excessively about suspicious bumps and rashes (while others take a wait-and-see attitude), about the details of their children's social affairs from kindergarten onward, and about what other people will think or say. They worry a lot.

CAUSES OF WORRYING

People become serious worriers in two ways: Some have grown up with worried parents, learning the worry pattern from them. Others become worriers via the genetic route (and both factors often coexist in the same family). Worrying can be a manifestation of an inborn anxiety disorder called generalized anxiety disorder, or GAD. In this case, a person is wired to worry. Her mind goes down the worry road without her consent. The diagnostic criteria for GAD include the following:

- **A lot of worry about a lot of things for at least six months.**

- **An inability to stop worrying.**

- **Three of the following symptoms (in children, only one of the following symptoms is required): feeling on edge or restless, being easily fatigued, having trouble concentrating, being irritable, having muscle tension, having sleep issues.**

- **The worrying causes significant distress.**

- **The worrying is not the result of another condition or substance.**

Intense worrying is not normal. It is usually upsetting for the worrier and for other family members who must live with the worrier.

HELP FOR WORRIERS

Some people will benefit from a cognitive-behavioral approach to worry. There are many self-help books that use this strategy. The work of Dr. Edmund Bourne (*Coping with Anxiety: 10 Simple Ways to Relieve Anxiety, Fear, and Worry*), for example, is very popular. In recent years, Dr. Bourne and many others have begun to recommend various forms of alternative therapy in addition to or even instead of cognitive-behavioral treatment. Bach flower therapy can safely and painlessly reduce the tendency to worry, for example. Energy psychology or EFT (Emotional Freedom Technique) is a do-it-yourself acupressure strategy than can help stop worrying in its tracks. Professional help can be extremely effective for intense worriers.

Because there is so much one *can* worry about in parenting, parents really need to know how to remain calm and positive. Worrying can be more than unpleasant; it can interfere with appropriate parenting. Reducing excessive worry can bring tremendous improvement in quality of life for the whole family. Self-help and professional help can be of great assistance.

MOODY, GRUMPY, AND IRRITABLE CHILDREN

There are some people who are chronically happy. Not too many, but some. These lucky folks have inherited "good mood genes" that enable them to maintain a sunny disposition, a flexible mind-set, an optimistic outlook, and a strong resilience to stress. They're always smiling and seeming to enjoy life.

Then there are the rest of us.

MOOD STARTS YOUNG

Even in the newborn nursery, mood is discernible. Some babies lie contentedly, while others are red in the face with rage. Once home from the hospital, temperament presents itself loud and clear: some babies startle easily, while others won't flinch at a power drill roaring near their crib; some are interested in everything and everyone and some just want to be left alone; some seem satisfied and at ease in their new world, while others cannot settle. In the early months and the years to follow, the child's mood profile and inborn character traits become even more evident. Now we see those who are shy and timid, those who are boisterous and outgoing, those who are easygoing and flexible, those who are rigid and strong-minded. Over time, parents come to know their child as "easy" or "hard." As the Torah states, they must find a way to educate each child according to his way—his inborn temperament and tendencies. Different strategies may be necessary for different types of children.

CONSTANTLY CRANKY

One group of children that often perplexes parents is the grumpy group. These kids always seem to be unhappy about something. They don't like their clothes, their food, their siblings, their activities, and whatever else that exists that can be rejected. Their glass always seems to be half full. They feel deprived, jealous, abandoned, and neglected. They can't seem to get what they want. Getting up on the wrong side of bed, they go through their day with one complaint or tantrum after another.

Children who are like this *sometimes* rather than *routinely* are "moody." This group is sometimes happy-go-lucky, but then under certain circumstance (like things not going their way or being tired or not well fed) they turn mighty sour mighty quickly. Or, they get this way for no apparent reason. The switch between moods happens often enough that the child will be described as moody, rather than even tempered.

Irritability and moodiness can occur in anyone once in a while. Poor physical health, stress, hormonal fluctuations, and trauma can result in an uncharacteristic bad mood of a sad or mad nature. Addressing the source of this negativity is generally sufficient to remedy it. However, irritability and moodiness that occurs as a regular part of a child's personality (with constant bad mood or with constantly alternating good and bad mood) may be caused by chronic health conditions (such as food intolerance) or inherited genetic traits. After food intolerance (and other medical conditions) have been ruled out by health care providers, a parent can assume that heredity is the culprit.

HELPING UNHAPPY CHILDREN

Chronic kvetchiness (of the constant or alternating varieties described above) in children may be a variety or precursor of adult depression. While depressed mood in adults generally involves a truly sad emotional state, depressed mood in children is commonly expressed as irritability and grumpiness. Although adults may sometimes treat chronic depressed mood with psychotropic medication, for childhood "bad mood," this is only recommended in extreme cases. In most instances, natural and naturopathic treatments are sufficient to help children experience greater calm and contentment. Consulting with a pediatric natural health practitioner (i.e., any practitioner experienced in treating children) can lead to a variety of interventions that involve nutrition, exercise, and natural supplements designed to improve mood.

Parents also need to be compassionate toward unhappy campers. It certainly does not help to tell children to "snap out of it" or "put a smile on your face" or "stop being so miserable." In fact, the opposite strategy of simply accepting and naming the child's feelings (emotional coaching) has a much better track record for helping children's mood improve in the long run. "You're not happy about this," or "You don't like this," or "You're upset" are simple statements that parents can make when their grumpy youngster is clearly displeased. There is no need for the parent to try to make the child happy by giving her whatever she asks for or trying to avoid displeasing her. Rather, the parent should behave normally, refusing to give in to an unhappy child's intense demands. Most importantly, the parent should understand that the child cannot help her bad mood and hates it as much or more than the parent does. Sympathy rather than disapproval is in order. When the parent takes the child to a practitioner to receive help with the bad mood, most children are intensely grateful and relieved. Instead of being seen as "bad," they are being recognized as victims of something they themselves cannot control. This in itself, is healing to some extent.

Parenting a moody child is challenging. However, with understanding and skill, parents can negotiate the task with greater confidence and success.

NERVOUS HABITS

Yitzy, age eight, has a twitch. His mouth curls up (on one side only) into something between a smile and a grimace—over and over again. It makes Yitzy look a bit odd, so his parents and siblings keep telling him to "stop it." Everyone is stressing over it. For his part, Yitzy claims to have no control. "I'm not doing it on purpose—I just can't help it," he insists. Mom is getting worried. "What's *wrong* with that child?" she wonders. "He looks like a nervous wreck!"

TICS

In fact, Yitzy may be no more nervous than anyone else, despite his "nervous habits." Repetitive movements or vocalizations are called "tics" and they have more to do with the wiring of a person's brain than with emotional conditions like nervousness or anxiety.

Whereas an anxious child may have fears and phobias or may worry incessantly, a child with a tic disorder may just have tics—no fears or worries included. The child may chronically sniffle; clear his throat; or make small grunts, squeaks, or barking sounds. Repetitive noises like these are called "vocal tics." Or, he may wrinkle his nose or pull his shoulder backward or twist his neck a bit, over and over again, as if he needs to straighten something out. Repetitive *movements* are called "motor tics." In the case of Tourette's syndrome, he may do *both* repetitive sounds and movements. A tic can be suppressed for a while, but then it *must* be released. While it's true that tics occur more frequently during periods of stress, they aren't caused by stress. They are caused by genetic factors. Some tic conditions are transient, meaning they appear for a time (commonly around age seven to nine in children), and then disappear on their own. Sometimes, however, tics can persist throughout life. A child cannot stop persistent tic behavior on his own; he needs professional assistance. Medical, psychological, and even naturopathic interventions (e.g., Bach flower therapy or homeopathy) have been known to help. Getting upset with a child not only *does not* help this condition, but it may increase the kind of stress that leads to an increase in tic behavior.

OTHER HABIT DISORDERS

Kids can have other behaviors that look like nervous habits, but are actually biologically based disorders. For instance, those who repeatedly pull out their hair (or eyelashes or eyebrows) may have trichotillomania. Those who compulsively pick at their skin (nails, scabs, moles, and so on) may have dermatillomania. These conditions are both characterized by an irresistible urge (something like an itch that must be scratched). Some kids who feel compelled to wash their hands, count their steps, say certain phrases, touch or tap things and so on may look like they have some strange habits—whereas they actually have obsessive-compulsive disorder. Most of these disorders not only lack spontaneous remission, but in fact worsen over time when left untreated. Repetitive behaviors should always be checked out by the child's physician.

BAD HABITS

Habits are repetitive behaviors that are subject to *voluntary* control. While a child may not be able to stop making that little coughing sound, he *can* keep that finger away from his nose. Parents can help children break their bad habits, using many kinds of interventions. It is often helpful to offer the child a replacement activity: "instead of chewing on your shirt or pencil, here is a fidget-toy to play with—just keep it in your pocket and pull it out when you want to chew on something." Parents should offer their child specific habit-fighting techniques. For instance, if the child bites her nails, parents can teach her to clasp her hands together or clench her fists to "hide" her nails. It also helps to explain to the child why he shouldn't engage in the bad habit (e.g., it's not healthy, or people are bothered by it, or it's not appropriate).

Since most voluntary habits are self-soothing behaviors (calming the nervous system), they will occur far less often when the child has other ways to calm and soothe herself. Parents can teach a child how to relax by breathing deeply and slowly. They can then encourage the youngster to do the deep breathing instead of the habit. EFT (Emotional Freedom Technique) is a stress-reducing self-help tool that can often decrease habit behaviors—parents can teach it to their child or take their child to a practitioner for treatment. In fact, mental health professionals have a range of interventions that can help kids break habits.

If, despite parental assistance, a habit is persistent, unhealthy, socially unacceptable, or very annoying for parents and others to live with, then it may be worth seeking professional assistance. On the other hand, if the habit only bothers the parent and no one else, maybe the parent should just wait quietly until the child outgrows it.

PHOBIAS

Phobias, fears, and worries are all part of the anxiety family. However, these three varieties of anxiety differ in intensity. One child might be a bit worried about having to deliver an oral presentation to the class. She thinks about it and frets about it for several days before the event. She may even experience a bit of sleep disturbance the night before the performance, as she tosses and turns with it throughout the night.

Every person worries at times. We feel anxious about something that has not yet happened or something about which we do not yet know the outcome. We don't worry about our worrying unless we find that we worry about a lot of things a lot of the time—in which case, we may be suffering from the worrying disorder known as GAD (generalized anxiety disorder).

The same oral presentation may provoke fear in another child. This child's hands sweat when she thinks about giving the presentation.

She's afraid to stand up in front of the class. Her parents listen sympathetically, knowing that their daughter will master her fear, give the presentation, and be all the better for it. Fear, like worry, is a perfectly normal human emotion. We feel it when our intuition signals possible danger (as when we find ourselves on a deserted road late at night in the middle of nowhere), or when we are encountering first-time experiences (like going to school for the first time or having a first driving lesson) or when we know from past experience that something might be painful or unpleasant (like getting a needle). Having fear is uncomfortable but acceptable to most of us, as long as it doesn't interfere with our ability to function. If we can operate under the motto "feel the fear and do it anyway," then we're acceptably functional.

Phobias, however, are a whole other story. Phobias are pockets of intense, debilitating fear. Someone who has a phobia of flying on an airplane may become incapacitated with fear just at the thought of having to get on a plane. A full-blown panic attack may ensue in which the person has a variety of physical symptoms, including some or all of the following:

- **Heart racing**.

- **Dizziness**.

- **Shortness of breath**.

- **Tightness in the chest**.

- **Light-headedness**.

- **Nausea or upset stomach**.

- **Trembling**.

- **Chills**.

- **Fear of going insane**.

Phobias generate instant panic when the person is exposed to a specific trigger (social phobias involve fears that relate to people; agoraphobia is found in adults who are afraid to be in places from which they cannot easily and quickly exit). For one person, the trigger may be flying, for another it may be having to make a speech. When confronted with the trigger, a phobic person feels out of control, helpless against the rush of adrenalin that engenders the panic symptoms. Without professional help, few people can master their phobia. Consequently, telling someone who is phobic to "get over it," "calm down," or "stop being silly" is not helpful.

PHOBIAS IN CHILDREN AND ADOLESCENTS

Full-blown phobias frequently first appear in adolescence, or even in adulthood. These phobias tend to be unremitting without treatment. When phobias appear in children under ten years old they sometimes do clear up by themselves; no one knows why this occurs. While the child is experiencing his phobia, however, it is as painful to him as the ones that adults later experience. Common phobias in younger children include fears of clowns, balloons, spiders, needles, dogs, cats, and elevators. Older children (and adults) are generally phobic toward something that has a realistic danger element, such as driving, heights, snakes, or dentists (people are not phobic of carpets or pencils).

TREATMENT FOR SIMPLE OR SOCIAL PHOBIA

While adults can take anti-anxiety medications like lorazepam (Ativan) to board a plane or give a speech, children's phobias are generally treated with behavior therapy. Cognitive-behavioral therapy is the most common form of treatment for phobias in people of all ages, although other treatments are available as well; all are best delivered by a mental health professional who specializes in the treatment of anxiety. However, before embarking on a course of therapy, some people try alternative treatments such as energy psychology. Emotional Freedom Technique (EFT) is an example of this modality, which is easy enough for kids to use on themselves. Another intervention that can alleviate phobias and fears is Bach flower therapy. The Bach remedies Mimulus and Rock Rose can be particularly helpful for these conditions.

Phobias need to be respected. Never mock a child or push her to "face her fear." Offer compassion and professional assistance. Phobias respond well to professional intervention.

DISORDERS OF IMPULSE CONTROL

I t's sometimes hard to draw the line between "personality" and "mental illness." Some of the things people do are clearly self-destructive but they cannot seem to stop doing them. Disorders of impulse control cause people to engage in activities that harm themselves and often others as well. However, people with these disorders do not mean to be hurtful. They are victims of their own brains. Nonetheless, when you are living with such a "victim" or parenting one, your own life can be turned upside down.

When a person has a disorder of impulse control, he or she has tremendous difficulty resisting a specific urge. Like an alcoholic, the

IDP (impulse-disordered person) is overpowered by an anxious inner itch that begs for relief. Like an alcoholic, the person can rarely resist that urge without some sort of specific rehabilitation program. There are five distinct disorders of impulse control affecting both men and women in every walk of life:

- **Kleptomania.** Stealing for the satisfaction of taking something, not because one needs a specific item. The person is responding to an inner compulsive urge that can be relieved only by the act of stealing.

- **Intermittent Explosive Disorder.** Unprovoked aggressive outbursts involving property damage or assault. The person seems to lose control on specific occasions but is otherwise pleasant, functional, and normal.

- **Pyromania.** Setting fires for pleasure and tension release.

- **Trichotillomania.** Involves pulling hair from one's own head, eyebrows, eyelashes, face, or body, and is more common in women than in men. There is an increased sense of tension before pulling the hair, which is relieved once it is pulled out. There may be noticeable hair loss. Trichotillomania often begins in childhood and can be associated with major depression or attention-deficit/hyperactivity disorder.

- **Pathological Gambling.** The inability to resist the urge to gamble despite serious financial loss. Five or more of the following symptoms must be present:

  » Preoccupation with gambling.

  » A need to gamble with more money to achieve the thrill of winning.

  » Repeated unsuccessful attempts to limit gambling.

- » Irritability related to gambling.

- » Using gambling as an escape from stress.

- » Lying to cover up gambling.

- » Conducting illegal activities, such as embezzling or fraud, to finance gambling.

- » Borrowing money to fund gambling.

- » Losing a job or personal relationship as a result of gambling.

MIND/BODY ILLNESS

One might have thought that a thief, fire setter, gambler, or a rage-aholic was just a bad person. As it turns out, these problems are not purely psychological. They have a physical basis in the brain centers that regulate control of impulses. It has been noted, for example, that people with serious head injuries, carcinoid syndrome (caused by carcinoid tumors), or epilepsy can be at a higher risk for developing impulse control disorders. Some people with Parkinson's disease develop impulse control disorders as the disease progresses. Some medications have been linked to the development of impulsive disorders as well. Moreover, there may be a relationship of impulse disorders to other physically based disorders such as obsessive-compulsive disorder and attention deficit disorder. Although it is not yet understood exactly how otherwise "normal" brains trigger disorders of impulsivity, the scientific community agrees that there is a specific, physical basis for the process.

TREATMENT

As one might expect for a mind/body illness, both medication and therapy are used to treat the disorder. Antidepressant medications have been found to make a positive difference for some of the impulse disorders when combined with behavior therapy. Trichotillomania may wax and wane on its own (like other tic disorders), sometimes disappearing for years at a time, and it seems to respond well to medication also. Some people have had success using Bach flower therapy (a harmless form of vibrational medicine) combined with psychotherapy. Intermittent explosive disorder usually requires a course of anger-management therapy along with medication. Pathological gambling often requires a twelve-step addiction program in addition to any other treatment.

DISORDERS OF IMPULSIVITY IN THE FAMILY

When living with a spouse or child who has a disorder of impulsivity, a person experiences stress, fear, shame, and anger. People with these disorders look normal; it is hard to understand why they engage in destructive behavior. It is crucial, therefore, to educate oneself about these disorders. Blaming a person for shaming the family is not a technique that is curative or positive in any way. Rather, taking the sufferer for treatment should be the goal; this is best accomplished when love and encouragement are the motivating factors. Firmness is also required, however. It is often necessary to let the sufferer know that treatment is not optional. This may require rabbinical or professional assistance. However, effective treatment is worth all the trouble it might take to arrange, because it offers an individual the prospect of a healthy, happy future, and it offers the family peace of mind.

TEENAGE MOODS AND MOOD DISORDERS

Teenagers are renowned for their moodiness. When teenagers are irritable, uncooperative, sullen, or otherwise unpleasant, we tend to chalk it up to their stage of life: "Teenagers are moody." But what if it turns out not to be a case of moodiness? What if the change from happy to moping and mournful represents something more sinister—like teenage depression? How can we tell the difference between normal moodiness and mood disorders?

ADOLESCENT ANGST

The adolescent years are stressful. Kids must deal with their changing bodies, peer pressures, academic and performance pressures, more responsibility at home, and other challenges of growing up. But then, no stage of life is stress free. It is obvious that stress itself does not cause depression, or we would all have to be depressed. In fact, stress hits us in our individual weak spots. When stressed, some of us succumb to headaches, some to stomach problems, some to colds and flus, some to anxiety, some to depression, and some to other symptoms. Teenagers who get depressed do so because they have the combination of a genetic vulnerability to depression and stress.

SYMPTOMS OF DEPRESSION

Whereas moodiness comes and goes, alternately between states that are "normal" and states that are grumpy, depression just stays. Bipolar depressions alternate like moodiness does, except that the alternation is between states that are very high (lots of energy, tremendous confidence, extreme passion and focus, poor judgment) and states that are severely depressed. Unipolar depression is a constant state of low mood and other symptoms (see below) that lasts a minimum of two weeks. Dysthymia is a milder state of chronic low mood and other symptoms that lasts at least two years. Regular low mood is not, in itself, depression. Some people just have a low-mood set point, whereas others are born with a higher-mood set point. Depression includes many more symptoms besides low or irritable mood.

Teenage depression is not exactly the same as adult depression. Whereas depressed women tend to be very sad, depressed men and teenagers tend to be irritable and hostile. Depressed teens also have more bodily aches and pains than adults. They are more sensitive to criticism and failure. And, whereas depressed adults often withdraw socially, isolating themselves from everyone, depressed teens almost always keep at least a few friends close to them even when they withdraw from the larger crowd. Characteristics that depressed teens and adults have in common are hopelessness, loss of interest and motivation, changes in eating and sleeping patterns, agitation, feelings of worthlessness and guilt, lack of energy, difficulty concentrating, and thoughts about death.

GETTING HELP

It's really important to help a teen through depression. Untreated depression can result in unnecessarily poor academic performance, eating disorders, Internet addiction, reckless behavior, increasing feelings of low self-esteem, substance abuse, religious problems, self-injury, and even violence or suicide. Kids who talk about wanting to die must be taken very seriously—most people who do commit suicide do talk about it beforehand or attempt to actually do it many times. Major depression is extremely painful. Young people need the help of parents and professionals to successfully negotiate this severe mood disorder.

Parents can help by talking to their teen about their concerns. They can let the child know what specific symptoms are causing them worry. They can offer unconditional love and support and important information. For instance, they can let their adolescent know that depression is a disorder and that there is help for it. They can also acknowledge that the child's behavior may reflect something other than depression but that a medical assessment can clarify this. Parents must be careful to listen without judging, criticizing, or lecturing. Rather, by naming feelings and validating thoughts, they can help the young person trust them enough to reach out for help.

TREATMENT

Treatment for depression includes options in medication, psychotherapy, and alternative treatments. Antidepressant medication has been found to have risks and side effects, especially for people under the age of twenty-four. Indeed, medication can increase the risk of suicidal thinking and behavior in this age group. Therefore, when medication is employed, very careful, regular medical monitoring is required in the first two months.

There are many types of psychotherapy that have been shown to be effective for depression. A teen needs to try out a few therapists to find the one whose personality and therapy appeal to him. Daily exercise and alternative treatments like Bach flower therapy, aromatherapy, herbal medicine, energy psychology, and many other interventions can also help in the recovery process, along with psychotherapy.

Parents should also look after themselves while looking after a depressed child, taking time to exercise, seeking professional support, and continuing to make time for relationships. Healthy parents are in the best position to help their child return to health.

HELPING CHILDREN DEAL WITH LOSS

Loss is a normal part of life. People are always losing things: a cherished ring, an important document, a scarf. Kids lose these kinds of things, too—mittens, a favorite pen, important homework. These kinds of losses are aggravating and sometimes very disappointing. Both children and adults appreciate sympathy—not lectures—when they lose something important.

However, these losses are minimal compared to those that involve relationships. A child can experience many types of relationship loss. If a child has a relationship with a pet, the loss of that pet will always hurt. A young friend moving to another school or to another country is a painful loss. A parent moving out of the house is heartbreaking. And then, of course, there are the permanent, devastating losses: death of a grandparent, sibling, or parent.

How can parents help children deal with loss?

REACTIONS TO INTENSE LOSS

Human beings of all ages have similar feelings when facing the loss of loved ones. Initial reactions may involve some level of denial, a sort of feeling that this isn't happening or hasn't happened. It can take the brain a while to really register the loss. However, once it does begin to sink in, there will be a jumble of feelings, each taking its turn in coming into focus: upset, grief, confusion, disorientation, fear, anger, abandonment, and rage. The feelings come and go, interspersed with times of calm and even happiness, typically cycling throughout the first year of loss.

Children have a special "advantage" in processing deep, painful loss: they dissociate easily. This means they can compartmentalize the loss—set it off in some storage container while they continue growing up. Many times a divorced or widowed parent will be asked, "How are the children coping?" Often the answer will be, "Oh, they're fine. They're real troopers." Indeed, the kids can appear to be fine, playing games, doing their schoolwork as usual. However, all the normal feelings of grief and loss are in their little psyches just waiting for the right time to be expressed.

When parents don't help their kids process the pain of loss, the stored feelings may show up later in strange forms: misdirected rage that seems to come "out of nowhere"; deep-seated fears of abandonment that interfere with forming significant adult attachments; numbing, panic, sleep disturbances, and other symptoms characteristic of post-traumatic stress disorder; addictions; and other problems resulting from unprocessed feelings.

HOW PARENTS CAN HELP

Even the loss of a pencil case deserves acknowledgment of the subsequent emotional upset: "I know you liked the pencil case—it's upsetting that you can't find it anywhere." Certainly more significant losses require all the more emotional acknowledgment and support. Emotional coaching—the naming of a child's feelings—is very therapeutic. The parent simply names what she thinks the child is feeling and then lets it be without trying to cheer the child up. For kids who don't want to talk about loss (and many have that reaction), a parent can initiate conversation. For instance, "It feels strange around here without Daddy. I'm not used to it." By opening a conversation, the parent is teaching the children that the topic of grief is not taboo. It is not too horrible to speak about. This is an essential message. Parents who don't talk about significant loss accidentally teach youngsters that sadness is something you must stuff deep down inside yourself, suffering it alone.

Parents can also use bibliotherapy (the use of children's books on the subject of loss) to help their children. Reading about how others feel and deal with loss can be therapeutic. Books can also stimulate discussion about the child's own experience.

Parents can also help a child create a memory book of the person who has been lost—to record photos, stories, life lessons, and messages. Of course, doing acts of kindness in memory of a deceased loved one is spiritually significant as well as emotionally sound. Professional grief counseling is especially appropriate for children who ask for help with their words or their behavior. In fact, since the parental model of grieving is also critically important, grief counseling can be utilized by the parent as well. It is essential to show children how full life can continue even after significant loss.

Parents can answer their kids' questions about loss with sincere "I don't knows." No one understands the mind of God. Knowing that something is good while *feeling* that it is bad is the human condition. Parents can affirm for their kids that life is in constant flux, and while loss is part of our experience, the really important part is our ability to enjoy what we have when we have it.

FESTIVALS
AND FAMILY–
SEASONS OF
GROWTH

GOOD SHABBOS

One would think that Shabbos would be a peaceful day of rest. And while it has many lovely moments, the reality is that Shabbos also produces numerous family tensions. The trick is to manage these tensions in such a way that the overall feel of the day is positive, warm, and loving.

BEFORE SHABBOS BEGINS

The challenges of Shabbos start long before the sun sets. Sometimes the challenge begins with shopping for Shabbos foods and ingredients. In some homes, a weekly battle ensues over the costs involved and the lack of available funds. In other homes, the struggle is more a logistical one—who will run to the five different shops and when? At last, when everything is in the kitchen and ready to go, the work begins in earnest: putting it all together into three festive meals.

And when *that* is finally accomplished, it's time to ready the house for Shabbos—a particularly tricky undertaking when little children are underfoot.

While some people flow easily through the preparatory stages of Shabbos, many others do not—and for good reason. These weekly stresses are *real* stresses. Entire issues of secular magazines are devoted to the stresses and difficulties of making *one* large festive meal once, or maybe twice, a year! Topics will typically include financial cost, time management, menu preparation, food preparation, presentation, and other aspects of planning. *We* step up to the plate every few days, and while this is our pleasure, it is also a very real challenge. Jewish homemakers need top-notch organizational skills in order to carry it off smoothly and efficiently.

Since we're not all equally gifted in the organizational department, we can certainly take advantage of the books, articles, and human teachers around us to help us find a way to prepare for Shabbos that works well for our own unique styles. We can learn tips and strategies galore, until we find the system and techniques that make this stage of Shabbos pleasant and peaceful for us. It is so important that children see Shabbos preparations as pleasurable, satisfying, and even fun. If they see us moan and groan under the "burden" of Shabbos, it can, Heaven forbid, leave them with aversive feelings toward this holy day.

THROUGHOUT SHABBOS DAY

Cultivating an awareness of the Shabbos mood can help people make adjustments in their routines before destructive patterns set in. For instance, what is the mood like during Friday night Kiddush? When the house is full of little ones, there are bound to be wigglers, teasers, droppers, and slouchers at the Shabbos table. Are misdemeanors handled calmly and lovingly? Or are there loud reprimands and altercations? When the family is alone, is the atmosphere as carefully constructed as when there are guests with watchful eyes? Utilize books, *shiurim*, courses, and professionals as needed in order to help establish peaceful order at your table.

Shabbos morning presents new challenges. Little slowpokes aren't ready for shul when Father needs to leave. Big-enough-to-know-betters are still snoozing when they should be long out the door. Not all children have reached a level of piety and maturity that allows them to fulfill their Shabbos obligations properly—how can a parent handle this without making Shabbos a battleground? It is helpful to connect to one's own feelings before attempting to deal with children's recalcitrant behavior. When rage is aroused, it is a signal that parental vulnerability has been triggered. This should be dealt with first (on one's own or with professional help). Then, a healthy parenting plan can be implemented. Remember: there are peaceful solutions to all parenting problems.

As Shabbos stretches forward into the day, there are still more potential hot spots. Though she knows she shouldn't, Wife feels irritated with Husband's *dvar Torah*: it's too long, too short, too complicated, too simple, too infrequent, or otherwise too frustrating. The children aren't participating. They're grabbing food. They're fighting. They're not helping clear the table. Spouse isn't helping. Spouse finally steps in with a raised voice. It's all wrong.

Actually, it's all right. It's family life. Everyone is growing up, including the adults. There will be time to reflect and correct; it's Shabbos.

SHABBAT SHALOM

It helps to keep in mind that we and our spouses are human and children are children. Shabbos, like the rest of life, is a *work in progress*. Each particular challenge needs to be addressed separately and over time, with the overall goal of achieving a peaceful Shabbos atmosphere. When the goal is clear, it becomes easier to see what is needed: more household help or better discipline techniques, easier recipes or a better plan, more marital communication or a better division of labor. Experimenting and fine tuning are all part of it. The peace of Shabbos is more accessible when we are at peace with ourselves and our learning process.

THE KING
WILL ANSWER ON
THE DAY WE CALL

In Psalm 20, we learn that we need to talk to Hashem. Even though Hashem knows exactly what is happening in our lives (and, in fact, has *caused* it to happen that way), His response to our situation depends in large part on *our* response to it. Do we run around frantically trying to get people and resources to help us? Do we sit passively and bemoan our fate? Or do we turn directly to Hashem to ask Him to mobilize a solution to our problems and *then* do what we can do ourselves?

Kind David advises us that "the King will answer us on the day we call." Hashem is waiting to hear from us and, as soon as He hears from us—"on the day we call"—He will respond. However, a closer look at the wording of this sentence provides us with an important caution. At the beginning of the psalm, there is a blessing that Hashem (called by the Divine Name that denotes Hashem's attribute of loving-kindness) should help a person in distress: "May Hashem answer you on the day of distress." Out of compassion alone, Hashem may come to our aid in times of trouble. However, at the end of the psalm, Hashem is not called by this attribute of mercy but by the attribute of kingship. "May the King answer us on the day we call." While it is true that we can always hope that Hashem will have compassion upon us just because we are helpless, it is chutzpadik to *call* Him for assistance when we haven't accepted His kingship. On the other hand, loyal subjects of the King can always *call* on Him and expect Him to come to their aid.

CROWNING HASHEM

On Rosh Hashana we crown Hashem as King. This is a bit odd, if you think about it. Isn't Hashem already King without us doing anything at all? Isn't Hashem the One who fashioned the heavens and the earth and who is responsible for every breath of each and every soul? And yet, it is our task to "vote" Hashem in, so to speak, to elect Him as our King. We actually *choose* to acknowledge (or ignore) Hashem's kingship. When we do decide to crown Hashem as King, we are voluntarily submitting ourselves to His authority. We accept that Hashem directs our paths in every detail. We pledge to obey the commands of the King.

LIVING IN THE PALACE

Hashem has filled our every waking moment with commandments. There are constant commandments of faith, commandments between us and Hashem, and commandments that direct our interpersonal relationships. Hashem has commanded us, for example, not to hurt people's feelings with words. This one commandment is very hard to keep when we live or work or otherwise deal with people! It is particularly challenging in the context of close relationships such as marriage and parenting.

If we look at this one commandment as an opportunity to crown Hashem as King, we can then also look at it as an opportunity for prayer. Let's say that we accept that the King has sent us our particular spouse and a houseful of children. Let's further say that the spouse He sent us is difficult at times and that one of the children He sent us is extremely challenging. Let's say that we sometimes feeling like screaming at these people.

But then we remember that the King has commanded us to guard our tongues. It is just at the moment when we feel we can't help ourselves that we can call out to Hashem and expect to be answered. Our King will save us from ourselves and from sin when we ask Him to.

Hashem will test us over and over again in our family lives. A spouse forgets to pay a bill (again and again), a child constantly hurts the baby, another one doesn't apply himself to his studies, another won't eat anything but cheese on bread, and on and on. And of course, there are much larger challenges in family life as well. Illness, abuse, disabilities, debt, legal issues—all of life happens to people. There are endless occasions for worry, grief, frustration, terror, and upset—all sent by the King Himself. When we crown Hashem as King, we acknowledge that everything that happens to us is sent on purpose for our own benefit, even when it feels bad. Then, instead of being outraged, we can accept the situation more gracefully, with greater humility. Having framed it correctly, having accepted Hashem's kingship, we can then follow the correct protocol: the first step to take in every stressful, distressing, and upsetting situation is to "call." For we know that the King will answer us on the day we call.

VICTORY

Family life has a lot in common with the holiday of Chanuka. Chanuka is the story of light over darkness, weak over strong, humble over arrogant. It is the story of faith in Hashem and all that's fair and right: the good guys win in the end. And so it is in family life. Goodness prevails.

THE WAR AT HOME

Chanuka—the story of war and of good over evil—has much to inform us about the war we fight in our family lives. Yes, war happens at home as well and often feels as if it involves a life-and-death battle. We are always "the good guy" and our opponent is the evil one (at least in our eyes). Sometimes it is our own mother we are fighting (the battle has been going on forever). After all these years she is still attacking us and we are still defending our fragile fort.

She is the strong, powerful enemy; we are little in comparison. Or perhaps it is Father who is still towering over us, intimidating and controlling, holding a supply of arrows strong enough to penetrate deeply when we are not vigilant.

Sometimes, the enemy is our husband. A cruel, domineering man of war, he crushes our spirit. (Or it is our wife—a cold, heartless queen who slices through us with her bitter tongue.) Sometimes the enemy is our parents-in-law. They use their power to pull our spouse away from us. They step on us. They demand absolute obedience and threaten to cut off our supplies should we demur.

The enemy can even be our own children. Disguised as innocents, they wield powerful tools of manipulation and tyranny, wearing us down day after day. They terrorize us, alarm us, exhaust us, and humiliate us.

Whether the enemy is close at hand or at a distance (the siblings and siblings-in-law can fire from afar, as can the cousins, aunts, and uncles), we must be prepared to do battle. But how?

WINNING THE WAR

The lesson that Chanuka teaches us is that Hashem is on our side. When we are behaving properly and calling out to Hashem to help us, we can certainly count on His salvation. We believers know that, no matter how things look in a material sense (the enemy appears large and all-powerful), Hashem can turn the tables and make us victorious. Therefore, we needn't despair.

In family life this means that we also shouldn't be deceived by appearances. While it may look like a relative is controlling our situation, it is none other than Hashem Himself. Therefore, Hashem can bring about a drastic change in circumstances. Knowing this, we can relax. No need to fall into depression. No need to lower our own behavior to the same cruel level exhibited by our enemy. We can fight a fair battle as the Jews did way back then, confident that when we do what we're supposed to do and put our faith in Hashem, the victory will be ours.

A PRACTICAL EXAMPLE

Let us say, for example, that a woman has a verbally and emotionally abusive husband. The social workers read her the statistics ("abuse gets worse, not better") and advise her to get a divorce. She's afraid to take the plunge but she is miserable every day. Her husband is always critical; she lashes back. He refuses to help her when she is in a rush; she screams that he is selfish. He slams the door in anger; she refuses to talk to him for days on end.

Her "enemy" has not only hurt her, but he has also brought out the worst in her. They descend together, each blaming the other for "starting it." However, had this woman chosen the mentality of Chanuka, she would have taken a different route. To begin with, she would have internalized that Hashem was with her. She would have been able to maintain her own dignity, knowing that Hashem would fight her battle for her and "win" it if He saw fit. Through praying, behaving properly in Hashem's eyes, and taking appropriate steps to set boundaries and initiate changes (i.e., fight the battle with counseling and/ or rabbinic guidance), she would have done what she could do in her private war. The outcome would be up to Hashem. Perhaps the marriage would dissolve anyway. In that case, she has at least maintained her good character—her soul remains untarnished by war, and this itself is a major victory. But perhaps Hashem would reward her trust in Him by turning the situation around for her.

Chanuka teaches us that the impossible is actually possible. Hashem can pacify the enemy even when this seems unrealistic to us. Faith, prayer, and good deeds are our weapons of war. Miracles do occur.

IT'S PARTY TIME!

Chanuka is party time. Eight full days of dreidels, gifts, doughnuts, chocolate coins, and latkes with sour cream and applesauce—what could be better? It's easy to understand why it's a holiday that children look forward to all year round.

Adults have a different experience of Chanuka. Of course, they appreciate the deeper significance of the holiday, the victory of spirituality over materialism. They light candles and sing songs celebrating freedom and closeness with Hashem. Some have noted that Jewish holidays tend to have a recurring theme: We were attacked, we fought, Hashem saved us. Let's eat! It's this latter part of the celebration that has many homemakers enthralled and leaves many others dismayed.

BALABUSTA CENTRAL

Some women love the opportunity to shine that holiday time brings. They enjoy the creative side of homemaking, the organizational challenges, and the opportunity to host company. They're in their element as they call up the family, arrange the place cards, leaf through the recipe books, and create memorable Chanuka celebrations.

Other women may be short on time or on the inclination to make Chanuka parties. Maybe they'll whip up some latkes for their own crew, but they don't want to serve up a storm for the extended family. For some in this group, catering will solve their problem. For others, the expense, the chaos, the mess, the family politics—it's all too much. And yet, not everyone can just bow out of it.

FAMILY DYNAMICS

Families have rules. In some families, having a Chanuka party is mandatory. Sisters and sisters-in-law must powwow annually, dividing up the responsibilities and chores. They must take turns hosting the family. Inevitably, there are those who take on more than their share and those who somehow manage to slack off. Resentments build year after year. Sometimes frustration rests quietly beneath the surface of the family gathering, and in other cases there is open fire. Cooperation and teamwork is always challenging, whether in the classroom, in the corporate playing field, in the international political arena, or in the living room. Not everyone lives in a group of reasonable, caring, and sharing adults.

NOT IN THE PARTY MOOD

Interpersonal challenges are part and parcel of family life. Parties raise unique challenges within family systems. For one thing, parties appeal to some people more than others. Some folks just enjoy being with people. Some just don't. Some enjoy people—but just not their own family members. Some may be going through a period of stress—financial loss, illness, depression, family problems—and are just in no mood for a party.

In the family, there may be adult singles who love the opportunity to nurture young nieces and nephews. They can add fun and warmth to the family scene. Other single or childless adults may feel intense pain during such gatherings, since it all reminds them of what they don't have in their lives. Some people stop coming to the Chanuka party because it just leaves them feeling so bad. Some teenagers also beg out of family gatherings because they're too old to enjoy it in the childish way and too young to enjoy the adult company. There is no one-size-fits-all Chanuka party. We need to allow for and understand individual situations and preferences. We need to refrain from trying to squeeze everyone into one mold.

CREATING A POSITIVE EXPERIENCE

With all this in mind, one can create an atmosphere that is relaxed and accepting at holiday time. Can't make it to my party? That's okay. Maybe next year. No explanations necessary. Need to leave early? Thanks so much for coming—it was great seeing you! Not up to making it at *your* house this year? Don't worry—there will be another time. You were only able to bring a bag of potato chips? Don't worry! The kids love chips and I forgot to pick some up. Whatever it is, it's okay. Parties are for fun and positive memories—not for stress and strain. Those who can't, won't, or don't do their share either have reasons or they don't. Right now, Hashem wants it to be this way for a good reason. There are growth opportunities for everyone all the time. Inner examination will reveal whether this situation calls for more action, less action, more positive judgment, or something else. It's all good.

Dealing with others in a pleasant manner, even when self-assertion is necessary, is crucial. An easygoing, loving attitude that allows everyone to be themselves will cause others to be more comfortable with themselves and more cooperative with you. You are an understanding, unthreatening person—to everyone, including yourself. After all, maybe it's *you* this year who isn't up to speed, who can't tolerate attending, contributing to, or making a party. Maybe you can handle the party but you're upset with certain family members. Your feelings are what they are—allowing them to just "be" is half the battle of letting them go. Self-acceptance is certainly as important as accepting everyone else. Let yourself off the hook; relationships change. There will be other years that can be different.

Keeping the big picture in mind can help make Chanuka parties what they're supposed to be: a celebration of Jewish values. "Love your fellow as yourself" is a primary value that can serve us all well at family get-togethers all year round.

LOOK AGAIN

Tu BiShvat is the new year for trees. Normally we don't think too much about trees or their birthdays. In fact, we tend to take trees and their fruits pretty much for granted. However, Hashem asks us to think again. He wants us to pay attention to trees, and to recognize that they have an important and even holy status. He wants us to take a second look—to see trees in a different, more appreciative light.

If this is true for trees, it is all the more so for people. Surely Hashem wants us to pause and reflect on the gift of people in our lives.

LOOK AND SEE YOUR CHILD

Part of our problem is that we don't see what's right in front of us. A child who does what he's supposed to do is almost invisible. Much like a tree that's providing shade, a properly functioning child is un-remarkable. A six-year-old brushes his teeth. Who cares? A ten-year-old is ready for school on time. So what? A fifteen-year-old calms the toddler down. Does she want a prize? These behaviors provoke neither parental shock nor surprise. They are givens. And therefore, many parents fail to notice them. As a result, these behaviors often go unattended.

However, attention and appreciation for normal behaviors can actually help bring out the best in children. While standing ovations are clearly unnecessary for normal, appropriate behaviors, positive attention to desirable behaviors often has powerful, positive effects. For one thing, it tends to increase the occurrence of those behaviors. Therefore, saying something like "thank you for calming the baby down" helps to ensure that the teenager will continue to want to help out this way in the future. In addition, showing appreciation for simple actions makes a child feel seen and recognized. This helps foster self-esteem and self-confidence in the child while it simultane-ously strengthens the parent-child bond.

Nonetheless, some people think that attending to normal, healthy behaviors might be counterproductive. They might feel that giving attention to regular, "normal" behaviors can develop an unhealthy dependency on positive feedback: "If I praise the child for doing something she is supposed to be doing, I'm train-ing her to be addicted to praise. Eventually she'll need it just to be able to breathe." Other objectors worry that excessive positive at-tention sends the wrong message: "She'll become insecure, think-ing that I have such low standards for her that I get excited about every normal thing she does. She'll think I have no faith in her." Still others worry that praise is a rare commodity that needs to be doled out sparingly: "I want to save the positive attention for be-haviors that really *deserve* it." Parents with these kinds of concerns may praise their kids for more "praiseworthy" behaviors, such as performing exceptionally well in school or doing a super job of helping out. However, they will refrain from commenting on the ordinary, everyday behaviors that are simply expected. To understand the consequences of this, let's look at positive attention from an adult perspective.

LOOK AND SEE YOUR SPOUSE

Miriam works part-time and is at home the rest of the time tending to the house and children. Her husband Yossi works and learns. Yossi's schedule is very busy; he is always running from one place to another. Every day, however, he manages to come home for a quick dinner before going out for his evening activities. Every day Miriam makes two dinners—one that the children will enjoy and a grown-up version of it for herself and her husband. Planning for, shopping for, cooking, and cleaning up after these daily meals takes hours of her time. But the results are worth it: Miriam is a great cook and everyone enjoys a great dinner. Every night.

And yet, busy Yossi never gives any attention to Miriam for these dinners. He gobbles them up and then leaves. If you were to ask him why he doesn't praise his wife for these delicious meals, he would answer: "The fact that I eat them is praise enough. Why should I make a big deal of it? Does she praise *me* for doing what I am supposed to do?"

However, Miriam feels not only unappreciated, but also invisible: "He has absolutely no idea of what goes into preparing each meal. He doesn't know what I do and obviously doesn't care. I feel very alone and lonely. We're in two different worlds."

Can a woman actually feel that wounded by lack of positive feedback? Yes! It happens all the time to both men and women. It's more than feeling unappreciated that is at the root of this kind of pain. It is feeling *unseen*. When spouses acknowledge the simple, routine behaviors of their partners and when parents acknowledge the small, expected actions of their children, then every family member feels recognized and celebrated. Just like the trees on Tu BiShvat—only more so.

PLANTING SEEDS

All parents are farmers. I bet you didn't know that. Yes, parents are farmers because they are busy planting seeds. In the fertile soil of the minds of their young children, parents plant all sorts of ideas and experiences which, over time, bloom into a garden of thoughts, dreams, attitudes, feelings, philosophies, beliefs, plans, and goals. The most successful farmer-parents are those who choose the best seeds to plant and do the best job of nurturing the garden.

THE INNER LANDSCAPE

What would you like your child's inner world to look like? The inner world is the world of thoughts and feelings. *You* have an inner world. Is it full of sunshine, smooth, clear and expansive space, colored with hope, optimism, and energy? Or does it tend to be tangled, dark, cluttered, tied in knots of fear, sadness, or negativity? If you're not sure, take a moment to check inside right now: close your eyes and "look" inside your head. Don't think about this exercise—simply note what sort of image first comes to you. If you see/feel "nothing," then check again later. It can also help to ask yourself a few questions, like "What color is it in there?" or "What's the mood in there?" or "What is the activity like in there?" Whatever you find is probably fairly typical for you at this point in your life. Are you happy with what's there right now? Or would you like to change it somehow? How did your inner world get to be the way it is today? What do you imagine your child's inner world looks like? What have you done so far to contribute to the way it is?

There are, in fact, so many factors that contribute to the way our inner world grows and develops. To begin with, there is the soil itself. Just as certain trees can only grow in certain soil, certain thoughts can take root only in a certain kind of mind. Hashem creates the "soil" of the mind as part of a person's mission in this world. For instance, the minds of some children will be ripe to absorb the anxious murmurings of their parents. The parent might wonder aloud if the food has spoiled, and this sort of child will absolutely refuse to eat it, accepting the anxious thought and digging it even deeper into his own inner landscape. However, another child overhearing the same remark may be totally resistant to it. "Looks good to me!" he says as he heaps a load of the questionable substance onto his plate.

The parents' words and actions as well as all the events of the child's life are seeds that are dropped onto the soil of the youngster's mind. Some will take root and grow and some will not. Moreover, seeds can be "blown in the wind" in addition to being consciously planted. For example, while a parent consciously desires to plant the value of self-control in her child's mind, the actual behavior of the parent may sow the seed of "when you're angry, cast self-control aside." In other words, both the words and the actions of parents are seeds that may take root in the child's consciousness, affecting his or her behavior for decades to come.

PLANT THE SEEDS
YOU WANT TO HARVEST

If you want your child's inner world to be positive and full of light, you'll want to contribute to this outcome by planting seeds of positivity and light! Both through your words and deeds, you can plant constantly throughout twenty developmental years. When you predict positive outcomes, say words of gratitude and appreciation, talk about Torah concepts, offer encouragement and understanding, express faith and trust, and clearly enjoy living, you are using your words to plant positive inner processes. When your face beams with happiness, you throw yourself into worthy projects and endeavors, and display your trust in Hashem through your actions, you are using your actions to seed positive inner processes. But what can you do to help ready the soil to receive and nurture these seeds?

Work the "land." In other words, parents can nourish the soil of their children's mind with constant repetition, consistent modeling, positive reinforcement, and occasional discipline. Parents can pull out the weeds that block healthy growth by constantly working on refining their own characters—raising themselves the whole time they are raising their kids.

Since Hashem will control all the factors beyond the parents' control, parents will want to do their best with their small share of the project. They certainly can't guarantee that every seed will flourish and bloom into the full expression of a fine *middah*, a correct value, or a healthy thought process, but that is not their job. Their job is to carefully plant seeds, tend the garden, and pray that Hashem creates a bountiful harvest.

THE JOY OF PURIM

Children experience the joy of Purim. They dress up and eat lots of treats—what could be better? Adults, on the other hand, may or may not feel the joy of Purim. The creative types may *love* the opportunity to create—costumes, food baskets, and Purim feasts. But those not so inclined may experience Purim as a series of stressful tasks. And yet, we're *supposed* to be happy on this holiday. We're not supposed to go around moaning about having to sit through Megilla readings, having to deal with relatives and *seuda*-politics, or having to deal with the high costs and intense efforts demanded by the festival. If nothing else, letting our kids see us "suffering" on Jewish holidays can give them the dangerous idea that living the Torah life is too difficult. But what if we *do* find it all too much? Should a parent just "fake it till she makes it"? In other words, is she supposed to put on a good show for her family while she keeps her actual feelings under careful lock and key? Or will her kids be able to see through her ruse—especially when they're a little older—inadvertently absorbing her true resentment? Can a parent ever really hide?

AUTHENTIC JOY

Even if a parent *could* hide her unhappiness, she would undoubtedly prefer to remove it for real. No one wants to be miserable. Moreover, when Hashem asks us to rejoice and be happy, it is clear that happiness must be a possibility. Otherwise, how could it be demanded of us? Hashem, who knows us thoroughly, knows that we are prone to stress and negativity. In asking us to be joyful, He is telling us that *we* can bring that state about. We just have to learn *how.*

BRAIN SCIENCE

Neuroscientists are teaching doctors, psychiatrists, psychologists, and everyone else that the principal of "neuroplasticity" allows for the rewiring of our brains. Even though we have genes, and habitual tendencies and enormous automatic brain processes, we can—when we know how to—override all that to create *new* neural pathways that will lead to new ways of thinking, feeling, and doing things. We can literally change our minds.

Hebb's Law says that "neurons that fire together, wire together." In other words, any two brain experiences that occur at the same time become linked in one neural pathway. If someone thinks about Purim and feels overwhelmed, the Purim-Overwhelm circuit is formed. It becomes bigger and stronger every time its owner attends to it, because *attention* strengthens neural pathways. Therefore, thinking about Purim and sighing a big "oy" (oy, so much to do, so much to spend, so much stress) enlarges the Purim-Overwhelm circuit. If one has sighed a sigh and then *continues* to focus on the issue, wondering where the money will come from, how all the work will get done, wondering if the *mishloach manos* will be good enough, stressing over the *seuda* menu and so on—giving it still more attention—the Purim-suffering circuit becomes a superhighway in the brain. Unfortunately, the suffering circuit releases unhappy chemicals into the body, infusing each cell with a generous dose of misery.

THE POWER OF ATTENTION

The good news is that a person has a choice over which circuits to build. By giving minimal attention to a negative thought about Purim and quickly turning one's attention to a positive thought about Purim and then giving that positive thought plenty of attention, one can build a positive Purim brain circuit. This new circuit will then trigger happy chemicals in the brain, which will then affect every cell of the body, causing the thinker to feel *genuinely* happy. The more attention the person gives to the positive thought, the stronger the circuit becomes and the more good chemistry it releases. Managing the brain this way allows the person to *feel good* about Purim. The whole process might look something like this:

Notice a negative thought: "*mishloach manos* are just too much work."

Move attention away from the negative thought to a positive thought: "I love how excited the kids get when they give and get *mishloach manos.*"

Give the positive thought lots more attention by thinking about it, expanding on it, picturing it, spending time on it: "It's really the highlight of their year. They have such a great time sorting out all the goodies and eating them right up to Pesach. I can picture the excitement on their little faces as they march up to their teachers' front doors! They're so happy to give treats to their friends, etc. etc."

Rabbi Zelig Pliskin points out in his commentary on the first line in *Tehillim* that sitting in the company of scorners includes sitting with our own negativity, while choosing good company includes choosing our own good thoughts. We have a choice. We *can* be happy on Purim—and every other day too—by leading our brain in the way we want it to go.

WHEN TO SAY NO

Purim is such a happy holiday—especially for kids. Youngsters of all ages look forward to the festivity and freedom of this special day. For young children, Purim is associated with candies, cookies, and other treats. For older kids, the day is associated with raucous behavior, parties, and liquor. When their kids hit the teen years, most parents look back with nostalgia on the junk food issue of yesteryear.

EVERYONE'S DOING IT

Parents are concerned all year round for the safety and well-being of their kids. They set (hopefully) reasonable limits on their youngsters' activities in order to reduce the possibility of danger or harm. For instance, they ask their kids to call home, give them a curfew, tell them what time to go to bed, and so on. In addition to setting such limits, parents provide a certain amount of guidance and education about lifestyle choices: don't smoke, don't drink, don't do anything worse than smoking and drinking.

However, when Purim comes along, it seems that the very structure of a home falls apart. All of a sudden, teenagers *are supposed to drink* (how much is open to interpretation by the local *rav*). It may not be a specific mitzvah to smoke, but lots of non-smoking teens seem to think that this normally forbidden activity enhances the joy of the day. And, to top it all off, for some youngsters, Purim is a stay-out-late party time. What happens when *your* adolescent asks permission to go to the overnight Purim bash and you don't think it's a safe idea?

PRESSURED BY YOUR TEENAGER

Kids of every age love to argue with their parents. Many are inexplicably unaware of the halacha within the mitzvah of *kibbud av va'em* that specifically forbids arguing with a parent. Kids particularly like to enter the debating mode when they are refused permission for an activity that they really want to do. Like go to an all-night or even late-night Purim party.

So parents may start off answering no. However, as the clever adolescent puts forth all sorts of (exhausting) arguments—"Everyone else is going," "So-and-so's parents are letting him go," "I promise I won't get drunk," "It's safer if I just sleep there instead of trying to come home smashed," "Nothing's going on; it's just fun"—parents may give up and give in.

How can a parent know if she is doing the right thing? What if it is true that all the other kids are going to this party? Will it be traumatic for the child if he is the only one left out? Does a parent of a teenager call the other parents of teenagers to find out what is really going on? Or is that only done when the kids are small?

PARENTAL UNCERTAINTY

Parenting causes confusion—and not just on Purim! Many times a parent must make a decision in a matter of minutes, without time to do research, think things through, or seek advice. It is easier for parents to feel confident about those decisions when the child is little; surely the parent *really does know* what's best for a six-year-old. However, when a sixteen-year-old is looking down at his mother or eye-to-eye with his father, the parents can become unnerved. The child no longer puts forth his thoughts in baby talk—he is quite articulate, even forceful in his presentation. Even when parents want to be firm, their inner confidence may be rattled. "What if I am being unduly harsh or restrictive? Will my child hate me forever? Am I making him a social outcast as he claims I am?" Some parents can no longer bring themselves to set limits with their teenagers—they are simply overwhelmed by them. Others try valiantly to keep to the old ways, sometimes finding that their kids become devious liars doing what they want behind the parents' backs. Some parents manage to set some reasonable limits without disrupting the parent-child bond.

KEEPING THINGS IN PERSPECTIVE

Being fair and pleasant can help parents continue to set limits with their adolescents. Parents must be perceived as being generous, understanding, and positive. Then if they have to say no on an occasion or two, the teens are still likely to love and respect them. Forbidding kids to do something that all the other kids really do is likely to invite trouble in the relationship. A parent can ask a teen to name several people who are going to this party and even provide their cell phone numbers ("in case of an emergency"). Kids of reasonable parents lie less often. Warning the child in advance of serious consequences for serious misdemeanors is important. "Yes, you can go. But if you get into any trouble with the law or with alcohol or with (fill in the blanks) such-and-such serious consequence will happen to you when you get home." If the parent feels that a particular activity is unsafe, the parent certainly has the right and the responsibility to say no—it will be well tolerated in a healthy, balanced relationship.

So do what you think is best, and have a happy Purim!

THE VIEW FROM
THE KITCHEN
WINDOW

Pesach—a dip into an alternate universe, far away from everything familiar: work, activities, and, particularly, food. Pesach is a time of complete celebration, a time to really *feel* our redemption from physical slavery to our elevation to the spiritual realms.

But if so, why does it feel mostly like a whole lot of work?

A WOMAN'S PERSPECTIVE ON PESACH

A woman's Pesach is typically filled with physical labor. In the days and weeks before Pesach, she is cleaning and sorting and shopping and cooking. Unless she has a full staff on hand, on the holiday itself she is cooking and serving and cleaning and cooking and serving and cleaning and cooking and...for a full week without rest. Where is her "elevation"? The only alternate universe she may be experiencing is the one found in her kitchen. Particularly if she is used to leaving her house on a daily basis to do errands, go to work, tend to children, or take care of her own needs, the new reality of seemingly endless kitchen work can make her feel confined and trapped. Where is the joy in that?

How can a woman *not* feel like a slave on Pesach? While feeding her household, entertaining her family and guests, and looking after her children who are all home from school (for the month!), how can she immerse herself in the spiritual energies of this holy festival?

COGNITIVE STRATEGIES

One thing that a woman can do to elevate her soul is to *use her head*. Hashem gave us our wondrous brains to help us achieve higher levels of spirituality. By learning and thinking, we can take ourselves out of the mundane realm into the spiritual realm. Since women are busy *making* Pesach and working even on *yom tov*, there may not be a whole lot of time for heavy reading. However, even the lightest perusal of a *Pesadig* Torah thought (in a magazine, in a newspaper) can offer perspective and inspiration. In addition, catching a five- or ten-minute audio class (available on tape or on the telephone) at any point before the holiday or during the intermediate days, can enlighten the mind and lighten the burden.

Reminding herself intellectually about *why* she is doing all this changes the nature and feeling of her service. It helps to remember that we were *freed* from Egypt in order to live a life of spirituality. We were freed from the slavery of doing hard, meaningless work for human beings, in order to do hard, meaningful work for Hashem. Knowing that every potato peeled and every dish washed creates a song in the celestial spheres can definitely help.

NON-COGNITIVE STRATEGIES

Spirituality can enter a person through many channels. While conscious intellect is one venue, unconscious knowing is another. In fact, when people connect to Hashem through faith alone, the connection is even stronger, since faith is a higher level than intellect. But how does one connect to faith?

Our sages advise us to use intellect as a path to faith—more study, more learning, more observing, more reasoning. As mentioned above, a woman in the midst of Pesach may not have much time for that particular road. However, she will have plenty of time for another path to soulful connection—placing herself in a state of mindfulness.

Essentially, the mindful state is a condition of being totally present in the present moment. It is a *holiday* from thinking, analyzing, worrying, planning, fretting, regretting, judging oneself, judging others, obsessing, and all other forms of stressful rumination. In fact, it is permission *not* to think! When peeling a potato, the mindful person uses her senses of sight, touch, and smell to enjoy the feel of the potato in her hand, the whoosh of the skin sliding off, the coolness of the vegetable, the glistening color of its flesh, the familiar smell, the *miracle of the potato*. When sitting at the table, the mindful person sees—really *sees*—her family and friends, the flickering candles, the flowers, the plates, the cutlery, every blessing that Hashem has bestowed upon her. She absorbs it slowly, fully, like she's never seen it before and may never see it again. She is totally, 100 percent there, soaking in the *gift, the blessing, the precious never-again moment of this very moment.*

Mindful attention is not only calming and highly pleasurable; it is also a direct path to Hashem. When one enjoys her world mindfully, Hashem's obvious hand in all aspects of it becomes immediately evident and her heart fills with gratitude and appreciation.

So this Pesach, give yourself permission to really concentrate on the soap suds as you rinse that stack of dishes. You may discover that those bubbles carry you high out of the kitchen, right into the heavens above!

STAYING ON TRACK

S taying on track is impossible unless a person knows where the track is. Indeed, many people waste a lot of time going nowhere because they can't find the track—the specific road that will lead them to their desired destination. Some people don't even realize that they need to *have* a desired destination! Just hopping on any old train at the station has a very small chance of taking you where you want to go. Think about it: *Where do you want to go? What track will lead you there?*

LOCATION: PESACH

Let's say you find yourself in Pesach. All around you there is chaos: a houseful of noisy, hungry children, long-lost relatives, please-get-lost relatives, other people, strange foods, reorganized counters, odd schedules, empty wallets, days that roll into one another, and more. What are you hoping to accomplish here? *Where do you want to go?* If you're not even thinking about these questions, chances are high that you're not going anywhere worthwhile.

Of course, some people, feeling stressed and overwhelmed, are simply waiting to go home—whether that is physically or metaphorically. They want to go back to where they came from: to a place that is quieter, saner, more familiar, and more comfortable. They want Pesach to be over. Others want to move through Pesach to a higher plane. They want to be further ahead at the end of the holiday than they are at the beginning. They want to progress, to move along their spiritual trajectory.

Naturally these two different directions necessitate two different tracks. The want-to-go-home group will be looking for the road *backward*—a track to take them back from where they came. The want-to-be-further-ahead group will be looking for a road that takes them further along the road they are traveling.

THE ROAD FORWARD

Since we all know where we've been, there is no point in describing that location. But what does the road *ahead* look like? From Pesach, where can one go? In fact, there are many possible roads forward. The important thing is to choose one in order to maximize the opportunity of the festival. Here is a small selection of possible roads one might travel:

- **The road to greater acceptance.** This road takes a person to a happier, more relaxed, more compassionate place than she is used to being in. The road has appeal for someone who is very particular, who needs things her own way, and who tends not to like the way the relatives and others behave or do things. A person who takes this road can watch the goings on around her with interest and curiosity. She can encourage herself to make peace with differences as she focuses on the thought "Different strokes for different folks."

- **The road to greater shalom bayis.** This road leads to higher levels of marital harmony. The road has appeal for someone who disintegrates under stress, tending to become irritable, snappy, and unpleasant. A person who takes this road makes a conscious effort to monitor her stress levels and address them every day of the holiday. She watches her own behavior and rates it, giving herself a daily score for maintaining calmness and kindness under pressure. She focuses on the bigger picture, insisting that her family has a right to fond holiday memories. She commits to keeping cool no matter what, focusing on the thought "The crazier it gets, the calmer I get."

- **The road to mental health.** This road takes one away from dysfunctional relationships into a land of healthy interactions. The road has appeal for someone who has played an active part in a dysfunctional family system, taking on the role of passive victim, explosive tyrant, sulking child, angry child, or any other less-than-healthy part. A person who takes this road maintains her current adult level of functioning no matter how anyone else behaves during family visits. She aims to change her role in the family and improve her own communication skills. She rates herself daily, using a special score sheet for particularly provocative family members, maintaining her focus on the thought "No one can make me behave in unhealthy ways."

- **The road to peace of mind.** This is the road to faith and trust in Hashem. As each event unfolds over the course of the festival, travelers along this road see Hashem's guiding hand. The road has particular appeal to one who feels stressed and overwhelmed during demanding times (i.e., most people). A person on this road allows herself to become a passenger, rather than the driver. As she sits back comfortably, trusting that the Driver knows the way, she concentrates on the thought "Hashem arranges all events for my benefit."

OTHER ROADS TO TAKE

Where do *you* want to go this Pesach? Pick a road and follow it. Stay on track and rest assured you'll get there in no time.

Appendix One

MARRIAGE-READINESS TEST

Not everyone is ready for marriage—including many people who have been married a long time. Marriage requires numerous skills and abilities. A lack of skill in any area means suffering for innocent spouses and children and consequently for oneself as well.

Take the following marriage-readiness test with your spouse. In fact, take it annually, perhaps on your anniversary. It can provide you with a snapshot of your progress in marriage competency.

You will each need a piece of paper on which you've drawn two vertical lines, thereby creating three columns. Name each column as follows:

- **My score: between 1 (poor) and 10 (excellent)**
- **My spouse's score**
- **The score my spouse will give me**

Place the numbers 1, 2, 3, 4, 5, 6, 7, 8, and 9 vertically in the far-left margin of your page. These indicate the skills you will be rating.

You and your spouse should now take turns doing the test. Give your spouse this test to read and have him or her do the ratings for each of the nine skill areas below. When your spouse is finished, you read the test and fill out your own ratings. Don't read each other's answers or discuss anything until you've both completed filling out all three columns for each skill.

When you've both completed the ratings, take turns reading your answers out loud to each other. You read your ratings first for skill number 1. Then your spouse will read his or her ratings. You should then discuss the ratings—why you rated yourself as you did, why you rated your spouse as you did, and why you thought your spouse would rate you the way you indicated. Talk about what you'd like from each other in terms of behavioral changes. Share all your thoughts and feelings about this skill area within your marriage.

When you've finished all of this, go on to skill number 2, this time having your spouse read his or ratings first. You'll then read yours and discuss the skill as you did for skill number 1.

Continue in this way, alternating who gives the report first, until you have completed the discussion for each skill area.

Finally, read the section on raising your skill level. Now start the test.

1. **The ability to handle responsibility**. The ability to handle responsibility normally begins to develop between the ages of six and ten. In childhood, the skill involves things like remembering to bring homework home, doing it, and taking it back to school—all on one's own. In marriage, responsibility involves doing what a spouse is supposed to do: hold down a job, run a house, look after children, get up in the morning, fulfill commitments and promises, fulfill spiritual obligations—all without needing to be reminded or supervised. Rate yourself between 1 and 10 on your ability to consistently handle responsibility.

2. **The ability to manage money**. The ability to manage money can begin by age nine. In childhood, this skill involves the ability to save money, set aside money for charity, and spend money appropriately. In adulthood, the skill involves running a household budget based on income and setting aside money for charity and savings. Those who lack this skill may chronically overspend, acquire debt, gamble, not know about their own financial situation, or allocate funds inappropriately. Financial mismanagement can be a source of tremendous stress, conflict, and suffering in marriage. Rate your money management skills between 1 and 10.

3. **The ability to manage anger**. The ability to manage anger starts to develop around age five, as a child learns to put words to feelings and uses those instead of more dramatic, bodily expressions of displeasure. In adulthood, this skill also involves the use of modulating (calming) emotion, anticipating consequences, choosing appropriate occasions and times for communicating displeasure, using sensitivity in verbal communications (thinking before speaking and choosing kind words), and keeping relationship goals in mind. Those who completely

lack this skill may operate at the toddler level—stamping feet, making faces, using gestures, screaming, throwing things, slamming doors, and so forth. Others may not be quite so dramatic but, lacking verbal self-control, use hurtful words when frustrated or upset. Some people withdraw from the relationship when angry, ceasing to engage or stonewalling for hours, days, weeks, or longer. Stemming from an inability to openly communicate one's feelings, it nonetheless delivers a punishing, even abusive message to one's partner. All mismanagement of anger leads to severe wounding in marriage, rendering the relationship either physically or emotionally (or in both ways) unsafe. Rate yourself on your ability to manage frustration, anger, and rage between 1 and 10.

4. **The ability to give**. The ability to give of oneself may begin as early as five years old. Children can make birthday cards for family members, bake cookies for a sick person, and give appreciative comments ("Thank you!") when appropriate. Grown-ups give all kinds of things in marriage: compliments, physical assistance, emotional support, gifts, attention, time, advice, nurturing, and more. The ability to give results in building warm, friendly, loving marriages. The inability to give in marriage results in cold, unsupportive relationships. Rate your ability to give between 1 and 10.

5. **The ability to speak nicely**. The ability to speak nicely begins around age three. At this point, parents can begin training children not to whine or scream to get their needs met. Marriage partners who speak nicely take care to consistently use a pleasant, respectful tone with each other. They use words like "please" and "thank you" and phrases like "would it be possible..?" and "would you mind..?" Even when irritated, such adults manage to speak nicely, phrasing their concerns with

respect. Adults who lack this skill may "bark" at their spouse, whine, grumble, mumble, use unpleasant expressions, use an unpleasant tone of voice that expresses impatience and irritability (even when not particularly angry) and otherwise sound harsh, cold, or unfriendly. An unfriendly facial expression may accompany the vocal communication. Rate your ability to *consistently* speak nicely between 1 and 10.

6. **The ability to manage stress**. This skill develops in adolescence or later. It is the ability to purposely bring one's own mood into balance. Everyone is affected by stress throughout life, and some days (and years) are more stressful than others. During stressful times, people may feel overwhelmed, irritable, short-tempered, sad, or otherwise "down." Because stress is an ongoing part of life, it is essential that marital partners know how to soothe, calm, and uplift their own moods so that they will not bring excessive negativity into the relationship. Stress management can include many activities, such as reducing one's workload; increasing time for fun, relaxation, and personal growth; getting more sleep; doing more exercise; seeking counseling or religious support; consulting a naturopath or medical practitioner; meditating; talking to and socializing with friends; improving one's diet; and so on. Each individual must manage his or her stress in order to protect the marriage. Rate your ability to manage your mood and your stress between 1 and 10.

7. **The ability to be neat**. The ability to be neat can start around age three as a child learns to clean up after himself. By age four or five, many children can put away their toys without being reminded to do so. Adults who possess this skill in marriage are capable of putting their clothes in a laundry basket instead of on the floor, hanging clothing in a cupboard instead of over

a chair, clearing their own plates off the table and counters, washing dishes they have used, organizing their papers in appropriate desks and drawers, contributing toward the cleanliness of shared household areas, and generally keeping things clean and functional. Adults who are neat are not "neat freaks," making everyone tense and uncomfortable; rather, they are organized and orderly, considerate of the needs of others in the house for a pleasant, uncluttered atmosphere. Those who lack the ability to be neat will often find themselves nagged and criticized by an unhappy spouse (who feels deprived of appropriate living conditions). Messy marriage partners should expect lots of conflict over their "lifestyle." Rate your ability to be neat between 1 and 10.

8. **The ability to take care of yourself**. Good habits of independent self-care can begin around age six. At this point a child may be starting to take a bath on her own, and brush her teeth and comb her hair without being told to do so. In adulthood, self-care involves having routines for cleanliness, health, and hygiene. Responsible marriage partners take care of themselves not only for their own sake, but also for the sake of their spouses and children. Adults who lack this ability may indulge in various health-threatening addictions, neglect their grooming, neglect to exercise or eat properly, lead unhealthy lifestyles, or otherwise fail to maintain healthy and attractive standards. The result may be a frustrated, anxious, critical, and disappointed spouse. Failure to take care of oneself is a form of abandonment and neglect in marriage. Rate your ability to take care of yourself between 1 and 10.

9. **The ability to share and negotiate**. The ability to share, compromise and negotiate begins around age three. At this stage children can give up a little of what they want, wait for

their turn, and work out deals with others. In marriage, sharing and negotiating are critical skills. People must comfortably share space with each other and negotiate compromises around their preferences, their habits, their interests, and their lifestyles. Being able to see the other person's point of view and act on their entitlement to an equal voice is crucial. The "my way or the highway" philosophy of toddlers simply will not work well in marriage. Those who lack this skill will try to dominate the marriage, call the shots, drown out the spouse, and otherwise run the show. Even when the spouse submits to such treatment, the inevitable result is an unbalanced and unhappy relationship. Spouses must be comfortable giving up and giving in at least 50 percent of the time. Rate your ability to act on your partner's wishes, compromise, and share power between 1 and 10.

RAISING YOUR SCORE

Acquiring these core skills is a must if you want to contribute to creating a happy marriage and homelife. They are also essential in parenting, as you will have trouble bringing your children to the required skill levels if you yourself aren't there. If your score is 5 or less in any one area, your marital happiness is being compromised. Indeed, the further away from 10 you find yourself, the graver the situation. If you have several low scores, you simply are not ready for marriage! However, the situation can be remedied.

Bring your scores up by working on one area at a time, using self-help techniques and/or professional counseling. Professional counseling may be the fastest, most efficient, and most thorough avenue of improvement, unless you are simply trying to raise yourself from an 8 or 9 to a 10. Whether you are working independently or with a professional, enlist the feedback of others. If you are already married, ask your spouse to rate your performance each month until you are consistently receiving 7 or more in that area. Then, work on the next skill that requires attention. Continue rating yourself and getting your spouse's assessment each month until you are at 8 or more in each skill—aim for 10 in order to achieve the greatest happiness. When you can achieve consistently high scores, you are ready for marriage. Good luck!

Appendix Two

THE PARENT'S TOP TEN

What makes a good parent? Apparently, there are currently about 40,000 parenting books on the market that attempt to answer this question. However, the Torah lens helps us to sort through them quickly. We have certain definitive answers about how to establish the correct relationship with children (the laws of honoring parents), how to communicate properly (the laws of speech), how and what to model for our children (as detailed throughout the Torah and its commentaries), and even how to discipline (from the wisdom of our proverbs, numerous Torah sources, and our sages). Interestingly, recent research on healthy parenting strategies very much confirms the Torah approach to child rearing (no surprise there).

For example, a study recently presented by Epstein and Fox at the American Psychological Association has isolated ten main parenting competencies. These competencies produce particularly good outcomes, such as better relationships between children and parents, and happier, healthier, and better functioning children. Although there are many things apart from the actions of parents that affect the development of human beings (including genes and other environmental factors), it is a given that parents will want to maximize the positive effect of their own actions on the development of their children. Let's look at the parent's top ten skills and see how we measure up.

THE TOP TEN

The following list is presented in order of most important to least important in terms of predicting the positive outcomes:

- **The ability to show love and affection**. Making children *feel* loved is a result of using words and actions that feel good to them. Parents can show love by giving positive feedback, cuddles, words of affection, and other "warm fuzzies" while simultaneously reducing criticism and punishment.

- **The ability to manage one's personal stress**. This skill is *second* to love and affection in its power to influence healthy, happy development. It refers to each parent's independent ability to stay calm while raising children. It involves a number of self-care and stress-management practices such as prayer, regular exercise, a healthy diet, downtime, therapy, and so forth, as well as any individualized intervention that will reduce stress, such as acquiring organizational skills, taking remedies or medications for stress, taking anger-management or time-management training, or taking parenting or marriage courses. In other words, when a parent does whatever is necessary for him or her to stay centered, calm, and positive, the kids turn out better.

- **Marriage skills**. This skill is number 3 in its power to influence healthy development. When parents live in harmony together, their kids do better. Happily married parents model healthy relationship skills. Parents can always improve their marriage by taking marriage courses or going for marital counseling.

- **Encouraging autonomy and independence**. This skill involves the ability to step out of the child's way to allow him or her to become self-sufficient and self-reliant. It means letting the child make mistakes in order to learn. It means being careful to avoid overprotecting, controlling, or smothering behaviors.

- **Encouraging lifelong learning**. You model and teach respect for learning. (This value is inculcated in the Torah mentality.)

- **Modeling life skills**. Children prosper when their parents are functional. Your own ability to independently carry out your responsibilities as a man or a woman, provide for your family, run your home, meet the needs of your children, fulfill your role in your community, and otherwise be a responsible adult correlates with your child's well-being.

- **Effective use of positive reinforcement**. Using various positive techniques to encourage desirable behavior and strictly limiting the use of punishment fosters healthier development.

As you can see, this is number 7 in terms of its power to affect development. The personal behavior of the parents has a stronger effect.

- **Modeling a healthy lifestyle**. Children are positively affected by parents who eat well, sleep well, exercise moderately, and engage in other good self-care habits (like brushing teeth, showering regularly, and so forth).

- **Living a religious and spiritual life**. Teaching children mitzvos and guiding them in a relationship with Hashem is a parental obligation. However, it is interesting to note that doing so can help kids become mentally and emotionally healthier. Nonetheless, as we can see from the number 9 power rating of this parenting skill, offering *religious education* to children is not sufficient for their optimum development. Children must also directly *experience Yiddishkeit* through the positive model and communication of their parents. Note that many of the aforementioned parenting skills are actually tenets of proper Jewish practice.

- **Pursue safety**. Protecting children is good for their development. This parenting behavior involves taking appropriate precautions, following the law, and observing safe practices in and out of the house.

Appendix Three

BACH FLOWERS— EMOTIONAL FIRST-AID

E motions are considered a "water medium"—in their healthy state, they flow freely. When emotions are working as they should, we can laugh out loud, we can cry unabashed, we can feel our fear and register our rage. We're not afraid of our own feelings or of anyone else's. We know that feelings pass through our awareness, providing us with important information. When we've got what we need from them, they move on.

At least, this is how it should be. Unfortunately, we are prone to emotional "problems." We can get stuck in an emotion, unable to shake it and move forward. For instance, we can get stuck in sorrow or in resentment. Sometimes we drown in unremitting fears or worries. We feel stressed, exhausted, burned out. Sometimes we hurt ourselves and our families with our chronic levels of irritation and impatience, or worse yet, our explosive temper.

We are clearly not the only ones affected by our emotions. Our families bear the brunt of any imbalance we are experiencing. Our moods may be uncomfortable for *us* but unbearable for our children. Our anger isn't a pleasant feeling to be sure, but for the family it is far worse; it can be terrorizing. What do our children learn from our negativity, pessimism, and low-grade depression? How does our spouse feel in the face of our overwhelm, our inability to cope well? Can our frenzied, tense, and harried energy really nurture our family? We do not struggle in isolation. We bring everyone along for the ride.

And there is something else to consider as well. As the Torah points out, negative emotions are bad for our health. Sadness, anger, and fear hurt us both emotionally and physically. Long-standing fear pours excessive cortisol into the system, which eventually can produce stress-related disease. In fact, 80 percent of illness is said to be stress related, including routine colds and flu viruses all the way to the most deadly diseases, such as cancer and heart disease. It's better for us to be happy and calm.

If only we could get there.

A GIFT FROM HASHEM

Although Hashem is the one who sends us our stressful challenges, He also sends us healing. For instance, Hashem has sent us a particularly gentle remedy for troubled emotions in the form of Bach flower therapy. Whether we find ourselves bothered by a genetic (programmed by Hashem) tendency to fall into anxious feelings, or whether we became anxious and troubled after a nearby terrorist attack, a Bach flower remedy can help ease the fear out of our system. As we will see below, Bach flower remedies can help address virtually any emotional issue or stress-related condition. Safe and healthy for pregnant women, nursing mothers, newborn babies, children, teens, adults, and the elderly, Bach flower remedies can be a first step in emotional first-aid.

WHAT IS IT AND HOW DOES IT WORK?

A Bach flower remedy is simply water. The water, however, has been heated for a few hours with the blossom of a certain flowering plant. The blossom is removed and the water is preserved with a bit of brandy (so as not to cause bacteria to grow in the bottle). Those who are allergic to flowers will not be allergic to Bach flower remedies—they do not contain traces of flowers. Through the process of heating the water and flower together, the water has been changed *vibrationally*. And it can now alter the vibration of our human emotions.

Some people will say it isn't so. Failing to find an active ingredient in Bach flower remedies, they will say that the water is just water and it can't do anything positive or negative to anyone. Others, however, endorse the vibrational theory wholeheartedly. For instance, Dr. Richard Gerber, in his book, *Vibrational Medicine*, explains the principles of quantum physics that underlie the healing power of vibrational preparations like Bach flowers. In Britain and Europe, Bach flower remedies have been used for more than seventy years. There are professionals such as cardiologists, psychiatrists, psychologists, and medical doctors who prescribe them the way our medical practitioners prescribe regular medicine. Perhaps they know something we don't know.

I don't know why the water remedies work. Perhaps it is the *placebo* effect—the effect of *thinking* they will work. That wouldn't bother me. I am a big fan of the placebo effect. Some recent research suggests that even psychotropic medicine such as antidepressant drugs may be effective primarily because of the placebo effect. Moreover, I'm not fussy about the mechanism that cures my pain or disease. Placebos have been shown to help everything from backache to depression to cancer and much more. One thing that is particularly nice about placebos is that, whether they help or not, they don't cause any harm. The same cannot be said for our traditional medications, virtually all of which have potentially serious side effects.

Nonetheless, I suspect that there is more going on with Bach flower remedies than placebo. They have, after all, been found to be helpful for animals, plants, and infants—none of whom are particularly suggestible. Moreover, many people who try them are actually surprised to find that they help. While they are willing to experiment, they are highly skeptical. I myself was the same for the first twenty years that I knew about these remedies. I just couldn't believe they could do anything. My skepticism eventually vanished, but it wasn't until I saw with my own eyes how they helped a small child's sleep-disturbing phobia of robbers completely disappear overnight, after the youngster had suffered from the fear for almost two years and no other treatment had helped. (This was one of my children, so I saw it up close.) That experience began my journey with Bach flower therapy, leading me to eventually become a certified Bach flower practitioner.

Does Bach flower therapy always work? No, of course not. *Nothing* always works—not back surgery, not headache remedies, not antidepressant medication, not mood stabilizers, not herbal remedies, not acupuncture, not cognitive-behavioral therapy, not occupational therapy, not…anything. But here is a tiny sampling of the cases I have treated successfully with Bach flower therapy alone (although one specific case is shown for each type of problem, I have treated many, many people with these same problems and many other problems, with similar results):

- **Public-speaking phobia**. A middle-aged man who blushed uncontrollably when delivering presentations at work had already tried many kinds of medicines, therapies, and treatments throughout his life—without success. The problem vanished completely when he treated it with Bach flower therapy.

- **Separation anxiety.** A seven-year-old child would not go to the second floor of his house (where the bedrooms are) without having someone accompany him. He wouldn't go to the basement at all. He wouldn't go to school on his own (one block from home) and he couldn't sleep over at anyone's house, including his grandmother's. Within a couple of weeks of beginning Bach flower therapy, the child seemed to forget his fears, happily going up and down the stairs at home and even accepting a sleepover invitation from a friend.

- **Tic disorder.** Sometimes Bach remedies help tic disorders slowly but surely, sometimes not at all, and sometimes quickly and dramatically. Tics tend to wax and wane, becoming more and less active on their own. This makes it hard to know when treatment is responsible and when other factors are at play. Having said this, it's been my experience that Bach flowers are worth a try for this condition. For example, I treated two young brothers with severe motor and vocal tics (Tourette's disorder). They had failed to respond to traditional treatment they had received from doctors, psychiatrists, and neurologists all over North America. Both experienced a seemingly permanent remission (at least so far—I have followed their progress for the past five years) of the disorder within only two weeks of starting Bach flower therapy.

- **Fear of animals.** Five-year-old Leah had such an intense fear of dogs that she could barely go outside. While none of her family or friends owned a dog, several of her neighbors did. Even if she spotted a dog a block away, Leah would begin to shriek uncontrollably. Amazingly, this same child made good "friends" with a small dog on the street just a few days after commencing treatment with Bach flowers. Her parents were astounded.

- **Temper tantrums.** A ten-year-old boy suffered from frequent, uncontrollable temper tantrums. He was a danger to himself and to the other children in the house. No amount of love, discipline, or professional therapy had made any difference over the past many years. As soon as he began taking Bach flower remedies, the intensity and frequency of the explosive behavior decreased. For the first time, parental interventions began to make a noticeable difference. The child continued to improve over the months of treatment that he received.

- **Addictive behavior.** Addictions are one way to distract oneself from inner states of pain, tension, and angst. Bach flower therapy can be helpful in the treatment of various addictions because it reduces inner turmoil. Less subconscious distress means less need for escapist behavior. Once he started Bach flower therapy, Myer was able to stop turning to alcohol to relax, calm down, feel happy, or feel normal. He was able to implement his conscious desire to lead a healthier lifestyle— something that he just couldn't make himself do earlier on.

- **Toilet training.** Almost four years old, little Yaakov was still afraid to have a bowel movement in the toilet. This was making life difficult for his mother and created problems at school. Mom had to go to school to change his diaper for him because he was too old for this kind of help from the classroom teacher. After one week on Bach flower remedies, Mom was instructed to begin the process of toilet training again. This time, it worked. Yaakov's fear had been reduced sufficiently that he was able to master the skill at last.

- **Abusive behavior.** A couple was on the verge of divorce due to the abusive behavior of the husband. The husband was an intelligent man, a pharmacist by profession. However, he could not use his brain to help him control his rage. Marital therapy and personal therapy had not helped him learn to handle frustration in a controlled manner. Anger-management classes had a very temporary effect that diminished over a six-month period. In desperation, the couple agreed to try Bach flower therapy before they ended their marriage. Neither really believed that the treatment could help (particularly the husband, whose training was in hard science), and so both were amazed when they saw a clear change in the husband's temperament. For the first time in their marriage, the husband didn't *feel* intense anger and therefore he didn't need to *control* or *manage* anything. Now, eight years later, this couple is still happily married and their home is intact.

- **Insomnia.** Mrs. G., a sixty-four-year-old woman with chronic insomnia, described herself as having an overactive mind. At night, she would lie in bed and either worry about what she had to do the next day or ruminate about what went on in the past twenty-four hours. Bach flower therapy can sometimes help this sort of problem very quickly, and in the case of Mrs. G., it did just that. There is a particular remedy that helps to quiet a "noisy brain," whether the person is just thinking things over or worrying intensely or even reliving traumatic memories.

- **Grief.** Bach flower remedies can help people resolve their grief more quickly. It cannot completely heal a broken heart—that is the work of Hashem—but it can certainly reduce the feelings that often surround loss: guilt, horror, anger, despair, emptiness, longing for the past, and so on. Mr. J. lost his world when his wife suddenly passed away. He could barely function, despite the fact that his children badly needed him to be there for them. Bach flower therapy helped Mr. J. break out of his stunned state of shock, get back on his feet, and begin the healing process.

BACH FLOWERS FOR YOU AND YOUR FAMILY

Dr. Edward Bach was a medical doctor in the 1930s. He developed the flower remedies in order to help people reduce emotional stress so that they could be physically healthy. While the remedies can certainly be used for that purpose by anyone who is weak or unwell, they also can be used just for their psychological benefits. Unlike psychotropic medications, they do not have to be taken forever in order to maintain their benefits. Moreover, one cannot become addicted to them in any way. In fact, one only takes the remedies when one feels emotionally out of balance. A person with low mood takes the remedy until the mood improves. A person with fear takes it until the fear dissipates, and so on. If the problem returns after a while (which it does at first), the person takes the remedies again until it dissipates again. This pattern continues, with the problem recurring for shorter and shorter periods, and not appearing for longer and longer periods, until it simply fails to occur again.

Bach flower therapy helps bring unbalanced emotional states into balance. The remedies are meant to address any of the normal, negative emotions and moods that people feel: jealousy, insecurity, upset, overwhelm, worry, perfectionism, sadness, hopelessness, anger, fear, guilt, boredom, irritability, impatience, and so on. They can help during periods of stress, like facing illness, experiencing conflict, dealing with financial problems, moving, starting a new school, going to camp, writing exams, getting married, dealing with aging parents, or starting a new job. They can help when the body is under stress—affected by hormones, illness, or fatigue. They can be used when one is having a hard day or a hard year.

Because the remedies don't act on the physical level, they do not interact with other medicines, herbs, or treatments. They can be taken internally (in any hot or cold beverage) or externally (directly on the skin).

Are there times when Bach flower therapy should not be used? While the remedies are harmless, they can never be considered the primary treatment for mental *illness*. The remedies treat negative *emotions*—something that every human being is prone to. Illness, on the other hand, requires professional assessment and treatment.

While Bach flower therapy may, if the doctor permits it, be used in conjunction with other treatments, the primary interventions for various forms of mental illness are usually psychotherapy, psychotropic medication, or both. Some adults prefer to avoid psychotropic medication and, when it is possible to do so safely, they may choose a combination of psychological treatment and alternative medicines, including Bach flower therapy. All of this is normally worked out with one's mental health practitioner. Anyone with severe emotional distress or inability to function well at school, home, or work should be seen by a mental health professional such as a psychiatrist or clinical psychologist. Do *not* attempt to treat mental illness at home with Bach flower therapy!

Once a person has been assessed with a clinical disorder, the mental health professional will recommend some form of treatment. While adults will often receive a combination of medication and psychotherapy, this combined treatment format is less commonly recommended for young people. Due to the discovery of severe negative side effects of psychotropic medications for people under twenty-five years of age, doctors are much more cautious in prescribing them for this age group, tending to restrict their use to more severe conditions. However, when symptoms are moderate or mild, Bach flower remedies may be an acceptable alternative for providing symptom relief for children and teens who are receiving psychotherapy or other types of intervention. It is something that can be discussed with the child's doctor.

WHICH REMEDIES TO TAKE?

There are thirty-eight remedies (plus a thirty-ninth remedy called Rescue Remedy, which is a mixture of several Bach flower remedies) in the Bach system. You can mix up to seven of them together in one treatment bottle. Treatment bottles (small, one-ounce glass bottles with a glass dropper) are sold wherever Bach remedies are sold. Simply fill the treatment bottle with water, add 2 drops of the desired remedies, add about half a teaspoon of brandy (to prevent bacteria) and the bottle is ready for use. Take 4 drops from the treatment bottle in liquid, 4 times a day (16 drops daily). They should be taken in the morning, middle of the day, afternoon, and evening, with or without food.

A professional Bach flower practitioner can select the most appropriate remedies to treat you or your family members. However, you can also try selecting your own remedies. To help get you started, below is a very brief description of each of the thirty-eight remedies and the type of emotional states they might bring to balance:

- **Agrimony**. Person appears outwardly happy but feels inwardly stressed, has bad dreams or nervous habits.

- **Aspen**. Has vague fears (of the dark, monsters, something bad).

- **Beech**. Is judgmental, critical, prejudiced, negative.

- **Centaury**. Gets bullied, abused, or exploited.

- **Cerato**. Is immature, insecure, indecisive—constantly asks others for advice.

- **Cherry Plum**. Fears losing control, going crazy, or becoming violent.

- **Chestnut Bud**. Is impulsive, fails to learn from experience, has learning disabilities, inattentiveness, disobedience.

- **Chicory**. Is easily hurt or offended, manipulative, overly motherly, has an intense need for involvement and appreciation.

- **Clematis**. Is absentminded, lacks focus, is inattentive and dreamy ("spacey").

- **Crab Apple**. Has a fear of contamination, desire for perfection, cleanliness, and/or purity, feelings of shame or self-disgust, obsessions and compulsions.

- **Elm**. Feels overwhelmed.

- **Gentian**. Is easily discouraged, gives up, tends to be pessimistic.

- **Gorse**. Feels hopeless and/or depressed because of the situation.

- **Heather**. Is very talkative, needy, self-absorbed, intense, "drama queen."

- **Holly**. Is angry, jealous, paranoid.

- **Honeysuckle**. Is homesick or dwells on memories of the past.

- **Hornbeam**. Procrastinates, is easily and intensely bored, lacks energy.

- **Impatiens**. Is tense, racy, on edge, impatient, can't wait.

- **Larch**. Feels inadequate, fears failure, lacks confidence.

- **Mimulus**. Has phobias, fears of illness; suffers from nervousness, shyness, blushing.

- **Mustard**. Is depressed, unmotivated, introverted, has seasonal affective disorder, hormonal depression.

- **Oak**. Overworks, doesn't take sufficient rest, has strong sense of duty.

- **Olive**. Is suffering from burnout; physical, mental, and emotional exhaustion.

- **Pine**. Experiences feelings of guilt or unworthiness, is frequently apologetic and self-blaming, may have obsessions and compulsions.

- **Red Chestnut**. Worries intensely about loved ones.

- **Rock Rose**. Experiences panic, phobias, nightmares.

- **Rock Water**. Is compulsive, perfectionist, dogmatic, hard on oneself.

- **Scleranthus**. Has changing moods, is indecisive.

- **Star of Bethlehem**. Suffers grief after loss, trauma symptoms, deep sadness.

- **Sweet Chestnut**. Suffers from despair, emptiness, unbearable suffering, anguish.

- **Vervain**. Is intense, fanatic, keyed up, hyperactive, highly principled.

- **Vine**. Is controlling, bossy, inflexible, aggressive, mean.

- **Walnut**. Is impressionable, has difficulty with transitions and change.

- **Water Violet**. Is lonely and reserved, tends to be aloof, may have feelings of superiority.

- **White Chestnut**. Experiences excessive mental chatter, constant thinking and worrying, "noisy brain."

- **Wild Oat**. Feels unfulfilled, lost, confused as to direction to take.

- **Wild Rose**. Feels apathetic, resigned, withdrawn.

- **Willow**. Is resentful, blames others.

- **Rescue Remedy**. For any sudden shock, fright, injury, or accident; for frightening experiences (like public speaking, flying, doing something for the first time).

Bach flower remedies are preserved with grape alcohol (brandy). As this ingredient is not certified kosher, the following questions are posed to and answered by Rabbi Pesach Eliyahu Falk of Gateshead, England.

BACH FLOWERS AND KASHRUS

In the following questions, the term "original Bach remedy bottle" refers to the Bach remedy bottle that one normally purchases from a health food store (for example, Mimulus or Hornbeam).

The term "mixing bottle" refers to a one ounce (30 ml) glass bottle that one fills with water plus two drops of each remedy that is needed. This is also known as the treatment bottle.

The terms "remedy" or "Bach flower remedies" refer, unless otherwise noted, to the traditional *liquid* form of Bach flower remedies preserved with grape alcohol (brandy). Today some of the Bach flower preparations (such as Rescue Remedy) come in different forms, such as chewing gum, candies, and sprays.

Rescue Remedy is a pre-mixed treatment bottle used for shock, injury, panic, hysteria, and other intense emotional states.

Rabbi Falk's responses are in bold italic letters below each question.

1. Is it permissible for children and adults to use Bach flower remedies?

   Yes. Anyone can use Bach flower remedies.

2. Is it preferable to drop the remedies onto one's skin instead of putting them into liquid?

   This method is not as effective for treatment and there are sufficiently strong heterim (halachic reasons) that we don't need to use less effective forms of treatment such as putting it on the skin.

3. Is it permissible to use Rescue Remedy in spray form, sprayed directly into one's mouth?

   The preferred method is to dilute Rescue Remedy in liquid. However, if you can't do that, it is okay to use the spray. In fact, it is better to use the spray than to take drops straight from the Rescue Remedy bottle itself. However, if there is an emergency and you do not have the spray but only the liquid tincture and there is no water available for dilution, in that case, you can take the tincture straight from the bottle.

4. Is it permissible to use Rescue Remedy or any other Bach remedy in the newer forms, such as chewing gum, tablets, or water that is preserved with glycerin instead of brandy?

Brandy is preferable to glycerin when the remedy is being used straight from the bottle. However, once the remedies have been diluted in a mixing bottle, there is no difference between the traditional remedies preserved with brandy and the newer ones preserved with glycerin. They are both permitted. Gum and candies should not be used unless they are certified kosher.

5. Can one drop four drops of the remedy straight from the mixing bottle onto one's tongue?

Yes. Once the remedy has been placed within a one-ounce (30 ml) mixing bottle, it is permissible to take it directly from the mixing bottle.

6. If the remedies are dropped into a glass or mug straight from the original Bach remedy bottle, do they cause the glass or mug to become *treif*?

Not when used in the normal way. Normally, a person puts some liquid in a glass or mug and then adds the remedy. However, if a non-diluted remedy sat in a container with no other liquid for a full twenty-four hours, then the container would become treif.

7. Can one drop four drops of the remedy from the mixing bottle into any liquid, hot or cold? Will the glass, mug, or bowl become *treif*?

The remedies can be dropped into any liquid, hot or cold. The glass, mug, or bowl does not become treif.

8. Can one drop the remedies onto moist food?

    It is preferable to mix the remedies with water or some other liquid. However, if this isn't possible, dilute the remedy in a mixing bottle or other container and then put it directly onto food. In case of an emergency, Rescue Remedy can be dropped directly onto food, even if it hasn't been diluted.

9. If the mixing bottle is boiled between uses, does the pot become *treif*?

    No.

10. Can the remedies be taken on Shabbos and *yom tov*?

    If a person is taking a seven-day or longer course of treatment, then he can take the remedies on Shabbos and yom tov. However, a person may take Rescue Remedy for an emergency on Shabbos even if he needs it only for that day.

11. Can they be taken on Pesach?

    Nelson's Bach flower remedies are fine for use on Pesach.

12. Can they be dropped into a Pesach glass, mug, or bowl? Does it alter the *kosher l'Pesach* status of the glass or mug?

    They can be put into Pesach vessels. The status is not altered.